A DIFFERENT LIGHT

Also by Helen Chryssides

Local Heroes

A Different Light

Helen Chryssides

Ways of being Australian

HarperCollins*Publishers*

Published by HarperCollins*Publishers* (Australia) Pty Ltd
(ACN 008 431 730)
22–24 Joseph Street
North Blackburn, Victoria 3130, Australia

Copyright © Helen Chryssides 1995
All rights reserved. Except as provided by Australian copyright law, no part of this book may be reproduced without permission in writing from the publisher.

First published 1995
Reprinted 1995
Designed by R.T.J. Klinkhamer
Cover design by R.T.J. Klinkhamer
Cover photo 'The Promised Land' by *Tomek & Eryk*
Back cover photo of Helen Chryssides by Matthew Nettheim

Typeset in 10/12 Minion by Alena Jencik, Grand Graphix Pty Ltd
Printed in Australia by Griffin Paperbacks

The National Library of Australia
Cataloguing-in-Publication Data:

Chryssides, Helen.
   A different light: ways of being Australian.

   ISBN 1 86371 446 4.

   1. Immigrants — Australia — Biography. 2. Pluralism (Social Sciences) — Australia. 3. Australia — Emigration and immigration — Social aspects. I. Title.

305.9069

The extract from 'The silent night of snowfall' by Elizabeth Jolley (p. 142) was first published in the Melbourne *Age*, 'Extra', 24 December 1994.

CONTENTS

INTRODUCTION *vii*

GROWING UP GREEK 3
Helen Vatsikopoulos

BUILDING CULTURAL BRIDGES 31
Dorinda Hafner

JUST A STORYTELLER 55
Bryce Courtenay

A MARVELLOUS ADVENTURE 81
Gosia Dobrowolska

GETTING THE PICTURE 109
Tomek & Eryk

A DIFFERENT LIGHT 141
Elizabeth Jolley

ALL AT SEA 165
Tenshi Ayukai

SCALING OPERATIC HEIGHTS 185
Hao Zhou, Wei li Xing, Xie Kun

INTRODUCTION

We are all immigrants or descendants of immigrants – whether our ancestors were Aborigines who came to Australia some 40 000 years ago from Southeast Asia, or whether we are part of the latest group of arrivals from China.

Our society – one of the most culturally diverse in the world – has swelled by five million since the Second World War, with settlers from over one hundred and fifty countries. Today, at least one in every five people in Australia speak a second language.

My interest in this area is partly personal. As someone who was born in England and raised by a Polish mother and Greek–Cypriot father, I found myself drawn to the experiences of others. Why had they come to Australia, and where had they come from? What were their expectations, and had these been fulfilled? What had been their first impressions of this, their adopted country?

When I first came to Australia in 1980 in search of improved job prospects, the clear and bright light made an immediate and dramatic impact on me. In complete contrast to the grey gloom of London, the colours here seemed vivid and vibrant, much more intense than I had seen previously. I was interested to discover that it was much the same for those I spoke with while putting this book together. The light, so different to that in England, persuaded Bryce Courtenay to remain in Australia, while Elizabeth Jolley came to incorporate the light and shade of her new environment in her writing.

In choosing Australia, these eleven individuals have joined more than a quarter of our population that was born overseas. Whether they came by choice or circumstance, to better their own future or that of a spouse or children, they have greatly enriched our community. They 'started from scratch' in an unknown country, arriving in many cases with little money, poor language skills or uncertain work prospects. Often alone, sometimes subject to racism, and more often than not away from the support of family and friends, these individuals saw their problems as challenges, and from those challenges created opportunities. It is a credit both to them and to Australia that they have each succeeded in establishing a successful life here.

I was fascinated to find that all eleven had a passion – a goal, a dream – which they pursued relentlessly. Eryk Fitkau took one menial job after another – using them as stepping stones – and ultimately resumed his career in photography, while Hao Zhou, Wei li Xing and Xie Kun supported their operatic studies working as dishwashers, factory labourers or kitchen hands. At times the goal seemed out of reach: a young Helen Vatsikopoulos in an Adelaide working-class suburb visualising a life of overseas work and travel; Gosia Dobrowolska unexpectedly, and unsuccessfully, auditioning for her first potential film role in Australia. Yet they persevered; highly motivated self-starters carried by an attitude of success.

Today, these individuals are contributing to and shaping Australia's future in their chosen fields – Dr Tenshi Ayukai's research is helping to maintain the Great Barrier Reef, Dorinda Hafner's self-proclaimed mission to eliminate racial prejudice with joy and humour is proving successful, and photographer Tomek Sikora's eastern European background is influencing his creation of innovative advertising campaigns.

Australia's multicultural society has given our isolated continent a global perspective. The diversity of views, languages, cultures and attitudes, and the variety of religions and foods, has produced a unique and complex society. As Bryce Courtenay observed when Australia bid for the Olympic Games: 'My country is the only one on earth that can bring a cheer squad, 10 000 strong, for any athlete you can produce for any country on earth.'

The eleven stories contained in this book are representative of the many different personal experiences of Australians. By assembling them together as pieces of a jigsaw – pieces with which we can all identify – we can form a bigger and better picture. Through these stories, we too can find the means and the inspiration to enable us to pursue our own dream.

And we can look on cultural diversity in a different light.

Helen Chryssides

For darling Panos,
You are a wonderful nephew and I love you very much,
Ciocia Helena xxxxx
London
August 1997

For Panos, Marylka and Andrew

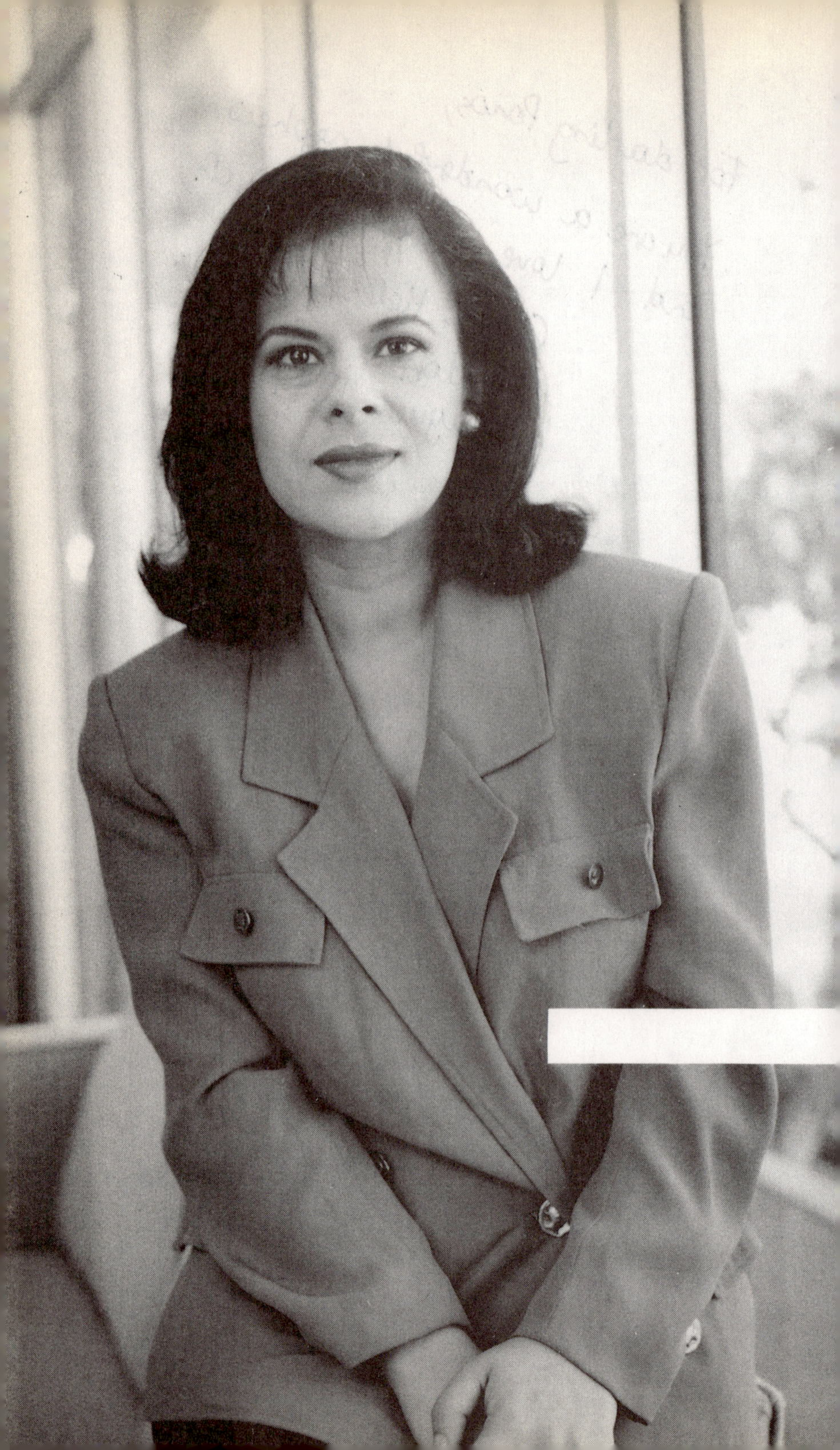

GROWING UP GREEK

'The editor said to me, "You've done well. Now don't get offended, but if you really want to make it in journalism, you are going to have to change your name".'

HELEN VATSIKOPOULOS
Journalist

When she's not interviewing global leaders or reporting from the world's trouble spots for Special Broadcasting Service (SBS) television, Helen Vatsikopoulos can be found working in Sydney, where she lives with her television producer husband Mark or, when she has some precious free time, visiting her parents in Adelaide.

This week she is at her parents' beachside home, relaxing with Mark for a few days. 'Enter the shrine,' she laughs, as she leads me into the front room, its walls adorned with photographs of herself over the years. The only child of Greek immigrants Victoria and Petros Vatsikopoulos, Helen naturally was always the centre of attention and there was pressure on her to succeed.

'When my mother was interviewed on radio recently, she admitted that perhaps she and my father had been a little hard on me when I was growing up,' says Helen. 'I can see now why that should be. And had they not been so strict, perhaps I would not have achieved what I have.'

We're sitting at a large table, with the traditional Greek welcome of *glyko* – small pieces of fruit prepared in heavy syrup – and coffee in front of us. I have been greeted by Victoria and Petros, and Mark, who has gone for a jog on this beautiful sunny day. Now Victoria is hard at work in the kitchen, busy preparing *dolmades* – stuffed vine leaves – for Helen to take back with her to Sydney.

Born in a small village in Greece, one of four children in a poor family, Victoria had always cherished a dream of a better, different life. She saw her own mother struggle to raise the family – alone after her husband was trapped in Albania when the borders were closed during a visit. At seventeen, Victoria had been married to Petros, a young man from a neighbouring village, and their daughter, Helen, was born five years later. But Victoria never forgot her childhood hopes. She wrote to her best friend, who had emigrated to Australia, and as a result of that letter, Victoria, Petros and Helen became sponsored immigrants. In 1965, they left Greece for Adelaide.

Helen remains close to her Greek heritage. It is a heritage she could never ignore, whether she chose to or not. From her early schooldays when she was teased for being a 'wog' to her later experience with a newspaper editor who suggested she change her surname to a simpler one, Helen always knew she was different. While these incidents may have shocked or unsettled her at the time, she came to develop an inner strength and resilience which she put to good use in later life. Hers is a story of a shy schoolgirl from an Adelaide working-class suburb who went on to become a highly respected journalist, producer and documentary film-maker, overcoming the difficulties and obstacles in her way with solid and steadfast determination. The recipient of prestigious awards for her work, Helen was applauded for her documentary on breast cancer, *Agatha's Curse*, and named 'one of the brightest visionaries on the Australian film-making scene' by *New Woman* magazine.

Her work colleague and superior at SBS television Paul Murphy describes Helen as one of the best and most talented foreign reporters that he's ever come across. Such a comment coming from a highly experienced ex–foreign correspondent is praise indeed. 'She writes and presents incredibly well, has a great voice, is pretty fearless and will go anywhere,' he says. 'She has a wide knowledge of world events, and the other important thing is that Helen has a strong streak of humanitarianism. Whenever she goes in to report a story, she really cares.' He considers her one of the best television all-rounders, as she is excellent also in the studio situation, and he sees her future as 'unlimited'.

Helen is just thirty-three years old. A petite and attractive woman with large brown eyes and long black hair, she is vivacious and engaging, dynamic and enthusiastic. When she speaks, there is a captivating lightness in her rich voice, coupled with an underlying firmness. She is supremely confident.

'My full name is Helen Vatsikopoulos,' she begins. 'Greeks don't have middle names but, as you can see, my surname makes up for that! I was born in a town called Florina in the north of Greece and we lived in Lemos, a small village nearby. We came to Australia when I was almost five. I remember that day very well – lots of hugs, getting on the bus and being told, "We are going now and not coming back." Naturally as a child of four, I didn't quite compre-

Seven-year-old Helen as a bridesmaid at a Greek wedding.

hend that. I remember thinking, of course we are going to come back. But we left and spent a couple of days, I think, in a hotel in Athens before we caught the boat out to Australia. That was a big thing. I don't think we'd ever stayed in a hotel before. I have vivid memories of being in that hotel room, eating grapes, feta cheese and bread.

'When I was seventeen, I went back to our house in Greece and it was exactly the same as my memories – a house made of huge stones close to a big walnut tree. We had a few cows then and we used to grow beans – broad beans, wheat, corn and potatoes. My dad was a peasant farmer, a shepherd. He had a flock of sheep and my uncle still does the same thing. Whenever I've gone to Greece, my uncle gets up at four in the morning and takes the sheep to the mountaintop to graze.' Her other childhood memories are of a large family. 'Grandfather, grandmothers, and lots of cousins. Of course that all changed when we came to Australia. We left them all behind.'

She was not to return until thirteen years later, when she did so unwillingly and as an 'awkward adolescent'. 'It's that cultural cringe, growing up to resent that part of yourself. "I don't want to go to Greece," I told my parents. But they said, "You have to go back. We will find out what it's like." So I went reluctantly and I probably didn't enjoy it as much as I should have.'

That rejection of her Greek background and culture – albeit only a stage – had started when she was fourteen. It is, she says, a phase common to many others with similar backgrounds.

'I went to Taperoo High School, very much a working-class school in a housing trust area. I grew up with lots of Aboriginal children and children of different cultures, more so than elsewhere in Adelaide. So the kids could say Vatsikopoulos as easily as they could say Smith or McDonald. But you reach that certain age when kids start listening to their parents, becoming influenced and, I suppose, racist ... Kids start differentiating. They know someone is Aboriginal – they've played with him since they were ten years old. But now, suddenly, he's a "boong".' It was then that Helen first started to see how she could easily become a victim of that racism.

'I had just turned fourteen ... In those days, we girls used to hitch up our skirts and pile on the mascara once we left home for school in the morning. It was also the age at which my parents had started becoming very strict with me.'

Helen recalls how the girls would stand in one corner of the schoolyard talking about the boys, and the boys would stand in the other corner talking about the girls. 'There was a boy called Ricky, a kid with big ears and buck teeth. He came up to me and said, "My dad told me you're a wog."

'Ricky meant to be hurtful. It was as if he suddenly had this revelation. I knew what racism was but it was never going to affect *me* – after all, I was friends with Lucy and all the others. My friends ignored the remark and told me Ricky was silly, but I was shattered.

'There were other Greek kids at school who perhaps were easy targets, with lots of brothers and sisters and a mother who used to pick them up. They were a much more obvious ethnic family, while I used to go to school by myself. Maybe they didn't belong to the right groups or gangs. A lot of them were teased but I never was – because I was cool with the coolest gang. Being an only child, I think I was a little introverted. I used to think a lot about these things. But I thought it would never happen to me. Ricky alerted me to the fact that I was different.' And over the next few weeks, he continued to taunt her.

Helen didn't tell her parents about these incidents. It was something she would never have discussed with them. But her mother would tell her how she and Helen's father were sometimes treated differently and resented for working so hard.

'My parents had jobs on the factory production line. When you have people of different nationalities, like the Greeks and Italians, working like crazy because they want to make more money to buy a house or put their children through school, and the Australian person doesn't really need to, then there is resentment. "These wogs and dagos come here and work really hard and take our jobs," they'd say. So from an early age I was aware of such things, that there were problems in my parents' lives, and I really didn't want to tell them that it was also happening to me.

'They both worked all the time, doing shift work. They each might even have held down two jobs at the beginning, in order to save up for a deposit to buy their first home. That house was in the same street as my school, literally five doors down.' It was a deliberate choice. 'I used to get up and go to school by myself – there was no one else in the house. The long-handled coffee pot, the *briki*, was there with sugar and a teaspoon of cocoa in it, already mixed by my mother. All I had to do was pour in the water – I never drank milk – put it on the stove, and that was my breakfast.'

The parents of Helen's classmates also worked in the nearby factories – the fathers in the asbestos factory with her father, or in the cement works next door, in the paint or sugar factories. Many of the boys she went to school with ended up working there. The mothers would also do factory work – perhaps at the fruit factory or Philip's Electrical with Helen's mother. And their daughters would become check-out operators at local supermarkets. 'No one's father was a doctor or a lawyer, that just didn't happen. There was one father who was an accountant and that was amazing.'

Yet somehow Helen knew she was going to do something else. She imagined herself as an architect, a journalist or a teacher, but whatever she would choose she wanted the experience of a university education. 'My parents had always drummed into me that I had to be educated. They may not have had that opportunity but I would.'

A handful of students from her school went on to university – two became architects, a couple social workers, and a few went to work for the public service. Helen received encouragement from her teachers as well as from her parents. 'They said, "You can do it, of course you can do it," but I remember one teacher warning us, "You might be one of the best in the school but when you get to university, you are going to be right at the bottom. There will be a lot of people there who have very well-educated parents and who have grown up with a different culture at home." That teacher was right.'

Going to university was a big jolt for Helen. 'It was not so much ethnic but more of a class thing. This was a very tortured time in my life because although I knew what I wanted to do, I didn't know whether I would get there.' She felt shy and a little inferior and withdrew into herself at university, suddenly realising that the world was very competitive and that others had had a better start. 'At the tutorials, the students were very well spoken. They had double-barrelled surnames and sounded really English, while a few of us had strong Australian accents as we had come from working-class schools.'

After studying Arts at the University of Adelaide, where she majored in English and history, Helen took a postgraduate degree in journalism at the Adelaide College of Advanced Education. 'Now I met other students – mature-aged and from different ethnic backgrounds.' Although, she says, it was difficult then to find a job in journalism, her lecturers – like her teachers at school – were encouraging. 'But there was only the ABC, and the *Advertiser*, where the people who got jobs had the same surnames as the major *Advertiser* journalists. It sounds funny but it was true. I suppose there was some nepotism and I thought I had Buckley's chance of getting into a place like that.'

This thought was reinforced after her work experience for a country newspaper, the *Renmark Recorder*. 'At the end of my two weeks, the editor told me I'd done well. They changed everything I'd written, mind you. I couldn't say, "The orange-picking festival was marred by rain," because they always wanted good news. That line became, "Despite the rain, it was fabulous." Anyway, the editor said to me, "You've done well. Now don't get offended, but if you really want to make it in journalism, you are going to have to change your name."

'I couldn't believe it – here was the grown-up version of Ricky. Maybe he thought my name was too difficult to pronounce, but it was also a racist remark. At the back of my mind, I could hear the little children at school saying Vatsikopoulos with no problem. If little kids can say it, I thought, then why can't big kids? I didn't believe this. I had a university degree. I had a postgraduate degree. I could achieve all that but I had to have an Anglo name to make it?

'I *never* considered changing my name. The editor's remark just made me angry. I know people who have changed their names but, to me, that's like erasing everything that has come before. So you suddenly become a new person and you are going to be successful because you have a different name? I'm still aware that in Australia we are a little behind – in terms of looking at someone like Helen Vatsikopoulos as being a Greek–Australian, and therefore different, rather than as being an Australian. We are only now, as a country, starting to become aware of these things.'

That comment made by the newspaper editor placed seeds of doubt in Helen's mind. 'By then I had spent twenty-one years of my life as a person with a Greek background. Was I now to become a Mary Smith? Would I ever look like a Mary Smith, a dark Mary Smith at that? How silly.' It also made Helen start to work harder and, she admits, she still does. 'Women often say that to be successful as a woman, you've got to work twice as hard as a man. Well, being a woman *and* ethnic is three times as hard.'

She was caught between two cultures. 'I was different here in Australia, open to prejudice, but I didn't fit in in Greece either. When I went back to Greece at seventeen, my Greek was at the level of a thirteen-year-old as the Saturday morning Greek school in Adelaide only went till then. That made things very difficult. I couldn't express myself adequately and things over there had changed so much. It made me realise that the Greek community here lived in a time warp. We were brought up strictly, just as our parents had been when they were growing up. But now I saw people of my own age in Greece going out, with the same sort of freedom that Australian kids had.

'That made me think, God, I've missed out again. You lose out here in Australia, you lose out there in Greece, and that's when you realise you're always going to be a little different.'

The strictness Helen refers to did not apply just to going out with boys but also with girls. 'At fifteen, I used to go out with the girls to the football at Alberton; we used to barrack for Port Adelaide. We weren't interested in the football but boys used to be there. Occasionally they would come and talk to us but, after a few matches, my parents stopped me going.'

Helen simply told her girlfriends that she was no longer allowed to go out. 'I said that my parents thought I should be going out with Greek kids. But at fifteen, where did Greek kids go? Nowhere. It was only a couple of years later that Greek kids got together and started organising youth dances. I was cut off socially from my classmates but we still hung around at school together. They started going out at night, to drive-ins with boys and, of course, that was out of bounds for me. So I was cut off from the people I went to school with.'

Helen now had to enter a new phase in her life, when the children with whom she had attended school from a very early age were not going to be the ones with whom she would spend her adolescence. 'It was like saying goodbye to them. I would see them at school but, a year or two later, most of them left and went to work.'

Her relationship with her parents also changed. She became resentful and had heated discussions and serious arguments with them. 'They were very strict with me. They wanted me to put my education first, which I was going to do anyway, but they were not going to give me any temptations – social or otherwise. We argued a lot, even when I did get into a different social group, the Greek one, and went to youth dances or on picnics.'

Helen went through the stage of being jealous of her school-friends and embarrassed of her parents, 'going to supermarkets and walking three paces behind them, pretending I wasn't with them as they were speaking in Greek. At other times, we'd be driving somewhere and I'd look into the next car and see my girlfriends. They'd be with their boyfriends while I'd be with my parents, off to my aunty's for lunch. I'd feel so uncomfortable. Now, of course, it's all different. It's fantastic, hilarious, and wonderful for my younger cousins. Everything has changed so much. I know girls who have lived or worked overseas, who are living with their boyfriends. I couldn't have done anything like that.

'At my wedding two years ago, there were girls hand in hand with boyfriends. I never could have gone to anyone's wedding holding hands with my boyfriend. For a start, I didn't have a boyfriend! But I look at those girls now and think, that's great, they've finally caught up.'

Being an only child, and a girl, had its disadvantages. 'I would have had a better social life had there been boy cousins of my age. But my oldest cousin was ten years younger than me so that was my bad luck. Other girls with strict parents managed if they had a brother near their age; at least they could drag him along and go out. So you had to find yourself a Greek girlfriend, from a family your parents knew, with a brother or a cousin of suitable age. My goodness – it was quite a trauma, and sometimes you just couldn't be bothered.

'I went to a few of the Greek youth dances but the boys were so macho and chauvinistic and I resented them as they were always trusted a lot more than girls. Boys were encouraged to be promiscuous, I suppose, as that was part of the sign of their manhood. But I used to resent them. There was that double standard – the parents didn't mind if the boys went out and were promiscuous with women who were not Greek. That was fine. But if they wanted to get serious about someone or get married, then they had to come back to the community and look for a Greek woman.'

As an only child, Helen was sometimes lonely and sought solace in reading. 'When I was a little older, say fifteen, I used to go to the Port Adelaide library and borrow magazines a lot – fashion and lifestyle magazines. I used to look through them and think, yep, I'm going to live in London, I'm going to go overseas. I lived in a world of my own, a world of escapism.' Her ambition to go overseas was a bold one, one laced with fear, but it was one she knew she would achieve. 'I didn't know how I would do it but I knew that I would.'

In retrospect, she is pleased that she was an only child, musing that perhaps things may have turned out very differently had she had older brothers or sisters. 'I think I would have been a lot more traditional, doing all those traditional things, perhaps finding a Greek boy and getting married. But being alone, you think about choices and you escape in magazines and realise there is something out there. I was not going to get hitched and stay here forever. I knew that's what was expected of me but I just never wanted to do that. Somehow I never saw my future as getting married and settling down. Had I thought of that as my lot or even an option, I would have given up any thought of becoming a journalist when Ricky said, "you're different", or when the newspaper editor said, "change your name".'

She chose another path – 'I have known when the timing is right to do things' – and pursued it vigorously. 'It's hard to say why. Journalism is just something I wanted to do.' Yet she was also something of a pioneer, a trail-blazer, being the first young woman in the Greek community to go overseas – to Europe – alone. How was she able to follow the path she chose? Perhaps by being a silent and determined achiever.

At school she was always the quiet one in class who didn't attract a lot of attention. Yet she was also the one who had always done the homework and had all the answers when approached by the teacher. 'But I would never show off because I knew that wasn't cool. It wasn't very cool to be smart. The smart ones were sometimes unpopular and I didn't want that. So I held back. I had a lot of friends, popular friends, ones who would make jokes in class and who everyone thought were funny. But I was very quiet. I didn't say much.'

Helen was a good student. She had to be. 'I couldn't come home without any As because I'd get into trouble.' She is still aiming for straight As and she is still shy. 'There is always this feeling that perhaps you are not good enough and that's what makes you work really hard, because you don't want there to be any doubt in people's minds.'

'At one stage I had two jobs at SBS, on *Face the Press* and as reporter and presenter on *Dateline*. It was ridiculous – I never saw Mark or had time to see my family. I had one day off a week for two years. When *Face the Press* was dropped, that was the best thing that ever happened to me. Mark was deliriously happy but even then I

14 GROWING UP GREEK

Helen with Bob Hawke, Malcolm Fraser and Gough Whitlam in 1991. *Courtesy of SBS Australia.*

Helen with Barry Humphries in 1992. *Courtesy of SBS Australia.*

was thinking – maybe I can start writing a book now!' Being a self-confessed workaholic also means that Helen sets herself high standards. 'When I do a story for SBS that may not turn out as planned, I get very upset – even though that may have nothing to do with me. Sometimes you go out on an assignment and the story just is not there or the talent may be awful. However hard you try to look for a different angle, there may be nothing you can do.'

As for the shyness she admits to, 'Mark laughs at that but I am shy. I am still shy when I have to interview really important people such as prime ministers. I think that sometimes people don't understand shyness. They see it as snobbery or disinterest. But my philosophy is, if I haven't got an interesting thing to say, then I just don't say anything. I am not the sort of person who walks into a room and starts talking to everyone, making chit-chat and small talk. When you interview people, you can feel a bit intimidated sometimes. You're sitting down and you have five minutes before the camera crew sets up and sometimes that five minutes can take forever. So what do you say? "Hello, Mr Prime Minister, nice day, isn't it? How's the government and how's the country?" I find that sort of thing excruciating.'

Sometimes, though, she says personalities just click. 'It's funny – sometimes the more important the people and the more they have achieved in their life, the better they are in dealing on a person-to-person basis. That has happened to me with elder statesmen. Then you can get ministers, who have not really achieved much, and they can be just incredibly rude. "How long will this take?" they ask. "I haven't got much time, you know."'

Helen enjoys working for SBS and believes it has the reputation of being an organisation that gives people a fair hearing. That can be an advantage. 'With *Face the Press*, we did get a lot of people who might not have appeared on commercial television stations, where an interview may have been sensationalised. But on the other hand, some people overseas haven't heard of SBS and, when you tell them it is funded by the government, they think it's a government propaganda channel as in their own countries.'

SBS is Australia's multicultural broadcaster and not only presents programs in different languages but also deals with issues that reflect the cultural and ethnic diversity of Australia.

Helen may well be a good role model for aspiring journalists, and especially for those of a non-English-speaking background, but she says, 'Sometimes people ask me whether I am working at SBS because I come from an ethnic background.' The response is a sharp no but the question concerns her. 'I didn't graduate, and then take my certificate and long Greek name to SBS saying, "I'm ready for you now." I started at the ABC, worked there for many years, and my background made me work harder. I think it still does.'

Her background also caused her conflict at times. She was the first woman in her Greek community to leave home, 'at the age of twenty-six, mind you,' she confesses with embarrassment. 'It was really traumatic; my parents were very upset. It was expected that I would live at home until I got married; that would be the only time to leave home. I left for Melbourne – it would have been unthinkable to leave home and go and live in another house in Adelaide. As it was, I was a working journalist at the ABC, living at home, not paying board and being able to save a lot of money. Kids these days think that is fantastic – being in touch with your family and ethnic background – but I didn't … in those days, it was get out and be independent.'

Helen's reasons for leaving home – in search of better prospects – were exactly the same reasons her parents had left their home in Greece some twenty years earlier. They had seen Australia as a land of opportunity, partly for themselves but mostly for their daughter. 'You always think of the children,' Helen explains. 'For as long as I can remember, my father always had a bank account set aside for my wedding. My mum always had a dowry she was working on – I've got some sheets she bought back in 1975, white with huge navy spots. I laugh and tell her the fashions have changed but she just says, "I bought them years ago and they were very expensive." And Dad, yes, he always had money put aside for what was going to be a big wedding. And it was.'

Helen may have had the big wedding her parents dreamed of but her life was very different to theirs in other respects. 'Had I stayed in my village in Greece, I may have married at sixteen or gone to live in the city where I was born and become a schoolteacher. Those would have been my options. I don't think I would have been able to achieve much more than that because of the social and class structure of the time. When you are a peasant, you don't get to become a doctor or a lawyer. You don't get much of a chance to rise above the class in which you are born.'

Helen's parents found the opportunity and the success they were looking for in Australia. The hard work that led to that success was measured, Helen says, for Greeks and Italians of her parents' generation, in real estate. 'You've really made it when you own one house and have another that gives you an income in rent.' For those of Helen's generation, attitudes and expectations are different.

'I am at a stage when I am re-evaluating the priorities in my life. Up until now it has been work, work, work. But I got married a couple of years ago and I now see a lot of my friends having children. I'm not ready for that yet but I'm feeling a little guilty – should I continue working? What do I want to do next?' Another consideration for her is the 'limited shelf-life' that she says women have in television. 'I suppose what success means to me is that I can say I've been to all those places in the world. I've seen the different ways people live, I've been to some war zones. I guess success to me is seeing the world.

'Mark and I have bought a house – with a huge mortgage. I've been working for all these years and I've nothing to show for it except perhaps too many clothes. I'm dreadful with money, exactly the opposite of my parents, and I think subconsciously that's probably the way I handle my success. My parents worked so hard and led a frugal existence, not wasting any money. They are retired now and when Mark and I take them out for a restaurant meal, Dad will look at the bill and say, "You could have eaten for two weeks with the money you're spending here tonight." They used to tell me they had to work so hard because they came to Australia with nothing much. I remember two trunks at home with some things from Greece – a tea set, some tapestries, and an old sewing machine.'

Helen saw how hard her parents worked in order to have the good life in Australia they had sought and she also saw, from childhood, the clear distinction between men and women in Greek society. When her uncle and other older male relations came to stay with them, her mother would cook and clean for them. 'They were always going out – with Australian girlfriends – and then marrying

Greek women and you would never see them cooking or washing dishes whereas I, as a daughter, had chores. But I didn't feel jealous of them. I think you have to be a fatalist. I think everything in this world happens for a reason. Had I had that freedom, maybe I wouldn't have been driven to do the things I have done.'

Her greatest work achievements to date have been the Gold Award for excellence in ethnic affairs broadcasting from the Walter Schauble Foundation and a Walkley Award – considered Australia's most prestigious media award – for the best international report of 1992, for her series on the former Soviet Union, *The Commonwealth of Disunion.*

'There are the As again,' she laughs. 'Someone in the industry gave me a few As for my stories. When I won the Walkley award for journalism and it was reported in the Greek newspapers, the Greek community radio station in Adelaide called up my mother and asked, "You've done so well with your daughter, can you give us a few hints on how we should be bringing up our children?"

'We have a lot of respect for each other and a very good relationship. I can see why she was so strict. I can see where my parents came from.'

It took a while for Helen to settle in Australia. She herself does not remember but her father tells of how, soon after she arrived in Adelaide, she would point to planes in the sky and say, 'Please come and take me back to Greece.'

Her first day at school was traumatic. 'There was another girl, Christine, from the next village, who had started a year earlier. We were chatting in Greek and the next thing I knew – I must have been distracted with something – she had disappeared. I didn't know anyone. Everybody was speaking a very strange language. I remember being very, very frightened. The next thing I remember is speaking English.'

Adelaide, by virtue of its size and traffic, was a big contrast to her village. There she had known everyone, and had been trusted to walk down the street by herself. In Adelaide, she had to be careful.

She lived a Greek lifestyle – attending church on Sundays, 'a corrugated-iron building full of beautiful icons and lots of candles dripping wax everywhere', Greek school on Saturday mornings, 'forty of us in one classroom with staggered grades, learning Greek grammar in silence', and observing Easter and Christmas in the traditional way. 'We'd dye the eggs red and we'd fast for Easter. We were not allowed to eat meat, eggs or dairy products. We'd survive on a diet of lentil soup.'

Namedays as well as birthdays would be celebrated. 'I remember the first nameday after we arrived was my father's – he was named after Saint Petros. This was in the 1960s and we were all dressed like extras in a Beatles movie – the men in white shirts, black pants, skinny ties and pointy shoes, and the women in slim dresses above the knee and with their hair up in beehives. Everyone came to the house and brought a present, an ornament for the house. We had Greek music and there was lots of traditional food like *tzatziki* – yoghurt dip – and *taramosalata* – cod's roe paste – and *toursi*, which we made with pickled capsicum, cucumbers and tomatoes. The men would have *toursi* with their beer or ouzo.'

The food served depended on the region of Greece the people had come from. 'We never really had a lot of seafood, like pickled octopus, as we were from the mountains. Instead we had lamb. One of my mother's specialities is pies – *pitis* – like feta cheese pie. When we finished the main meal, the women would clear up the tables, but not the men. They would sit there and drink and continue having a good time. Then the women would serve the sweets, like *baklava*, *galaktobouriko* or *kadeifi*, with Greek coffee.'

Helen believes her cultural background not only enriched her life but gave her more insight and even greater depth in her work. She recalls one of her first stories when working for the ABC in Adelaide; the topic was a retirement home planned by people from a certain ethnic background. 'I was one of a very few from a non-English-speaking background at the ABC and I found I could bring my knowledge of extended families to this story.'

For her the assignment reinforced cultural differences. 'In Greece you would never bundle off the old people to a home; this was a whole new concept for me. My parents worked hard in their early days to be able to enjoy their retirement. Now, when they are older, they are seen as valued members of the community because they have something that young people don't have – and that's wisdom. They, and the others of their generation, are people who have endured a lot. They have fought in wars, they are proud of their community, and they are respected.'

When doing voluntary work at fourteen, Helen found it distressing to discover what happened to the elderly in Australia. 'I used to visit an old folk's home where one lady used to show me photographs of her grandchildren, and her husband who had fought in the First World War. I used to think how sad it was that she was here now – lonely, eating horrible food and not even allowed to drink real coffee but drops of chicory in water.'

Yet Helen's own life – with its extended family and regular large jovial get-togethers – had its own disadvantages. 'You were always tied to your family – sometimes there was no escape.' She was anxious to wait for the right time to assert her independence, for fear of hurting her family. 'When I got a job with the ABC in Melbourne, that was a way of saving face for everybody. For myself, it was a very good career move but there was a lot of heartbreak nevertheless. It was devastating for everybody. There was a great sense of guilt, especially being an only child.

'I loved living those couple of years in Melbourne, being truly independent, and coming to Adelaide on weekends. That's when I truly started appreciating my parents, realising how fantastic they were and how they really loved me. I had relations in Melbourne, more than in Adelaide in fact, but I was as independent as possible.'

She mentions a poem, 'The City', by her favourite poet, Constantinos Cavafy, a Greek who had grown up in Alexandria. 'He wrote of the city pursuing you wherever you go. I used to think that Adelaide was dragging me down and I had to get out but it's you, it's the baggage you take around with you. You can go to a million cities but you take the same baggage with you. Now, when I come back to Adelaide I think it's a great city.'

Helen's career had started at *Nationwide* for the ABC in Adelaide. She was offered a job there as researcher, and after a period of work experience went on to work in the newsroom. 'In those early days, it was very WASPish at the ABC. It was eastern suburbs, red wine and cheese, and the Adelaide Festival. I wasn't any of that. I was Port Adelaide and *dolmades* and the Magpies football team. I would talk like someone from Port Adelaide. Max Harris once wrote a piece about standards slipping at the ABC and I've never forgotten it. He wrote, "Somebody must have stepped on Helen's foot because suddenly an 'hour' became an 'ower'." I remember reading that and thinking, oh my God, what am I supposed to sound like? There were a lot of nice people there – they are still close friends – but I had the feeling for a long time that it was a bit toffy.'

A few years later, Helen went to the Melbourne ABC newsroom and then *The 7.30 Report* before coming to SBS television in Sydney.

'What I enjoy most is what I'm doing at the moment. In the early years, you're working towards something and, even if you're doing that early shift – getting up at five in the morning to do radio bulletins – you know it's not going to be forever. Hopefully you'll move on to something more challenging. I really enjoy my work now – it's like being a foreign correspondent but you get to come home in the end.'

Coming home means coming back to her Greek heritage, and Helen's own wedding reinforced for her the positive aspects of that heritage. Although she was then living in Sydney and her husband and his family came from New South Wales, there was never any question of the wedding being held anywhere else but Adelaide. 'There was the whole Greek community to invite!' And Helen had no intention of ever doing otherwise. 'There were some girls in the community who went through a complete denial and total rejection of anything Greek. Some left home. I saw that but realised that for me it would mean totally jeopardising my future. Was I going to be totally Australian – leave home, get a job and then what? What sort of job could I get at that age? I didn't want a job. I wanted a career and security and I wasn't going to cut off my nose to spite my face.'

There had never been any pressure on her to marry someone Greek. 'Not at all, never at any stage, which was fantastic. My parents had seen Greek girls marry Greeks and they hadn't turned out to be the right one, and Greeks who married Australian men who just doted on them. All they wanted was for their daughter to be happy, no matter what the nationality of the husband.' And while Helen was aware of arranged marriages, these had been for women some ten years older than herself.

It was on a visit to Adelaide a few years earlier that Mark proposed to Helen while the couple were walking on the beach. 'I said yes and we went back home because this was the moment Mum and Dad had been waiting for all of their lives. Mark suddenly turned to Dad and said, "I've asked Helen to marry me and she said yes." Dad's a bit deaf and he said, " Who did you ask?" "Helen, your *daughter*!" Then the tears came and Mum rushed into her room and got Mark a present – a lovely gold cross and a beautiful gold chain – and welcomed him into the family.'

There were over two hundred guests at the wedding and it was as traditional as possible – with a male relation placing bank notes in her shoe to make it fit snugly, and the bride kicking over and smashing a glass for good luck on leaving the house. 'But someone had left a rubber mat outside the door, the glass merely bounced and the expression on everyone's face was one of horror. Luckily someone moved the mat, I was able to smash the glass and everything was fine.'

The ceremony was in both Greek and English. 'We prayed at one stage, not just for a happy wedding but for world peace, for unity of the churches and for the well-being of Archbishop Stellianos of Australia. One of my friends said afterwards it was quite an ambit claim!'

While she was growing up, Helen felt sometimes she was trapped but now she thinks otherwise. 'The trappings are good and these days you really do appreciate them. I'm going back to Sydney today and I'll be taking back some beautiful freshly made pies and *dolmades*, kalamata olives and barbecued red capsicum, all the favourite foods that my mother knows I love. I'm always given parcels of food to take back to Sydney. Mum even sent me a feta cheese pie once through the post. This is really an extension of the Greek kids leaving the village – they go to work in the city and the parents constantly send them things. They go back to visit the village and end up leaving with baskets of eggs and lots of food.'

She has more than fulfilled her parents' expectations. They had encouraged her to get an education, 'all the time, the more the better. They always used to say, "If you get an education, then you can get a job, sit in a clean office and come home at the end of the day when you've finished."' She laughs. 'They don't realise there is no rest – it's even more work than in their day, it never ends ... And sometimes my aunt says to me, "You've been to all these places – enough," inferring that it's time to stop and have a family. I told her yesterday, "I'm not ready yet, maybe in three years from now." She looked at me: "You will be thirty-six then."'

❄

A few weeks later, I meet Helen in Sydney and discover her work persona. She has just completed her documentary on breast cancer, *Agatha's Curse*, and is contemplating her next overseas assignment for *Dateline*. We talk in the vast central area at the premises of SBS at Milsons Point. We are surrounded on all sides by editing suites from which emanate sounds of constant activity. Helen sprawls comfortably on a sofa, becoming more and more animated as she speaks about her work. It immediately becomes obvious that she is intensely passionate about her assignments.

I look through a selection of photographs: Helen in Sri Lanka standing alongside a Tamil Tiger soldier armed with a machine-gun, Helen with Barry Humphries, Helen sitting next to rock singer Jimmy Barnes, with comedian Lenny Henry, Helen standing in the midst of three ex–prime ministers – Gough Whitlam, Malcolm Fraser and Bob Hawke. The last was the highest-rating locally made program on SBS. I have watched her television reports on subjects as diverse as Bosnia, Tibetan Buddhism, and the merits of 'ethnic humour'. She has covered events in Israel and Greece, Malaysia, Japan, and Papua New Guinea. She was in India when Rajiv Gandhi was assassinated, in East Germany when the Berlin Wall crumbled and she interviewed Poland's Lech Walesa when he was still leader of the illegal Solidarity movement. Her knowledge of world politics is immense and her reporting experience likewise.

Helen is well aware of the dangers her work can sometimes involve. 'When I was doing my research for the piece on Sri Lanka, I called a woman in London who had been able to get into the northern town of Jaffna, cut off by the army. "How did you do it?" I asked. "I want to go there too." "If you want to go to Jaffna, you must be prepared to die," she said. I was really thrown. There I was, sitting on my lounge room floor in Sydney, and she is telling me that I will be fired on and must be prepared to *die*.'

So why, despite these dangers, did Helen go? She seems taken aback at the question. 'Well, it's not necessarily going to happen,' she says eventually. 'Those are the risks.' Her story on the ten-year battle of the Tamil Tigers with the Sinhalese attracted interest from even the Immigration Department. 'No one had been able to get there for over two years and they wanted to know what was happening there. At times like that, your report can make a difference.'

It was a frightening assignment, her most dangerous to date. 'We flew to a military base in the north of Sri Lanka, got in with their blessing, and then travelled for a couple of hours on a Red Cross ship. Then we had to start making friends with the Tamil Tigers. One night we went to the lagoon where their suicide squads were assisting illegal crossings, and the military started bombing. There were three of us – the camera operator, the sound recordist and myself. That was a very frightening time. We kept thinking, "The military let us come here, they know we're here," but once they started bombing, we knew they were not going to stop their campaign for the sake of a few journalists. But we were fine.'

She has never turned down an assignment because of the risks involved. On the contrary, she has volunteered for jobs that had been cancelled by the producer because of the danger. One such assignment was Bosnia. 'More journalists have been killed there than in the whole Vietnam War. It's very dangerous because it's not a matter of being in the wrong place at the wrong time – in Bosnia they actually try to kill journalists. I was ready to go and, at the same time, a colleague was going to Cambodia to cover the elections, so we both had flak jackets made. They cost $1500 each. Mine is still in the office down there,' she points. 'The producer turned the assignment down because Lloyds of London were quoting something like $20 000 per person to insure us for a week in Bosnia. The insurance would have cost much more than the entire trip.'

What makes her go so far as to have a flak jacket made? 'Because

I'm a journalist,' she states, simply. It's as practical a reason as that. 'Journalism to me is not just the glamorous stuff that we do in the studio ... I admire *real* journalism, the journalism of Ryszard Kapuscinski and Oriana Fallaci. Someone has to bring back these pictures and these stories to all of us sitting in the comfort of our lounge rooms.' She feels priviliged to be able to do so.

Her husband Mark is as adventurous as she is. 'He's just like me; he'd love to go to Bosnia tomorrow.' Helen can be away for anything from two to five weeks, perhaps six times a year, in her work for *Dateline*, and the separations can be hard on the couple. 'But he understands, we're both journalists. It might be different if he worked in a bank or something but he'd love to do half the things I do and so we both think the same way. He's a producer for the ABC's *Four Corners*.' Helen's job takes her all over the world and she now thinks she would not be content staying in one city or even one country. 'I'd get a little bored. If I didn't have a job like this, I'd need a good income to travel.'

She sees the role of a journalist today, at the time of so much change in the world, as a very important one, as the 'forerunner of recording history – if we're actually good journalists, if we're not biased and don't try to twist facts for the sake of a good story.

'Sometimes you come back to this world after having been in that world and you tend to put it all into a compartment, saying, "I'm home now." But then I look at the news and the places I've been to and I get angry. I've been to Sarajevo when it was peaceful, when people were saying, "This will blow over, this will be fine." The politicians aggravated it and made it into a war. What makes me angry is that it was as plain as the nose on your face what was going to happen – if I could see it, why couldn't the leaders? Then you have to look back and say it's just history repeating itself – time and time again. Maybe it takes exceptional leaders to avert that.'

She has also become cynical. 'Of course, you become very cynical. But you don't get despondent, because sometimes things can turn around for the better. I went to cover the Japanese elections and the Liberal Democratic party fell after thirty-eight years. Suddenly out came this new generation of Japanese leaders who weren't in their seventies – they were young, in their fifties, and they apologised for the war and they had a new way of thinking, a new mind-set. I was there, I saw it happen and that's great. That's really satisfying.'

She experiences no problems as a woman. 'I'm amazed at that. You might think it would happen in some Islamic countries but it doesn't. I am always treated with a lot of respect, and I in turn am sensitive to their traditions and religion, by way of dress and behaviour. Going from a mosque in Baku, Azerbaijan, to being with fundamentalist rebels in Kashmir, it's never been a problem.'

As a journalist, the value she holds highest is believing in your own judgement. 'You can send ten people to the same place and they might each come up with a different analysis. You have to see things straight down the line and you've got to have a bullshit factor. There's nothing worse than coming back and saying, "They lied to me." When we were in Sri Lanka, there was a military build-up. Many people were recruited; it was as if they were getting ready for a big assault. I asked them. "No, no, no, we're just replenishing the troops," they told me. Two weeks after we returned to Australia, there was a massive assault on the Tamils in the north. They lied to me.'

Success for Helen professionally is recognition, keeping her integrity and never compromising. 'Yes, and having autonomy in my work.' Therefore she enjoys the editorial freedom she has at SBS. 'You are true to your work here. What goes to air is what you saw when you were there. No one says to me when I come back, "Look, can you make this a bit sexier?" and I wouldn't anyway. No one says, "That's a bit dull. Cut it out and let's have more action." Maybe that happens at other places. But here, you're not going to cut the grab into thirty-second digestible bites just to make sure someone's not going to change over to another channel. If they're more interested in watching the commercial channels, well, then they're not interested in what's happening to the Tamils and Sinhalese in Sri Lanka or the Kashmiris in India.'

Work assignments may have taken her on many hazardous missions to the world's danger spots but none has affected her more deeply than working on her documentary on breast cancer, *Agatha's Curse*. It was not in Rwanda nor in a chaotic India after Rajiv Gandhi was assassinated that she felt her life was threatened. That happened, ironically enough, back on home territory – in suburban Sydney when Helen sat face to face with a young woman.

'She was thirty-three years old. She didn't have children. And she was Greek. It was like looking at a mirror image of myself.' A mirror image with one difference. 'She had breast cancer. It was a chilling moment. I was both deeply shocked and scared. I had to keep reminding myself: I'm a journalist; I have a job to do. I can't allow myself to become emotionally involved. But I did.' So much so that Helen later consulted a medical specialist to allay her personal fears of breast cancer. 'Research had told me that breast cancer was no longer a disease of ageing and this woman, Maggie, vividly demonstrated that to me.'

Helen's documentary – named after Saint Agatha, the patron saint of breast cancer sufferers – included interviews with high-profile individuals. 'Olivia Newton-John told me how breast cancer had changed her life. She realised she was taking care of others and not herself. She's learned to say no more easily now and only do the things she really wants to.' The three months during which Helen was involved on the project also saw her life change for the better. She started to look after her health more and joined a gym. Her outlook changed and she found she was no longer becoming upset at life's minor irritations.

She rationalises her emotional involvement, saying she could not have made the documentary without any sort of compassion. 'Then Maggie died and that caused me a great deal of pain. I attended her funeral.' The experience caused her to confront herself as someone who was 'almost an Australian, growing up in a Greek family'. For at the funeral she saw the outpouring of grief and open distress of the Greeks in direct contrast to the response of Maggie's 'Anglo' friends.

'I joined her friends as they went back to her house and drank champagne and ate her favourite kind of cake while looking at photographs and talking about her life. They were celebrating her life and looking at her in a good light. Perhaps they were more philosophical about life and had a better concept of death being part of life. All Maggie's relations went to her parents' house and I can imagine it was a very sombre occasion. Maybe it is healthy to show emotion more, to weep and wear black, but it's also important to come to terms with death.' It is a dilemma she has to this day.

One of the most important aspects of Helen's life is family. 'The older you get, the more important it is.' Family and friends are more important to her than fame, income or even professional success. 'To be frank, it's a cruel and competitive world out there. I'm lucky enough to be able to work semi-independently. I've been burned a few times and you come to realise that politics rather than hard work can get you further in your career.'

There is a lot of pride in the Greek community at Helen's success, her parents are constantly being congratulated on her stories, and – paradoxically – she is often asked at the talks she gives, whether her Greek background is an advantage in her work. 'It can be and then again it may not be,' she replies. 'It can be because you've experienced a lot in your life, including prejudice, and so it can make you very aware and sensitive. And my "baby" Greek has come in useful at times when interviewing. But it can also stop you looking at things objectively. What if I had to do a story on Macedonia – I could find that very difficult.'

Her husband Mark has forced her to look more closely at her background. 'He asked me why everything was always such a tragedy for us Greeks, the other day. "Why can't you be like the Irish who laugh at everything?" he said. So I listened to the lyrics of some Greek music: it was all "no one loves me; I don't know what love is". I suppose it's a dark way of looking at the world. But if you look at what can't be achieved, then you're surprised at what can,' she laughs.

'When Mark made that observation, I thought about it and he's probably right. He thinks the Greek comes out in me a lot, the way I'll look at an issue and question it. Mark tells me that Greek people shout all the time. I keep saying, "We're Greek, we're just talking!" Actually a lot of Greek men who have worked in factories with noisy machines all their lives have lost a bit of their hearing, so there's also a very good reason why Greek people shout.'

She laughs again. 'Mark tells me I'm very Greek. I have a Mediterranean temper. I do believe in being honest and expressing myself, which gets me into trouble a lot of times. Yet, when I go back to Greece and see the people there – uninhibited in every way – I think I'm not like them at all. When the Greek government decided to help increase productivity by closing the nightclubs at two in the morning during the week, there was a huge uproar; people were demonstrating in the streets. That tells you a lot about what is important to them! They certainly know how to live for today, forget about tomorrow. Maybe we need to do that a little bit more in Australia.'

As for Helen, her future plans include looking more closely at her travels. 'I'd like to do some writing. I've got all the notebooks from my trips and all the interviews transcribed. One day I'm going to drag them all out and write a travel–journalism thing based on all the countries I've been to, looking into the people there and what they've represented, from the leaders to the person pushing the cart in India who speaks the truth and has an amazing amount of wisdom. I'd like to do that and I'd like to write down stories from my family.'

Her parents and their experiences have taught her many things, not least of all to be on her guard. 'I think that comes with being a migrant and being in a different country. When my parents were working here, they were scared to belong to unions for fear of being sacked … When I wanted to change jobs, they advised me not to. They said, "Don't move, you never know what might happen." They were always very security-conscious. Perhaps that's why I like going overseas all the time. It's a constant break but then you come back to a sort of nest.

'It's funny – when I go back to Adelaide and I'm at my uncle's place, I can just sit there in the corner and listen to them, or watch television. I don't feel I have to do anything or say anything. I only feel that in Greek company. You don't have to try hard at all, because it's your home. It might be your uncle's but it's yours and you're one of the family, the same as your cousins. It's a sense of real security.'

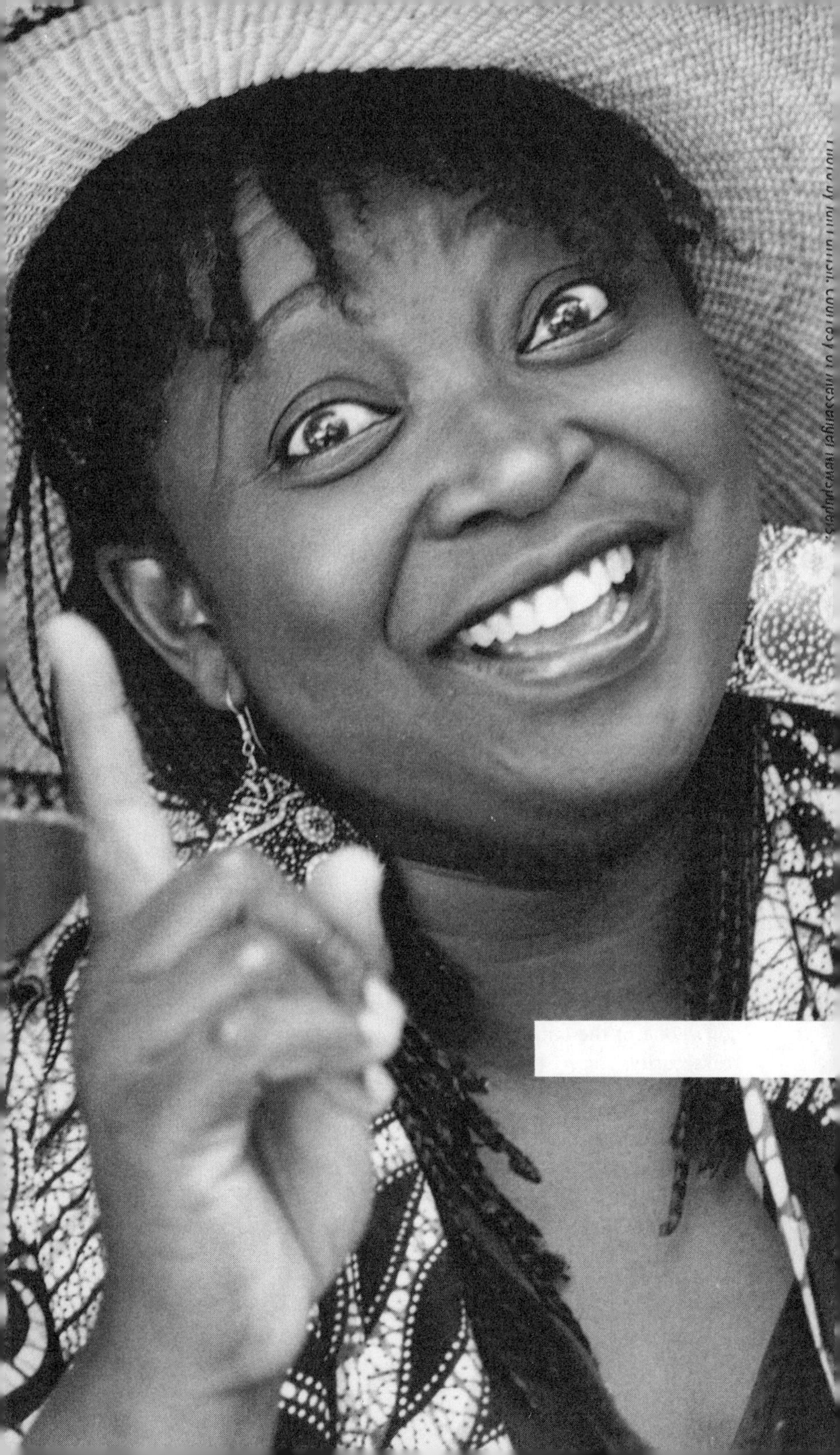

BUILDING CULTURAL BRIDGES

'I was eighteen before I realised I was black because I had grown up in a culture where colour had never been an issue. It had never been significant to describe people specifically in terms of colour. There was class prejudice but not colour prejudice.'

DORINDA HAFNER
Performer

The man in the grey suit hesitated and then cleared his throat a few times. Sitting upright in his chair, he fixed his gaze beyond the couple on the other side of his desk and began.

'I would be negligent in my duty if I were not to warn you ...' but before he had even completed the sentence, Dorinda knew what would follow. His nervousness and red face had given him away. She flashed him a smile of encouragement, feeling she had to help him in his uncomfortable task. Meanwhile her husband Julian, sitting beside her, looked perplexed.

'This is a sensitive issue but I have to approach it sooner or later,' continued the man. 'I hope you don't mind me saying this but ... mmm ... we have a few racial problems in Australia. Now, if you were intending to go to New South Wales, or even Victoria, I'd say that your wife's problems, your family's problems, with relation to colour, would be diminished somewhat. But South Australia ... mmm ... that's a worry ... South Australia.' He paused, then, 'The good news is that it's not Queensland, Tasmania or the Northern Territory. The situation is even worse there,' he added.

'Well, if there are problems in Australia to do with race, I'm probably the best person to go there,' offered Dorinda.

'Madam, many have been there before you and not made it.'

'That's true, but I dare say Queen Boadicea would say the same thing,' she chuckled.

Today Dorinda Hafner sits in her Adelaide home and laughs heartily at the memory of that immigration interview held at London's Australia House in 1977.

'It was a serious conversation but there were lighter moments. He was dealing with a very serious issue and didn't know how to approach it, so I felt I had to make him feel comfortable and realise that for me it's no big deal to talk about blackness. After all, I *am* black. The moment he started clearing his throat, looking sheepish, and going bright red, I knew he was going to talk about colour. But I made him laugh with my comment about Queen Boadicea and then he told us he was from Tasmania. I thought that was amusing.'

Dorinda did not find the content of the conversation completely unexpected. 'I knew about the racist image Australia had but as soon as he started talking, it was like a red rag to a bull. Had he told us Australia did *not* have any problems and that it was all nice and quiet, I would have thought, I'm not going, what's the point? I would have been less determined to get there. But the moment he said there are difficulties to do with race, then I thought that's *exactly* the place I want to go to. Because they need someone like me, who has a positive self-image and whose whole attitude to life is optimistic.'

Dorinda explains she came to Australia as the 'appendage of a white man'. Her psychiatrist husband Julian was taking up the position of senior staff specialist and senior lecturer at the Flinders Medical Centre in Adelaide. But far from taking a minor role as someone else's attachment, she has forged for herself status and a successful career in her own right. Originally trained as an ophthalmic nurse and then a state registered nursing sister and dispensing optician, she now brings joy and light to many through her public image.

Well known to thousands of Australian schoolchildren as a versatile and delightful performer, Dorinda has revealed her culinary skills all over the world with the television series and accompanying book, *A Taste of Africa*, and her home-entertaining business *Cuisine Africaine*, and has charmed theatre, radio and television audiences with her acting and storytelling skills. She refuses to be categorised in her work – to be described as a performer, an author or a cook – 'that's a Western concept; in Ghana and in Africa you are brought up with a whole range of expertise' – and so she describes herself instead as 'a kaleidoscope of vibrancy' and 'a walking mural of arts'.

To be with Dorinda is to experience the phenomenal and boundless amounts of energy of which she boasts, to enjoy her quick wit and wicked sense of humour, and – most of all – to revel in her zest and enthusiasm. 'I love life,' she pronounces. 'My epitaph will read, "Here lies Dorinda. She has lived. She has lived for herself and for others." For I *have* lived, I have experienced life in all its forms – its atrocities, its romanticism, its pain, its laughter, its tears and its excitement.'

She chooses, however, to dwell on the positive aspects and is passionate about her undertaking to channel any negativity, including racism, towards a positive end. And the means by which she does this is – in one simple word – fun. Whether she is acting, singing, cooking or storytelling, the aim is the same. 'I feel like I am in Australia with a mission and, although there have certainly been improvements in the seventeen years I have been here, I haven't finished my work. People have always said to me, "What's an optician, a dispensing optician, doing in the arts?" And I say, "Because there are so many short-sighted people around and I need to help them see." That is still very true.'

This quest of Dorinda's began soon after the family arrived in Adelaide, in November 1977, when her two young children, James and Nuala, were teased and bullied at kindergarten because of their colour. 'Other kids would throw things at them, hit them or snatch toys away saying, "You're black, you shouldn't have this." One time a child smeared brown and black paint all over his piece of paper, making a mess, and said to them, "This is horrible, just like you." I happened to be there at the time and I was astounded that a four-year-old should have that attitude.

'I spoke with the kindergarten director, who had noticed what was happening and was wondering what to do about it, and she invited me to come and talk to the parents.' But this was to be far more than a talk. Invitations were sent out for an African night. 'I brought along music, food, artifacts and fabrics,' says Dorinda. 'The parents were welcomed with Ghanaian music playing gently in the background and I spoke to them about the different countries in Africa, sang songs and played music from each part. I explained to them how we as Africans see the rest of the world and especially Australia. Then I brought it closer to Adelaide and talked about my children.

'As all these parents were sitting and looking at me, I said, "You don't look like the sort of people whose kids would pick on somebody because of the way they look – and especially my kids who are not even as dark as me – so why have they been picked on?" They expressed horror at this and of course none of them admitted that it was his or her child, they would never do that. It didn't matter. The point was made.

'Then they ate. I explained the food – different-flavoured chicken pieces, *moi-moi* (a Nigerian savoury bean pâté), traditional banana fritters, a spinach dish with seafood, *jollof* rice – I did a whole spread. I showed them calabash sculptures, bronze, copper and wooden carvings, traditional gold jewellery, and fabrics such as *kente* cloth. It took about three hours and was well worth it. Everyone liked it and wanted more and we decided to do it with other cultures as well. We'd have a Greek night, and Italian, Japanese, Chinese and Irish nights. So we started booking nights and that was a wonderful way of making cross-cultural contacts.'

As she had made her point and initiated communication, Dorinda would have been happy to leave it at that. But her telephone started ringing. 'Within a week, I had offers to go and do the same in other schools.' She did this for three years on a voluntary basis, travelling to metropolitan and country kindergartens and primary schools. 'Nobody paid me and I didn't expect them to. I couldn't afford to cook each time so I reduced the show to include music and games, some dancing and a talk and, whenever possible, a dish or two.'

So it was that Africa-in-Schools was formed, successful from the start. 'After I had spoken to the parents at kindergarten, there was a dramatic change in the children's behaviour towards James and Nuala, a truly dramatic change, and that's when I knew I was onto something. It really warmed my heart. I suddenly realised that I could do some good and change what could have been a negative energy – and anger and frustration on my part at having my kids bullied and feeling helpless. I could channel that into something positive. My aim was to build cultural bridges, to eliminate prejudice through understanding, breaking down those barriers through positive contact. I wanted to kill prejudice with kindness.'

Dorinda's ninety-minute show proved so popular that it became almost a full-time commitment as she soon found herself performing three days a week, travelling as far afield as Murray Bridge, Gawler or Kadina. 'Then the Education Department asked me to join their artist-in-schools program and so I was able to make a small charge.'

At the start of her show, the children are curious but somewhat shy and wary. 'At the beginning, they sit far away from me – "the big black lady" – and even hold onto one another for support but by the end they are all over me, dancing with me and hugging me. They ask me all sorts of questions. "Why are your palms white and the rest of you black? Do you use fingers or cutlery to eat? Did you learn English here? Do you sleep on a bed in a proper house?" I don't get offended – why am I there if not to answer these questions?'

Far from taking affront, Dorinda responds fully, even to the extent of pricking her finger to prove to the children she has red blood! 'I've taken it for granted that I am black, a woman, and capable, and now I'm having to realise that a lot of people find me odd or different. I feel it's my duty to provide information so that we can operate from the same vantage point.'

It is also vital to Dorinda that such work is done with children, for she believes the hope for the future lies here. 'I have been able to keep my pride and self-respect, despite what I have been through, because it was ingrained in me from childhood. It is just as the Jesuits said, about having a child before the age of seven and then having the adult.' She therefore believes that it is vital to talk to young children before racist attitudes, as clearly demonstrated in her children's kindergarten, become permanently etched or ingrained in their minds.

※

In Dorinda's case, those early years in Ghana, West Africa, helped form her strong character. 'I was born in Ahenboboano, in the Asante New Town district of Kumasi, just 200 metres from the Ashanti palace, close to my ancestral roots on my mother's side. My mother had been born in Accra and came north to Kumasi to work. People thought she was from the Ga tribe and didn't realise she was partly of royal descent. Princess Yiadom from the Ashanti royal family was my great-great-grandmother.'

Dorinda's mother Elizabeth, a district nurse and midwife, ran Thelma's Maternity Home together with its founder, her cousin Thelma, and her father was a theatre superintendent who later trained and worked as a bush doctor.

A natural performer – 'a little show-off really' – Dorinda would dance for the royal wives, from the age of three. 'I had a broad forehead, an admirable trait of the Ashanti royals. Some playfully accused my mother, who was midwife to the palace, of stealing one of the royal babies! The royal family took a liking to me and wanted to educate me; they trained me in traditional dance and performance. They dressed me, putting clay and charcoal on my body and then adorning me in *kente* cloth, handwoven silk, heavy gold jewellery, family heirlooms, and leather sandals, for tribal dancing. I absolutely adored this. I went to school with one of the royal children, Gladys Prempeh, and spent many hours at the Kumasi Cultural Centre watching dances and sometimes joining in. But there was no chance of me taking this up professionally – you do this as part of your culture, not for money.'

But there was no stopping the exuberant youngster. 'When my mother and cousin were busy consulting, I thought the other antenatal patients were bored so I would entertain them. I would come out into the waiting room and put the radio on. I'd sing along to the songs I knew and dance to the others – Glenn Miller, rock and roll. I'd come out with a little saucepan but I'd put it upside-down because I thought it was a bit rude to start collecting the money first. Then I'd buy myself little things like sweets and ice creams, give some to my little cousin or save up for something special like a pair of fancy shoelaces.'

Was her mother cross when she found out? 'Cross is not the word. She used to be absolutely ropeable!'

Performing was in Dorinda's blood and at other, more suitable family occasions, Elizabeth would encourage her enthusiastic daughter. 'When friends came to the house, I'd be asked to show the latest dance steps. When I was a little older I used to talk to my Aunt Sophie, who was very understanding and sympathetic. I said I wanted to go on the stage and perform and she told me that respectable young ladies did not do that, only prostitutes, and that I had to study hard and get into a good profession.'

A precocious child, Dorinda was reading by the age of four and so her parents decided to send her to school early. 'This is an early memory, being taken to school in Accra. I remember seeing all this grass and wondering why no one was cutting it because there could

Three-year-old Dorinda in Kumasi.

Dorinda, aged nine years, in Ashanti New Town.

be snakes there, and hearing all these children and thinking I would not be able to cope with all this shrieking. They seemed to be thoroughly disorderly.

'"Don't they know they shouldn't shout like that all day?" I asked the teacher, who was really taken aback. She asked me what my name was and I thought, "This lady's really silly, my mother has just introduced me to her." So I condescendingly told her, "Charity Dorinda Naa Tsenkua Bannerman Addy." "Oh dear, that's far too long a name for me to write in my roll call book," she replied. So I opened her book and said, "Look, there are lots of lines. You can write Charity Dorinda Naa on one line and Tsenkua Bannerman Addy below and then you have my name." I remember her whispering to my mother, "Oh my God, you've got your hands full with this one. She's far too bright, she'd better start next week."'

The first-born – 'I was an only child until the age of six' – Dorinda feels she was brought up to be highly responsible and to be an example to her siblings, Susan, Lynda and Sam, six, eight and eleven years younger than herself. 'It was a big responsibility and

I didn't have room to be naughty. I wish I had now.' Instead she was a quiet and studious child, in complete contrast to her adult persona. 'I was also high-spirited and my mother was a strict disciplinarian. Most of the time I was quiet. I didn't really have a lot of time to play – I had to go to the market, help with chores and then study. But I also danced. I danced for everybody.'

Dorinda's home environment was multilingual, with family members being fluent in English, Ga, Ashanti and Fante. 'We would respond in the language in which the conversation was started. I was brought up with a healthy self-esteem, with confidence and with the attitude that I could do and achieve anything.' Here, unlike other African nations, being female was not seen as a disadvantage. Far from it. The Ashanti culture is matrilineal.

'The most important person at that time in the land was the Queen Mother, and we had women judges, chief justices, doctors, architects and politicians. Ghana is very progressive and has been a leader among nations for a long time. Matrilineage is part of traditional Ashanti and other tribal culture.' Women were encouraged to contribute, Dorinda says. 'If you stayed at home and relied on your husband to bring in the money, without making an effort to have some sort of business on the side, the community would frown on that sort of behaviour.' And she has been highly impressed with how resourceful these women have been.

Visiting Ghana for the filming of her cookery series *A Taste of Africa* in 1993, she came across a group who had invented an oil-extraction machine. 'We have a saying in West Africa, "Give an idea to a man and you give it to an individual, give an idea to a woman and you give it to a whole nation." I was so impressed by these enterprising women.'

Dorinda enjoyed a good relationship with both her parents. Her father was away a lot, due to the peripatetic nature of his work, but when home they would enjoy their time together. 'He's a very funny man, a natural comic and impersonator, and tells wicked jokes. I think my sense of humour and storytelling skills come from him.'

Dorinda's mother gave her a sense of confidence, impressing on her daughter that nothing was beyond her reach. 'It only depended on how much effort and hard work I was willing to put into it. She used to tell me, "*Ahwenepa Nkasa*", which means good beads don't talk. This refers to the beads women traditionally wear around their hips and tuck their underwear into. Good-quality beads don't make a sound when you walk. In other words, "empty barrels make the most noise". My mother was also fond of sayings in Latin, which she had studied at school. She would often say, "*Regimentus opportunitatum*" – make use of your opportunities, or hate what you do but never give up, because that experience might build up your character, make you a stronger person.'

Dorinda's background includes Scottish and Dutch ancestry. 'My mother's maiden name is Bannerman, her ancestors helped shape Ghana in political and legal fields, and my paternal side is a mixture of Ga, English and Dutch.' Both her parents were trailblazers in their respective medical fields. 'My father became a first-aid worker when the British doctors were sent off to Burma during the war. After training overseas, he helped establish the huge Central Sterile Supply Department in Ghana, which reduced post-operative infections dramatically.' Working as theatre superintendent at Accra's major hospital, he later trained as a bush doctor and designed his own instruments, which included disposable bamboo scalpels. A West German manufacturing firm subsequently used some of his designs for instruments.

'He went into private practice with a medical doctor and has been "retired" for about twenty years. He's eighty-four now and has set up a little room at the end of the garden where he consults daily, on anything from stitching people up, to medicals or circumcisions for boys.'

Elizabeth became president of the Ashanti region Midwives Union and worked hard, using both education and encouragement, to stop the practice of female circumcision. 'My parents don't believe in this practice. I must emphasise that only a very small proportion of Ghanaian tribes, especially from the north, circumcise girls. Generally this probably happens more in north and east Africa. The circumcision takes place at a certain age, either at ten days or in other tribes at puberty, and so my mother believed if she hung onto the girls long enough to educate the parents, then they would be safe. She would explain to the mothers how septicaemia was killing some of the babies and how those that survived would, like their mothers, have difficulties when giving birth. She tried hard to convince them that their daughters did not need to suffer in this way.'

Elizabeth would keep the babies until the ten-day deadline had passed. 'Their mothers would come in and feed them and my mother would insist they needed to remain with her, that they were jaundiced or something. She looked after them well and the mothers were happy because they were able to get a bit of rest at home.'

Growing up in Kumasi, the second largest city in Ghana, was for Dorinda a noisy and extremely colourful experience; tradition was mixed in with modern customs. 'At all times in the street, you'd see very chic dressing alongside very traditional. You'd see a woman in a gathered skirt with a belt and high-heeled shoes, with straightened hair, big shiny earrings, a watch and a little handbag, next to a woman in the wraparound garment – the Ghanaian *ntoma* – draped over one shoulder rather like a Roman toga, with leather sandals, with short hair shaved at the bottom and dyed with yoomo-pomade, which is black.'

Her family lived in a two-storeyed brick house with a domestic staff and a nanny. 'We were well-off by Ghanaian standards and it was normal for the middle classes to have servants – someone to do the laundry, a manservant and two women who helped with the cooking and cleaning. My mother brought us up so that when they had days off, we would take over their duties and do for them what they did for us.'

Dorinda's childhood, like her surroundings, were a mixture of traditional and modern ways and beliefs. 'My mother was Church of England and my father Methodist. We'd go to church on Sundays wearing Western clothes – smart dresses and frilly socks, polished shoes, hats, handbags, and sometimes I'd even wear white gloves. Then I'd come home and change out of my Sunday best into wraparound cloth, *ntoma*, with *kaba*, matching blouse.' She later attended Wesley Girls High School, a Methodist boarding school, with its strict discipline and religious background. 'I was very lonely and very unhappy initially but I couldn't complain as I was the one that insisted my parents send me there. I thought it would be really exciting living away from home but found I suddenly had to leap from a very free environment into a very regimented one. I had a very eclectic childhood and I was exposed to the broadest range of people – from very traditional to those in the public eye, from professionals to village people. It was not a narrow upbringing by any means, far from it, and I felt like a sponge soaking up different cultures. It's a wonder I'm not schizophrenic, what with the debating society, Shakespeare and scripture at school and traditional storytelling and tribal dancing at home!'

Her interest in ophthalmology stemmed from an unfortunate incident in her childhood. 'My paternal grandfather was a merchant seaman who got river blindness. As a child I could not understand how he could be blind when his eyes were open. I thought he was just pretending. So one day, when I went to visit him, I rearranged the furniture in the lounge, including his favourite chair. I watched as he came in and kept bumping into things. Then he went to sit down, missed the chair and fell, hurting his back very badly. He had to be in traction for weeks. I got a hiding and felt so guilty, I vowed when I was older I would do something to help people who were blind or who had poor vision.'

When show business proved not to be a realistic option, Dorinda persuaded her reluctant parents to let her study nursing in England – they wanted her to stay in Ghana. England came as a shock for the shy eighteen-year-old. She was suddenly and abruptly forced to confront racism in all its forms. While some encounters were humorous ones, others left her staggered by the insidious prejudice of a hostile society.

'When I first saw a white Santa Claus in a department store, I stood there gazing in astonishment. In Kumasi, when we used to go as children to Kingsway, the equivalent of Harrods, Santa was always black. Then I thought, well I suppose they must come in different colours. I had seen white Santa Clauses, depicted on Christmas cards from family and friends overseas, but I thought these were caricatures.'

Another incident was more personal. 'I had gone to Marks and Spencers to buy some flesh-coloured underwear and when I was unable to find some, I asked the shop assistant to help me. "Here you are," she said, picking up an item. As she lifted it up, my face came side to side with the knickers. She looked at me and then at the salmon-pink underwear and we both laughed. I had come in automatically expecting to see chocolate-brown underwear. While we were giggling, a little girl stared at me and said to her mother, "Look at the lady with the black face." Instinctively I turned to the shop assistant and asked, "Has my mascara run? Do I have something black on my face?" "No," she smiled, "but *you* are black." I suddenly thought it must be so. I'd never thought about it.

'So I rushed home, stood in front of the mirror and then took off all my clothes. I wanted to get a full look at myself. "I'm actually brown. Why do they say black?" I thought that was a strange expression; I would not describe people as white but as pink. I wrote a letter to my mother. "Why didn't you tell me that I'm black?" I admonished her as a joke. But I was also serious – I wrote explaining that here they looked upon colour as something derogatory ... When I thought of my nursing colleagues, it never occurred to me to think of them in terms of colour. They were Sue and Christine and so on.

'I was eighteen before I realised I was black because I had grown up in a culture where colour had never been an issue. It had never been significant to describe people specifically in terms of colour. There was class prejudice but not colour prejudice. Even at Wesley Girls High School where most of our teachers were white, we didn't see this as odd. We just didn't think along those lines.'

She soon learned that things were very different in England. Acceptance into a general nursing course was the first hurdle. Although her educational qualifications exceeded those required for entry, she was rejected several times before finally obtaining a place at a London teaching hospital. 'They told me I was the first black to train there as a state registered nurse – they usually trained as enrolled nurses – and so they would be monitoring my progress with the utmost interest. By now I was becoming aware that my blackness could work for or against me. And I was never one to resist a challenge.'

Dorinda accepted her lot stoically. 'I got given all the bedpans and was put on the more difficult wards. I was informed that I had to get 80 per cent or more in my exams while the others passed with 50 per cent. They said, "You have to work harder; your people always do."' Far from discouraging Dorinda, this spurred her on. 'I was homesick and wrote letters to my family three times a week but

I never thought of chucking it in. I remembered those words of my mother's, "Hate it but finish it." I arrived in England very shy and naive and became confident through my experiences. I realised I had to stand up and fight for myself.'

Yet then, as now, she did so with good humour – using her artistic talents to organise a review for hospital and staff, with herself as compère. And academically she was one of the few to pass their examinations with credit. 'That freaked everyone out, especially as I had had marks taken off for handwriting – the prejudice really amazed me.'

She became popular – 'I kept killing prejudice with kindness' – and so endeared herself to her superiors that she was given the responsibility of taking over the eye ward when the sister-in-charge fell sick. Some patients, however, were not as impressed by Dorinda as her superiors. 'Take your black hands off me!' one yelled and Dorinda was delighted to hear the response by another nurse and to know she had finally been accepted: 'She is the most qualified person here so either you let those black hands put those drops in your eyes or you do without.'

Acceptance maybe she had earned but there were other cultural differences. When a boyfriend greeted her with a bunch of flowers, she reacted in horror. 'I opened the door to see him standing there with a bunch of roses in his hand. How dare he! I refused to take them. "Put them on your own grave," I told him and he was most upset. You see, in Ghana flowers are only for funerals. They are never given as gifts. We give flowers to the dead and food to the living.'

The couple were able to reconcile their differences and three years later in 1973 Dorinda married him. He was British psychiatrist, Julian Hafner.

While still studying, she simultaneously took up a modelling career. 'I was very slim, with an eighteen-inch waist. The hospital sent me for three-monthly X-rays and put me on a fattening diet; they thought coming from an African country I must be carrying tuberculosis or something. They could not accept I was naturally thin. My friends kept telling me to try modelling and they gave me a six-week course as a Christmas present. I graduated in second place and landed a photographic modelling contract. I did magazine and television commercials, record covers, and I was plastered over billboards. Of course I was modelling under a pseudonym, moonlighting on my days off. I was meant to be married to nursing and I was in a very precarious position.'

By now her face was well known to consumers of Right Guard deodorant, Heineken beer and Jamaican Blue Mountain coffee. 'People would look up at the billboard and say, "That lady looks amazingly like you." "You're the third person to have told me that," I'd reply. "I must get to meet her one day".'

※

Her business card simply says Dorinda – the name that her mother told her comes from the Greek and means 'gift of God'. Dorinda sees herself as a determined woman, a woman determined to 'grasp life firmly with both hands and squeeze it for every positive drop'. Tonight, however, she is grasping the delicious food at a Thai restaurant – with cutlery rather than hands – and enjoying it in every aspect: the flavour and texture and, most importantly, the aesthetic appeal. For, in Dorinda's opinion, 'Food should tempt all the senses and amaze the eye as well as the palate, so that you don't know whether to eat it or paint it!'

Her meal adequately satisfies all such criteria and the staff are delighted, if a little overawed, by this effervescent customer who jokes readily with them and happily joins in conversation with other diners who recognise her. This is the public Dorinda Hafner, 'a big black woman, all 117 kilograms of me. I'm not embarrassed about my size. Back where I come from, this is seen as a sign of affluence,' she jokes.

Yet there is also a quiet side to her, seen only by a few, when at home with her children and a few close friends she can be the real Dorinda, the quiet Dorinda. These times of solitude are vital to her, to balance the public image, the image that is public property. 'I dislike the fact that I'm still seen as an exotic curiosity by some, that people will approach me and have no qualms about touching my hair. I'm a forty-seven-year-old woman, for goodness sake,' she says, pushing aside her long intricately plaited braids. She is protective of her children and, the more popular and well known she becomes with the public, the more retiring and reclusive she becomes in her private life. Away from the public gaze she is calm, even subdued, enjoying her increasingly rare breaks at home. 'In Ghana we don't go away for our holidays,' she explains, 'we relax at home and visit friends. I can't understand this compulsion to get away. From what? My home is my domain.'

Her son James, now a twenty-year-old medical student, describes life with Dorinda as 'being on a roller coaster, riding the big emotional highs and then sweeping down to the big lows as well. She lives a twenty-five-hour day, sometimes sleeping for three or four hours, and you know when she gets up, she'll need some support – whether it's just a little note to say, "I love you, Mum, have a good day," or whether it's doing the washing or taking out the rubbish bins. That's a side of her a lot of people don't see and it makes me angry sometimes that people always expect her to be happy and full of energy, that they always take from her and don't give anything in return. So I see that as part of our family's role, part of my role and my sister's role, to give her the emotional and practical support that other people don't provide.

'In Australia I think black people are still a novelty and, if you're not Aboriginal, then some people will either envy you or worship you. But there is still discrimination – people feel they can always approach a black person; you don't often get given a lot of status. Australians are a little more forthright in their dislike of you and strangely enough that's much better. It's easier to deal with someone who hates you and says so. Racism as a visible opponent is much easier to combat than racism that is less open or implied.'

Dorinda was prepared for racism in Australia, as was made clear in the immigration interview, but she was not prepared for the extent of it. 'It is so overt here. People will imitate you in pubs and call you nigger. My friends have been called nigger lovers. I've been pushed and shoved in the street and told blacks should not be driving cars. I've been told I speak very good English, and asked did I go to college to learn? And, when I went to buy a sewing machine, the man told me, "You'll love this model. It's very simple to use, all the Aborigines buy it." I had not anticipated this level of overt racism and neither had I anticipated the level of ignorance – of international affairs, of other countries and cultures and even of this country.

'I reacted in one of two ways: by dealing with the situation comically and sending people up – I'd encroach on their personal space and hug them, "How nice to meet you", and etiquette would get the better of them – or by a supercilious attitude. My background and education gave me an inherent confidence. Yet when people used to tell me to go home, I used to think it was too late, and anyway, where was that home? The children were settled here and would have to start again culturally in Ghana. Sometimes I used to think perhaps it would have been better to have remained in England. There were no role models for my children here. Racism exists there certainly, but not so openly and the children would have had peer support. Here they are alone.'

Now a single woman – Dorinda and Julian separated in 1987 – Dorinda sees family happiness as far more meaningful than career success. 'The support and love of a family, having a platform of care, shelter and love from which to launch one's foray into life is, for me, the most important of all. Success to me is being able to shut my door at the end of the day and say, I have done some good things. My yardstick for success is quite small.'

※

Dorinda today is a far cry from the young woman who arrived in Adelaide eighteen years ago. Juggling her various commitments, determined not to be typecast, she makes increasingly adventurous sallies – into print, film and performance. Writing books, preparing for the second series of *A Taste of Africa*, she still finds time to fly to Canada and America for a few days to entertain schoolchildren with her storytelling skills at national festivals.

But in 1977 Dorinda, despite her protestations, was not expecting to find work. 'We agonised over coming because it seemed that I was expected to be a housewife, not that there is anything wrong with that, but there were other things I wanted to pursue. I was trained as a general nursing sister, an ophthalmic nurse and dispensing optician and wanted to work in that field but the immigration officer told me Australia had enough nurses and that there was no such thing as a dispensing optician here.'

They had decided to leave England for the sake of Julian's career – 'he decided the National Health Service was not serving our purpose' – and for their daughter's health: 'Nuala had respiratory problems as a baby and we thought a warmer climate might help, which it did.' Expecting an outdoor lifestyle with barbecues and trips to the beach, they parted with their warm clothing. 'I gave away a stunning winter coat, thinking Australia was hot and that I wouldn't need it,' laughs Dorinda. 'I saw myself not working initially, but spending time with the children. So I invested in a number of books with black people's imagery and role models. I thought there would not be many black people in Australia and so I didn't want my kids growing up feeling negative about themselves and thinking that white people were the only role models. I wanted them to feel they could achieve anything they chose.' Looking back, she is well pleased with those purchases for she found nothing equivalent in Australia at the time.

While Julian had also had offers of work in the United States and New Zealand, the family chose Australia 'for the challenge – it was a place neither of us had visited before' and it came as a surprise. 'I expected the buildings to look more weatherbeaten, something like colonial Africa or the India of the Raj, with verandahs, boiling hot sun and people in hats and desert boots. That's the sort of clichéd nonsense that was going on in my mind. Instead I saw brick houses and Italian-style villas, modern dwellings, tin roofs and some verandahs but I thought the buildings would be much higher.'

When the plane landed first in Sydney, Dorinda was both shocked and amused at what happened next. 'I'd been sitting in an aircraft for hours and now suddenly two men, in safari suits with knee-high socks, went down the aisle with arms outstretched and a can in each hand, spraying. I thought they looked very silly, imitating an aircraft inside an aircraft, with what looked like smoke spewing out from the engines. The visual image amused me enormously.' Finding it peculiar that the men were wearing long socks in the heat, Dorinda decided one of them was unwell. For why else would he be wearing a vest under his shirt?

As the family changed planes for their flight to Adelaide,

Dorinda discovered the Australians in Sydney were not very healthy. 'When I asked someone where we were to collect our luggage he asked very slowly, "W-h-i-c-h f-l-i-g-h-t w-e-r-e y-o-u o-n?" Poor man, he obviously had a speech impediment. At customs, I was standing with the cases and the children and I was asked whether we were immigrating. But the i-m-m-i-g-r-a-t-i-n-g was really hard for him to say. Another one, I thought: they're obviously not very well here at all.

'Then Julian came up to me and suddenly this man's speech impediment disappeared when he asked Julian to open the cases. So then it dawned on me that maybe it was *me* that was making them speak like that. Obviously I had some electromagnetic force around my person that caused them to react in that way! I was shell-shocked with all the travel but shocked all the same. I thought Australians knew better than that.'

Communication continued to thwart the Hafners, in one form or another. Shortly after their arrival in Adelaide, Julian received an invitation that almost caused an argument. 'It was for a Chrissy Barbie and I thought it was from a Chris and a Barbie, two women inviting my husband out,' Dorinda shrieks with laughter. 'We'd barely been here five minutes and the man was already off someplace! Julian didn't understand what it meant either and he told me he had been given it at the Department of Psychiatry and that maybe it was to do with some social gathering. "Who are Chris and Barbie?" I demanded. "Are they work colleagues? Are they staff?" He said he didn't know and we had to ring up the hospital to figure it out. What a relief to discover it was just a Christmas barbecue.'

Dorinda felt isolated for her first few months in Australia. 'And I was surprised that Adelaide was full of white faces because London has people from all over the world. I recall coming back from playgroup one day, sitting the children down on the carpet and saying, "We're going to have to work very hard, you know kids, because we're on our own now. There are no other people around here like us." I remember saying it out loud.'

Not only did she feel isolated but also unwelcome. 'I told Julian one day I could no longer take the children to playgroup because as I walked in, I heard someone say, "There's a wog going around."

Like me, he thought this was very rude, since wog is a derogatory term for a black person in England. He told me to complain. The next day, I sneezed and one of the mothers said, "Oh, you've got a wog." I looked at her. "What do you mean? I *am* a wog," I replied.'

Little things made Dorinda feel uncomfortable. 'There were no black hairpins for black hair, no hairdressers and no make-up for black people. The other thing I remember from that era is that every time I opened my mouth, people were surprised. Now, in retrospect, I realise that they didn't expect a black person to speak such good English, to be so articulate and well-read.' She shakes her head sadly. 'It's still happening, to this day. When people look on someone from Africa, they see either the exotic or the mendicant. They may see you as a strange creature from some far-off place they dream of visiting or else they see you as poor, needy and uneducated. It is not often that they equate education with Africa.'

Dorinda works towards changing this perception. At public talks, she tells astonished audiences, 'I'm the result of your Red Cross parcels and overseas aid. I am the product of one of those generous acts of giving, one of the fortunate ones,' and she goes on to talk about the importance of communication between the recipients and the givers.

Now a public figure, Dorinda is often asked to speak to groups. Yet she almost missed out on the career which has given her such a prominent profile. Shortly after arriving in Adelaide and still knowing very few people, she and her husband were invited to a party. 'A man looked over at me and said, "That's the face I want in my movie." I thought it was a wonderfully original pick-up line. So when he told me his name was Bruce Beresford and that he was a film director, I put out my hand saying, "My name is Sophia Loren and I'm pleased to meet you," thinking the whole thing was a big joke.

'We chatted and he told me about his films and the one that he was now making, *Breaker Morant*. He wanted me to be in it. I was convinced he was having me on – I had never heard of Bruce Beresford. So, when he said he'd get a script to me, I just laughed and agreed. "Your friends are amazing," I told the hostess. "Someone just tried to pick me up. He said his name was Bruce Beresford and he wants me in his movie." "He's one of the leading lights in our film industry," she told me. I was so embarrassed!'

All was not lost. Dorinda was sent the script and had a role as a featured extra. On the set of *Breaker Morant*, she met Bruno Knez of Adelaide's *La Mama* theatre and as a result she staged an African cultural show. 'I found people from Kenya, Sudan, Nigeria, South Africa, Lesotho and Ghana and we put together a ninety-minute show of dance and song.' The show, choreographed by Dorinda, was an instant hit as part of the Adelaide Fringe Festival and its two-week run was extended to a month. 'Then we got more bookings and decided to formally set up the African Dance Troupe. We toured widely interstate, to city and country areas, even as far as the Northern Territory.'

Her career started to take off, with appearances on ABC television and radio and in theatre. She choreographed for Magpie Theatre and the Margaret Walker School of Dance and appeared in *Akwanso – Fly South* for the 1988 Adelaide Festival.

While this new career of hers blossomed, nursing and optics faded into the background. 'I had applied to work at Flinders and had kept in regular contact but it was three years before a position became available. After a short stint on the combined surgery and eye ward – as the only eye-trained nursing sister – they wanted to transfer me to men's medical as part of the regular rotation. That seemed ridiculous, not to make use of my ophthalmic skills, and so I resigned.' She was always, however, the centre of attention. 'I felt like an exhibit. Staff would come from other parts of the hospital to look at me, this black nursing sister in a white uniform. "Keep looking today," I'd tell them, "because the price will go up tomorrow," and they would get very embarrassed.

'People also used to stare at me a lot in the streets in those days. That has all changed over the years. Now when people look at me and approach me in public, it's for a completely different reason. I'm now nationally recognisable, a television personality, and they feel happy that I should know them or talk to them. I am probably an extreme example of somebody different – I'm black, I'm big, I'm short and I'm single – everything that Western society defines as negative about women. So I feel it is a wonderful achievement to be able to challenge those stereotypes and help break them down.'

The breakdown of her marriage in the process was distressing to her. 'We both suffered enormously. You don't end seventeen years of your life with someone without a lot of pain. There are a lot of women like me who went off to Britain in the 1950s, 1960s and early 1970s and, as part of our need to be accepted and to succeed, we buried our African-ness and took on a pastiche of British-ness. It is only as you get older that you realise you need to be more and more of your own person. What finished my marriage off was when I decided to pursue my deep buried self, to get into performance, read African literature and be in touch with my heritage. Julian and I have a good relationship now but it took time; I was angry for many years.'

Now she is poised on the brink of international stardom. Her television series *A Taste of Africa* is being screened by London's Channel Four and has been sold to Canada, New Zealand, Hong Kong, Malaysia, Egypt and Bahrain. There are more books in the offing for England, America and Australia.

Meantime, Dorinda has undergone another image change. Her long braids are gone, replaced by closely cropped dyed hair. 'I like to be my own person. It seems that every other performing black person has braids these days. Besides, I can't afford the time or money – $250 and twelve hours. I prefer my hair short and chic and I've always wanted to go ginger!'

Her home may now be Australia but Dorinda visits her parents in Ghana regularly. What she misses about Ghana is the good humour. 'I miss that ability to laugh – to have a really good belly laugh, to laugh at our misfortunes, to use laughter as medicine. People here are too frightened to share. I miss that sharing.'

Sharing is something she does much of. In recent years she threw her considerable energy into an innovative and highly successful venture, *Cuisine Africaine*, providing Adelaideans with an evening of 'tasty bits and spicy tales'. Transporting her delicious food to the comfort of their homes, she entertains with Ashanti battle cries and traditional dancing after the sumptuous feast. Audience participation is the order of the night. 'Why should I have all the fun?' she teases, her brown eyes twinkling and her husky voice encouraging the diners.

Much as she loves Australia, her adopted country, Dorinda does not feel truly accepted. 'I have Australian citizenship and consider myself an African–Australian. Australians won't let me be Australian and that's my frustration. Every time I say I'm from Australia, they say, "No, but originally?" We are constantly being told by politicians to think of ourselves as Australians but the public won't let us.'

She is very grateful to the immigration officer at Australia House who had warned her about racism. 'That man did his job brilliantly and I would take my hat off to him if I saw him today. He was absolutely right. There were changes that I had to start effecting. Racism continues to live and breathe in Australia, in all strata of society,' she concludes, 'and I continue to fight it with humour.'

These are changes she is still working on, even though she says attitudes have mellowed in the years she has been in Australia. 'Many years ago if you put garlic in a dish, people thought you'd gone foreign. Now many restaurants of different nationalities have opened up. When people start eating, they start asking and learning about that culture. You can use food as a medium – you can start to change people's attitudes through their taste buds. And the arrival of the black American basketballers, now the envy of many, has improved the image of black people.'

The cultural bridges she is forging are still uppermost in her mind, an altruistic aim she admits, but one she considers to be of vital importance. 'The world is only a small place so let's make it a better place in which to live. If we speak a common language of humanity, hopefully we will fight less and share more. Altruism is not dead.'

After all her experiences, Dorinda now considers herself a mixture of cultures, 'born and bred in Ghana, extended and advanced in England, and matured and artistically nurtured in Australia – just like a fine cultured cheese', she grins. And just like that fine cheese, the ingredients and influences have complemented each other to produce an outstanding result.

Dorinda has become a role model now. 'I would like to do more Australian film and television work,' she says, 'as we don't see nearly as many black faces on the electronic media as there are in the community. My presence would remind people that Australia is full of different colours. You don't want a garden of red roses alone – you want pink, yellow and white also, because it's more appealing, more exciting. That's how I see Australia and that's why I get excited when I think of myself as part of that unique picture.'

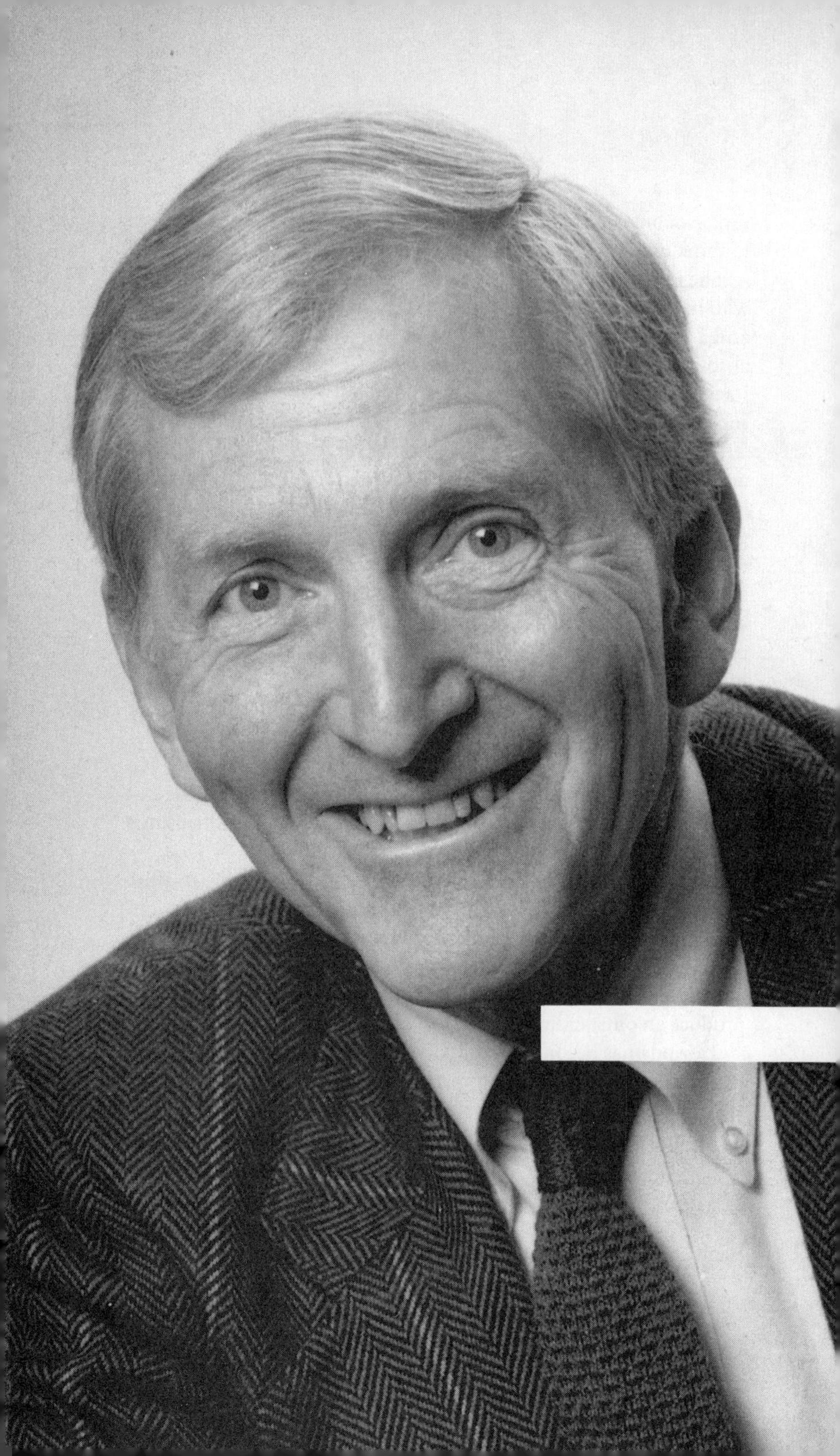

JUST A STORYTELLER

'I knew instantly that this would be my new country. I took one look at the Australian air and light and knew I'd really found the country I wanted.'

BRYCE COURTENAY

Author

The five-year-old boy stood in the playground of the Northern Transvaal school, a paper bag containing a spare pair of pants in one hand. He stood alone in the playground, sheltering from the hot sun in the shade of an old mango tree, for three long hours until someone found him. 'The woman asked, "Who are you?" and I didn't know who I was. And then she took me by one ear, grabbing it between her fingers, and pulled me inside the building.'

That five-year-old boy was Bryce Courtenay and, fifty-five years later, he returned to South Africa to that same school and that same playground with a film crew. 'As soon as I walked through those gates, I just started to shake. Can you imagine, a man of sixty *shaking*,' and he shakes his head in disbelief at the memory. 'I had to tell the film crew to give me ten minutes. I went and sat under the mango tree where I had stood for three hours, and pulled myself together.' The school was at a place called Duiwelskloof. 'It means Devil's Canyon,' says Bryce with an ironic smile.

The scene he has just described is one of the opening moments in his first novel, *The Power of One*, a story he describes as largely autobiographical 'inasmuch as any novel written by a writer about a child would have to be. I don't think you can invent that unless it comes from your own experience.' Written over the space of a year, while he was working full-time in advertising, this was Bryce's trial run as a novelist.

This 'practice' book, *The Power of One*, has spawned a Hollywood film, been translated into eleven languages and sold over three million copies, making Bryce Courtenay, hugely successful advertising man, also Australia's largest-selling author on his first attempt at writing. For Bryce, it has been a long journey from the poverty and hardship of his childhood and formative years in South Africa to the comfortable lifestyle he now leads in Australia. Along the way, he has learned many lessons.

Life, according to Bryce Courtenay, is not about success. Life is about failure. For it is only by failing, he says, that we can succeed. 'You can never succeed from success. Success makes you careful. You have to fail. How else do you learn?' Life is not about having, but about doing. Life is about having a dream and going for it. Life is a journey, an adventure – one that will be hard but one that's fun. 'If it's not hard, it's not fun,' says Bryce, his blue eyes sparkling with exhilaration and excitement as he sits in his eighth-floor office in Sydney – at the top of the building and at the top of his profession.

It is a small office, one that is cluttered with papers, photographs of family and friends, a personal computer. He sits in one corner on a swivel chair, beneath a print of a rugby game played a hundred years ago. He is like the players above him, fit and lean and – as always – enthusiastic and seeking a challenge.

Small in stature, Bryce is big in personality. Dressed simply in a light yellow shirt, dark grey trousers, and a colourful tie, his clothes contrast with his silver-grey hair. He is friendly and welcoming and speaks rapidly, intensely, pausing only to contemplate some important point.

He's just returned from South Africa today – two trips in the last ten days – making a television segment to tie in with the forthcoming elections. Instead of resting, he's put in a full day's work and still has the energy to talk. 'I'm suffering from jetlag,' he announces, and then proceeds to have an eloquent, lucid and in-depth conversation.

A man who believes that each one of us should have three careers – 'the brain is insulted with only one, that's too easy' – he himself has had to make many journeys and turning points. He remembers well his first impression of Australia, in 1958, when he was twenty-five years old.

'I came into Sydney by ship and I remember standing on deck, passing those large limestone cliffs. It was one of those halcyon Sydney mornings when the harbour was like a millpond, the sky was beautiful and I knew instantly that this would be my new country ... It fitted even before I talked to an Australian. Everything about it was right and I've never changed my mind. I took one look at the Australian air and light and I knew I'd really found the country I wanted because it had the same light as South Africa.'

Bryce had come from England, where he had studied after leaving his home in South Africa. 'I'd finished university in England but it was too cold a place for me to settle there. It was not in my bones, not in my blood, and I felt England was an alien place for someone like me who had been brought up in Africa. I had to find a place where the sun shone and the sky was high enough. And English sky is not high enough; it sits on your shoulder and the light is a miasma. It doesn't have a clarity that allows you to see into yourself.'

Prepared to settle in any country in the world other than South Africa, 'because I'd left there under a political cloud and was told I couldn't return', he chose to come to Australia because of a woman, Benita, whom he had met in London. 'She had me promise that I would come out and look at her country. I said I would – but I was just on my way to look, and then move on until I found what was right.' It turned out that Australia was right for Bryce. He and Benita married two years later and they made Sydney their home.

'There was no difficulty in staying: that was an automatic right within the Commonwealth. I think you had to wait three months before taking out citizenship. So I waited three months and a day and it was that precise.'

He admits he did not know a great deal about Australia before he came. 'I'd met a few Australians in London and played rugby against them. I liked their attitude, the fact they were a casual people, an open people. I liked their egalitarian attitude because I came from a country where there were bosses and peasants and I deeply resented that, even as a child. And suddenly I found a country where every man was as good as his master. That intrigued me and I loved it. That certainly wasn't true of England. So it was the very nature of the people and the national characteristics that I found myself attracted to.'

In that first instant of glimpsing Australia, Bryce not only made the decision that this would be his new home and his new country, but he even spotted the exact location of that new home. 'The boat passed a little beach that turned out to be Camp Cove, then another one called Parsley Bay and there was a large white house with a brilliant splash of bougainvillea across it. I thought, "This is it, just like my home country, this is it," and it took me seventeen years to buy that house.'

By the time those seventeen years had passed, Bryce had become a highly successful and wealthy advertising man. His outstanding career saw him win most of the local and international advertising awards. Yet this career had all started after a bad work experience, but it was one that motivated him to use his initiative and perseverence in more rewarding ways.

'I arrived here with sixteen and tuppence and I got a job in a chemical factory in Botany. I had to stir and take care of these huge paint vats and, every half hour, we had to stop and have a pint of milk because of the lead poisoning involved. We had a totally repulsive foreman but I stuck that job for two months. Then, when this chap gave me a really bad time, I threw him into a paint vat. And left.' Television had just started in Australia. 'During the day I watched television frantically. I had trained as a journalist in England but I had also done a course in television at the BBC. So I desperately wrote television commercials, thinking I could do better than the ones I saw on air, and I started selling them to advertising agencies. Then one day, in fact on the same day, two agencies offered me jobs as a copywriter.

Faced with this difficult and important decision, Bryce made his choice merely by flipping a coin. He ended up working for McCann Erikson – then the world's largest advertising agency – and five years later became the youngest creative director in the country, and a director of the company. 'So it worked for me,' he laughs. 'Everything in this country's worked for me.'

Along with the sixteen and tuppence that Bryce brought with him to Australia, he also brought along a bright and burning ambition – not only to succeed but to be the best. And he's happy to pass on to others how he has done that. When a group of second-year university students asked to meet with Bryce a few years ago, he readily agreed. They told him how much they had loved *The Power of One*, but were themselves unsure of what they wanted to do in life. Tell us what we have to do, they said to Bryce. 'I don't know what to tell you,' was his response, 'but I'll think about it.'

It was a Friday. 'All day Saturday I wrote,' Bryce recalls, 'and then I photocopied what I'd written and gave it to the students, saying, "I don't know *what* you have to do, but this is *how* you have to do it." Then my publisher saw it and asked, "Why don't we print it?" It's now sold 150 000 copies. Well, they've given away 150 000 copies and the money goes to charity.' Donations for *A Recipe for Dreaming* went to the Haemophilia Foundation. Bryce's son Damon was a haemophiliac who died of medically acquired AIDS. With this one small book, filled with Bryce's thoughts and observations on life, he has kept his son's memory alive while helping many others.

Bryce is a man who gives a lot – in his time, his writing and his motivational and inspirational talks. A dynamic and charismatic speaker, he combines the confidence and expertise of a polished performer with the fervour of a religious evangelist.

Picture the scene a few months earlier in Adelaide ... When he strides into the packed room at the Adelaide Town Hall to deliver a speech at Marketing Week, there is a sudden hush as all eyes are fixed on the man in the smart suit. His reputation is as a doer and high achiever and the audience is here to learn just how to do and how to achieve. To start with, Bryce advises, look for a challenge. 'I asked myself at the age of sixty, what was the most difficult thing I could do? Run a ninety-kilometre marathon in South Africa.' So Bryce set about training in order to achieve that goal. He tells the story of the marathon in vivid and captivating detail, building up the interest and tension. 'A few kilometres from the finish I saw people stopping, giving up. "There's no point in carrying on," they told me. "The eleven hours are up and you only get a medal for completing the marathon in eleven hours."' Bryce's eyes blaze with fury as he recalls the moment and he slams his fist down on the wooden podium to emphasise his point. 'A medal? I'm not doing this for a medal! I'm doing this for myself!' And, running on, he urged the other runners to follow him.

Bryce is silent for a moment. Then he starts to speak once more, softly. 'Can you remember when you were a kid,' he asks, 'lying on your back in the grass, looking at the clouds above you and saying "I'm going to do this"? Well, what happened?' His voice builds up in a crescendo. 'If you can think it, you can do it!' he pronounces, explaining how, to the brain, imagination is reality. 'If you can visualise it, you can achieve it. The brain interprets this image as reality.'

The audience remains captivated as Bryce talks of 'daring your genius to walk the wildest unknown way'. 'You have to follow what you believe you can do.' He urges each individual to become the best, to become world-famous at what they choose. 'Set yourself deadlines, go for it, and don't break those deadlines. Approach your dream with panache and with confidence. When you're skating on thin ice, you might as well tap-dance. The ice will crack anyway; it always does.'

Bryce's speech is interspersed with strong visual images and with metaphors, illustrating the points he makes with powerful stories. Those stories gave him his dreams and his fate.

'I'm just a storyteller,' Bryce is fond of saying. He said it in Adelaide and he repeats it now in his Sydney office. He states the fact directly and simply as if this were a direct, simple and straightforward process. The process may work well for him now but the apprenticeship has been a long one. Bryce's storytelling skills stem from his childhood, from his Zulu nurse. 'I was pretty well brought up for the first five years of my life by a nanny who was much more than a nanny to me. My first language was Zulu and my first instinct was to hear things told in a story-like manner. From the age of four, I always had a book on my lap but I never really associated reading with writing.

'The Zulus have a language which is made for storytelling. Zulus make everything into a story. Even a daily greeting turns into a story. In fact, it's an exasperating language because if you say g'day to a Zulu, you have to say it in such a way that you might get round to the subject you came to visit them about, half an hour or so later. You have to describe the day, the climate, even the cattle, and everything else. Storytelling is just the way the Zulus do everything.'

With such an upbringing, it was natural that the young Bryce became a storyteller. 'I always wanted to tell stories and I had this capacity to do so. Even small kids would gather round me and say tell us a story. I equated stories with writing, with telling these stories, but never with books. I knew I was a storyteller but I didn't see myself as a writer in the literary sense of the word. I would be appalled, in fact, if I were to win something like the Booker Prize, because it would mean that the writing had taken over from the story. My job is to be a storyteller.'

While he sees his books as having literary merit, Bryce thinks that is quite incidental. 'That's because I care and because I love words. My books are well written in order to carry the story. They're not well written just to be well written. I think modern literature is about post-modern deconstructionism and that's exactly what I'm not on about. That, to me, says that the story is subordinated to the style and the language and the importance the writer has in him or herself. So it's a cathartic or evolutionary thing whereby the reader is privileged to come in and witness what is happening to the writer.

'I find that totally absurd. I come from the opposite side. I believe the reader is a character in the story and you can't remove the reader from the writer or the reader from the story. So the writer becomes the least important of those three. The story and the reader are the two important factors and the writer is simply the messenger.'

Bryce used his storytelling skills to ensure companionship throughout his schooldays. Bullied mercilessly at primary school, he became hugely popular at high school. Storytelling ensured his survival and sustained him throughout those years. Yet even his storytelling and resulting popularity could not overcome other well-ingrained barriers. 'When I was eleven or twelve, I read in the paper that a professor of anthropology in Alabama had come up with the conclusion that the negroid brain pan was smaller than that of the Caucasian. So this definitely established that Africans, or the negro people, were inferior to white people because their brains were smaller.

'I read this and I was appalled because, even at that age, I knew this was bullshit, absolute nonsense. So at recess, I went to the headmaster and stood there in fear and trembling with this piece I'd cut out of the paper, and said, "Sir, you have to say something about this because it's not true." And he said, "Oh, why is this not true? Are you going against this famous professor?" And I said, "Yes, I am, Sir." "Good, son," he told me, "you will put your case at the School Debating Society next Friday."

'I was in form one. The debating society asks fourth or fifth formers. I'm really shitting myself. I've got no pocket money and so I borrow the money, threepence or so, to phone the Department of Anthropology at Witwatersrand University. The guy that answered was Professor Louis Leakey, the world-famous anthropologist. He'd discovered the first man in Central Africa, was doing a sabbatical in Witwatersrand and he answered the phone!

'So I told him what I had read in the paper and he said, "Son, wait there. I'm coming over." He came to meet me, gave me a lecture on how stupid this idea was and I wrote it all down. When Friday came, I gave a talk – backed up with facts and figures – on why this American professor's conclusion was impossible.' Then came Bryce's biggest test. 'The whole school and assembly voted. Two kids out of 600 voted for me.'

He pauses. What was his response? 'I just knew that South Africa was stuffed. I had won hands down. I had won a million times over. I had beaten the School Debating Society but I couldn't beat the prejudice. The prejudice was there.' He does not see that action as a youngster as a courageous one. 'No, I think it was a conviction, rather than courage, that spurred me on. I've always had this absolute conviction that there couldn't be any difference between human beings. Yet here there was a newspaper telling a terrible lie and I had to fix it.

'I think it was the fact that I was born in Africa but I was never able to see that one colour was different to another. Never. Remember that for the vital early years of my life, the first five years, I considered myself black. It wasn't as though I morally told myself these things. I just simply couldn't see any difference; it didn't make any sense to me. And that has never changed. Not for one second have I thought that colour or where a person comes from has anything to do with who they are. So I was alienated from day one in that sense.' He may have been popular at high school but he was still set apart from the others.

'My family were really poor. I got my first pair of shoes when I won a scholarship to an important school, a high school in Johannesburg. So we're not talking about little poor but really poor. Here I was, a fairly quiet country kid, in form one at an enormously rich boarding school. That first night the housemaster said that pocket money would be on Wednesdays. "This is a classy place," I thought. "They even give you pocket money." So on Wednesday I queued up and when I got to him, the housemaster said, "Your mother didn't leave you any." My mum had never left me any pocket money in my whole life. I didn't know that mums did that.'

As well as being poor, Bryce was also born illegitimately and this is where the alienation he speaks of began. He sighs. 'I come from the deep north and, when I was very young, the local preacher made me understand that because I was illegitimate, I had sinned against God, and that I would be punished very severely for this. And I was punished by the community. I was pointed out in public. I was English-speaking in an Afrikaans community of deeply charismatic religious people and God didn't tolerate people who were illegitimately born. All was forgiven when I started winning scholarships but by then it was too late ... I came out of the situation feeling inferior, just as a coloured person or an African person feels inferior – because of what's happened to them, not because they *are* inferior.'

Bryce's mother worked hard as a dressmaker to take care of him and his older sister Rosemary. It is only in the last couple of years that Bryce has discovered who his father was. 'I knew his name and I ran an ad in South Africa which simply said, quite presumptuously, "World-famous author wishes to know the whereabouts of ... " And people came out of the woodwork. I pounced on them and said, "Tell me." There isn't a great deal to know. He was an alcoholic and had been dead for years and years. He came from a very old-established and distinguished South African family but didn't amount to much himself. I come from quite old English-speaking stock, maybe a hundred years old on my mother's side, and since the 1840s on my father's side, when my great, great grandfather came out with Bishop Colenso to found the colony of Natal.'

What he lacked materially as a child, Bryce made up for with skill. 'I realise that now. I wanted to be popular and a nice guy because that sort of made up for my poverty. Most poor kids will tell you this. Poor kids go in one of two ways – they get very bitter or they become clowns. And then they have to grow out of that, but some of them never do. As clowns, they please people, they're pleasing and they're nice to be with. What they are covering up for, what they are really saying, is, "I haven't got any money, I haven't got any clothes, I haven't got any possessions, but I'm great myself. You've got to love me for who I am." And being bitter is the resentment that life has thrown you this bad curve. I never felt that.'

In his own case, Bryce realised very early on in life that he was very bright. 'I could out-think most of my peers. But I had to conceal that I was bright because, particularly in that part of the

Bryce Greer (grandfather), Pat Roberts (mother) and Rosemary (sister) in Barberton in the early 1940s.

world, people resent bright children. So I had a secret brightness that I kept burnished and that was the Power of One.' Just like young Peekay in the novel, Bryce hid his brightness in the belief that mediocrity is the best camouflage.

'There are two types of camouflage. You can be so far ahead that nobody can ever understand where you are and that's what I chose to be. But as a youngster, you can't do that. As a young child, you have to do it through mediocrity – be like everybody else … As I grew older, I realised that the better camouflage was to be so far ahead that everybody had to speculate about you. You became an enigma. And that's the way to hide, a very good place to hide – as an enigma.'

As a poor, illegitimate and intelligent eight-year-old boy, Bryce came to the realisation and the decision that it was only by his own efforts that he would be able to change his situation. 'There was nobody else to do it. And so I won my first scholarship to a very important private school in Johannesburg, carrying all the burdens of people who are very poor. When I finished school I won a scholarship to university. I was determined that whatever it was I did, I would be a huge success to prove that poverty wasn't a stigma.

'It's a weird thing but people tend to do that. It took me nearly forty-five years to get rid of the chip on my shoulder. When I finally realised that it didn't mean anything, I was a huge success in life. I had two continental cars and a huge house, with a pool and garden, in Vaucluse. I was a very rich man. And I was overweight. I was smoking one hundred cigarettes a day and drinking seventeen cans of beer and two bottles of wine on an average day.

'I suddenly realised that this wasn't what I set out to do in life. What I set out to do in life was to be a famous writer. I wanted to be that at nine, I wanted to be that at eleven, I wanted to be that at sixteen. I'd lost the dream and become a very important so-called something else, which wasn't important at all. All that I was doing was killing myself, so that's when I stopped.'

This turning point came in a dramatic way. 'I'd been working hard all night and the next morning I found five empty cigarette packets on the table and seventeen empty beer cans in the bin. I looked at myself in the hallway mirror. I was 168 centimetres, a hunchback, with my belly spilling out over my gut. I would be dead in five years. So I resigned from my job at J. Walter Thompson's that day and I have not had a drink or a cigarette since then.'

This was the first day of Bryce's second career. He had warned his wife Benita when they married, that he would have three lives, three careers and perhaps change into a different person. 'The poor boy chip on my shoulder told me, "I can be as good as everyone else", "I can beat them all at their own game", "I can be important", "I can be a millionaire". And so I chose to do those things rather than the things I had to do. I let ambition ride me, rather than the other way about.

'Here I was, a good writer who could walk into a business and they could afford to pay me to live in the manner to which I had absolutely no right to become accustomed. I just fell for the three-card trick, that's really what it's all about. I only woke up to myself at the age of forty-five when I realised that this was absolute total nonsense. I was never meant to be a corporate man. I was essentially a storyteller. That's who I was and that's who I was going to be.'

He doesn't see his experience as an unusual one. Far from it. 'Everyone I have met has a desire to do something else. In all of us, we have the factor "if only I could have, I would have". So we stay in dumb jobs because our parents taught us about security. We have to pay the mortgage, bring up the kids. But there is nothing in it for us. We need to do something for ourselves. Do something for yourself. If you don't, you let yourself down.

'I think there are three ages of man. There's the business of growing up till you've had your children, that's the first age. Your second age is from about thirty-five to sixty and that's the acquiring of wisdom, and the third age is from sixty onwards when you use that wisdom.' So began his second life, his second career, as a storyteller.

'People don't write books suddenly. Books are things for maturity. Books are things that come later in life. Books are really things where you have to put in a fifteen- or twenty-year apprenticeship.' Perhaps best known for creating Louie the Fly to advertise Mortein insect spray, Bryce had initially put his writing skills to good use with McCann Erikson and then J. Walter Thompson, before setting up his own very successful advertising agency. He sold the business ten years later and is presently working as creative director at George Patterson advertising.

'My plan on resigning from Thompson's was to take ten years building up my own organisation and then flog it to become a world-famous author. I thought that I would need five years to write a book that was good enough to be published.' It took him, in fact, just one year to produce an international bestseller. And the circumstances under which he did this are no less remarkable.

To hone his storytelling skills, Bryce used self-hypnosis. 'It was simply an exercise in writing to get back into the mind of a five-year-old.' This was Peekay, the main character and hero of *The Power of One*. 'I went back and age-regressed myself and what a traumatic experience that was. I didn't do it in order to get back into *my* mind – although in fact that was inevitable – but ... to try to understand how a five-year-old thinks and works things out.'

The self-hypnosis was a technique he had developed for Damon many years previously. 'I taught myself self-hypnosis and I used it for pain control with him when he was very young. Then I learned age regression because things were pretty miserable for him and I'd take him back to pleasant incidents and actually make him re-live them precisely so that we could pass the hours and do so joyously. And it used to kill his pain because the pain wasn't in the incident.'

To write *The Power of One*, Bryce also needed incredible self-discipline, determination and stamina in order to follow the gruelling schedule he had set himself. 'I said I would write the book in one year.' The first sentence came into being at 2.15 in the morning on 8 June 1986. Bryce got out of bed, wrote the words "This is what happened", and went back to sleep.

Thereafter he would rise just after four each morning and write for almost four hours. He'd shower, dress, have breakfast and be in the office by nine to put in a full day's work. Back home, he would work well into the night, pausing only for an hour. 'I'd call that my quality time with Benita. She'd call it dinner.' At weekends, Bryce would work from early morning until midnight, stopping only for meals and a thirty-kilometre run on Sundays. 'I was working ninety to one hundred hours a week and sleeping four hours a night.' Each time he would go back to writing, he would merely re-read his last paragraph and continue.

He did not find it hard to switch from writing to work in advertising during the day and then return to his book in the evening.

'There's no magic in this. These are habits that every human being should have. According to the well-known theory of right-hand brain and left-hand brain, the left-hand brain is the logical part that computes everything and the right is creative. An awful lot of *The Power of One* was written using the right-hand side of the brain. Writing is really daydreaming, isn't it? You're sitting there and the plot is going on in your head, you're daydreaming it. The characters come alive and start to talk to each other and all you are is a sort of intellectual stenographer. It's all right-hand brain stuff.

'Right-hand brain thinking has been hammered out of us. And it's not naturally out of us, it's naturally *in* us. But, from the age of four or five, our parents say, "Stop that, stop dreaming, don't do that, you're dreaming again, that's stupid," and they teach us how to evaluate things with the left-hand brain. An average five-year-old kid spends 70 per cent of his or her time in the right-hand side of the brain: it's the most natural place to think. And we hammer it out of them. All I've done is reclaim what is basically mine. It was not hard to do what I did. If you did think about it, it would be strange to have an overlap, because you're using two doorways. The left-hand brain is one doorway, then there's another doorway. You close that door and open this one. Advertising was pretty much left-hand brain but none of these things are precise. They're a mixture.'

The pages of his book were building up rapidly. Bryce admits, with some embarrassment, that he did not think it would be a book unless it was at least twenty-five centimetres high. When completed, the manuscript of *The Power of One* was twenty-nine centimetres high and weighed three kilograms. Yet the end of the year found Bryce 'blubbing at my desk at midnight. Benita heard me and came to ask what was wrong. "My year is up and I haven't finished the book," I told her. "But you didn't start until 2.15," she said. She was right.' An elated and invigorated Bryce continued towards his goal. At 2.17 in the morning, *The Power of One* was finished.

The story of its publication and subsequent success was yet another triumph for Bryce. He had not thought of submitting this practice book to a publisher; in fact he had not even read it all the way through. He just put it away in a drawer and forgot about it. It was only when a jogging partner asked how Bryce's book was coming along that he took up the suggestion of sending it to a well-known publisher. He glued together the corners of a couple of early pages to see whether it would be read. The manuscript was returned, pages still stuck together, with a letter of rejection.

When his friend suggested an agent as his next step, Bryce thought of Jill Hickson. He was undeterred by the information that this highly respected agent took on very few new writers, but instead worked with well-established authors, and did not personally answer the telephone. He called her.

Just as with Professor Louis Leakey, the vital person picked up the phone and spoke to Bryce. Jill Hickson asked Bryce for a synopsis of his book – which he wrote furiously that night – and then for the manuscript. During the couple of months of waiting, Bryce assured his family that he didn't mind if it was rejected. This was, after all, his first attempt and he would write another book. So he was stunned to be contacted by Jill Hickson and told he had written a 'marvellous book'. *The Power of One* was bought in London and a publisher offered US$175 000 for it in New York. 'Never before had an Australian's first novel been offered that kind of money. But I told her to turn it down.' Jill Hickson was stunned but Bryce was adamant. 'It did not matter what money I was offered; I would have been happy to let it go for $1000,' he says, 'but I would never have sold it to those particular publishers. The money was immaterial. They were the ones who had rejected it without even reading the book.'

So, in an unprecedented move for a first novel – let alone one by an Australian writer – *The Power of One* was auctioned. Twelve publishers bid and it was sold for US$500 000 in America. It went on to sell over three million copies worldwide. It may not be important to Bryce to win the Booker Prize but it is important to him to have a big readership. 'Yes, it's important for the storyteller to have an audience. Now, I don't know that I would be content with an audience of ten. I really do consider it important to be a world-famous storyteller but that comes from a completely different impetus. I believe that as a human being, I have a right to do it as well as I know how. And I have this vision that our potential is so enormous that we have no idea. So if I do it with all the talent I've got and with all the genius I've been given – which I don't believe is greater than anyone else's – then it's inevitable that I'll become a world-famous writer. It's not a question of ambition, it's a question of inevitability.'

※

If you ask Bryce whether he could have been as successful in life anywhere other than in Australia, he will tell you it's a perspicacious question. 'I could never have made it in South Africa. I had too much hate and fear in South Africa and too much inferiority. I felt inferior. The day I left I felt different, as though this enormous yoke had come off my shoulders. I was eighteen and I felt light and clean and as though I could do anything. Within that atmosphere, even though I was considered to be brilliant, I had terrible fear.'

On leaving school, he had – just like Peekay in *The Power of One* – worked in the mines in Zaire, now Zambia, in order to earn enough money to enable him to take up a scholarship to study law at Oxford University. 'I did go to England but I changed my mind and went to the London School of Journalism instead.

'When I was still at school, I started up a school for Africans. I was arrested for that and labelled a Communist, which I wasn't. There were several occasions when I had stood up for Africans under certain circumstances and had been involved with the police. Africa is absolutely paranoid about Communism ... When I went overseas, they said, "If you come back, you'll be banned." I realised then that if I studied law – as had every first-born son in my family for 600 years – that my life would be finished if I came back. I'd be in prison more than I was out. Seeing that very clearly, I ran away.'

He has missed certain aspects of South Africa. 'I miss the black people enormously but that's like missing your family. I don't miss the country and what it stands for and I don't miss the nature, it's too rapacious and greedy and cruel. It has blood on its teeth. But I miss the song. I miss the journey, and I miss the creatures that dwell on the land.'

After he has been there watching and reporting on the build-up to the first democratic elections, does he have any hopes about the future? His response is immediate, sharp, and final. 'No.' Yet there are positive indications, ones that Bryce personally observed on that trip. 'I met an orphaned black man who started as a garden boy in prison. He's now a brigadier and the only black man in the entire prison service, in the stronghold of what has always been the most ignorant part of the Afrikaans nation. He runs Barberton Prison and is an enormously charismatic man. This one black man is now in control of prisons under a white regime. Impossible, you may have thought. Nothing is impossible if you believe it.'

When they met, the brigadier said to Bryce, 'When I read your book, I thought this is a guy who thinks like me.' Thinking like Bryce involves having a dream and applying yourself to it ruthlessly. 'I don't think it is just possible to achieve anything today. I think it is inevitable,' says Bryce. Notwithstanding the news that today's youth are bombarded with – recession, high unemployment – he says, 'The worse it gets, the easier it becomes, because everyone else has given up. Therefore, by definition, the dreamer must win. It's not the determined myopia that wins, it's always the dreamer and people don't understand that …

'There's only one thing you have to understand and that is to never compromise your dream. Never. There will be some hairy moments in the process, but there will be hairy moments anyway.'

He even goes so far as to say that if he were an eighteen-year-old today, he would do well. 'The climate is better now than it's ever been for success. You only see negativity if you feed it to yourself as negativity. Why not look upon it as opportunity? With our intellectual capacity, both the means and the potential for change are well within our reach. I think there's a whole universe in our heads and that's the country in which we really live. But we never actually explore it.'

As Bryce writes in *April Fool's Day* – his book about his son Damon – '"The need to dream is critical, to visit the private country in your head". I believe passionately in dreaming. Every person who has had a dream has collected around them a whole heap of very happy people – families, people who love them – because a dream is magnetic. It cannot be stopped. Anything can happen with any dream. It is the Power of One.

'The Power of One creates intellectual satisfaction and happiness, for that person and others. I've never known anybody who was happy who didn't make others happy. So be true unto yourself. Very few of us are and I think it is a perfectly valid idea. The rest takes care of itself.'

The rest may also include wealth which, to Bryce, is immaterial. 'I've never wanted money. I've made a great deal, lost it and made it again. Initially it proved something to me – that I could make money – but money itself and buying expensive things has never ever meant anything to me. I've never bought anything because it was or could be valuable but because to me it was a thing of beauty that I could afford at the time, and gave me joy. What's important to me is not things but journeys – touching, feeling, smelling, loving.'

While Bryce talks of the internal country inside his head and its potential, he has also seen many developments in the external country he has chosen – Australia. 'The changes I have seen in Sydney have been astonishing. When I came into the harbour thirty-six years ago, someone on board pointed out the Unilever building, which has since been pulled down. It was about seventeen storeys high, the highest building in the southern hemisphere. There were no high-rise buildings in Sydney at all and where the Opera House now sits, there was hardly a building.

'I've seen Sydney grow but, more importantly, I have seen the effects of immigration. That started in 1952 and I got here in 1958 so it wasn't under way to the degree that the generation of migrants had started to change Australia. It was still an Anglo-Irish community and hadn't become the polyglot community that it is now. To see it change the way it has, has been astonishing, wonderful.

'To me, the idea that we are multicultural is the most enchanting thing that there can possibly be. I take enormous pride in the fact that we are a multicultural society. We are the most mixed-up people on earth, the freest country on earth and an example of what other countries could be. There's no question about it. We are. Despite the appalling conditions of Aboriginal people, we are still innately the freest people on earth. By arriving when immigration had only been going six years – so the last big migration hadn't really started – I became part of the most extraordinary human adventure.'

There are many advantages that Bryce finds in such a culturally diverse society. 'One of the positive benefits is that it destroys racism. Racism is the most destructive element in society. And when you're confronted with the fact that all human beings laugh in the same places, cry in the same places, care about the same things, worry about the same things, and scratch their bums in the same way – it's very hard suddenly to think of somebody as being inferior, superior, a wop, or something else. Racism is based on fear and we've largely eliminated that fear. That's not quite the case yet with Asian people but that will come.'

Bryce loves the other aspects of multiculturalism – 'the languages, the culture, the points of view, the cooking, all those things that everybody talks about' – but these are subsequent considerations. 'We are all confronted daily with the fact that racism is a stupidity and that in itself keeps us a sane, honest and decent people. So only a fool can conclude that one person is inferior to another in this country. There are no dichotomies.'

He considers himself more than Australian. 'If there were such a thing, I would consider myself 110 per cent Australian. I have no loyalty to anyone else. My love extends passionately to this country, with such a passion that I can't even begin to express it. So now I would think of myself as Australian in every circumstance, under any circumstances. Being Australian means being part of the most splendid human experiment that has taken place. There is no country that has more successfully integrated all the nations on earth than this one. To be part of that makes me feel very special.

'You see, I hate nationalism of any kind … Nationalism is what people march in the street for. Nationalism is what's happening in Croatia right now and in Sarajevo, and most countries embrace nationalism. America has nationalism. Britain has nationalism. Germany had it and it destroyed Germany. One of the few countries that jumped over nationalism was us. We never had it.

'Eighty-seven per cent of this country don't know the lyrics to the national anthem. People say that's appalling. But that's one of the most splendid indications that these are a people who are free and are not going to die for country. You die for humankind, you die for principle or something else, but you sure as hell are not going to die for a flag with five stars in it.' His voice rises in volume as he speaks with intensity. 'That's an absurdity! That's an inanity!'

It follows that an Australian is 'a part of everybody else on earth.

When Australia pitched for the Olympic Games, I had some small part in that and this is how I put my argument. I said, "My country is the only one on earth that can bring a cheer squad, 10 000 strong, for any athlete you can produce for any country on earth." Everybody was astonished – they'd never thought of it like that.'

Positives about Australia include the attitudes here. 'I like the attitude that we instinctively suspect politicians of being basically dishonest and power-hungry. To give you some idea, I met P. W. Botha about ten years ago, when he was prime minister of South Africa. I was introduced to him and the next time I referred to him as 'P.W.' There were ambassadors, generals and other dignitaries there, and the room just went totally quiet. I realised I had done something terribly wrong but I didn't know what it was. So I said, "What did I do, P.W.?" And he was crimson by this stage. Then an aide came up to me and said, "How dare you refer to the prime minister as P.W.?"

'Well, I referred to Gough Whitlam as Gough. I referred to Bob Hawke as Bob. I referred to every single one I'd met by their Christian name and that's how I felt. That's how it was. That's my country. You see, we don't have nationalism. The prime minister isn't the most important party. He isn't God. He's just a guy like me. That's what it means to be Australian.'

Yet that egalitarian attitude does not always make things easier in Australia. 'You're more easily accepted here for what you are but I don't really think it's easier. We have a tall poppy syndrome, which is a very negative idea, and I'm not suggesting that Australia is the perfect country. That tall poppyism is a disaster for this country, because we are not founded on excellence. We have a shoddy way of doing things and that's a shame ... Yet there are some aspects of Australia that are excellent simply because they're not powered by the need for things. The whole democratic capitalist mercantile world is based on the need to have things.

'I think life is not about having things but about doing things, and there's more of that in Australia than almost any other country. We're still a materialistic people because most Western people are, yet there is still that sense of have a go, there is still that sense of life is a journey, it's not a destination. Australia is the lucky country only in the sense that somebody was smart enough to open up its gates and say, "Welcome, world."'

There is one group of people, however, to whom this does not apply. 'Having been urbanised and working in advertising, I was busy with my career. I went for a long, long time being quite oblivious. I was enormously shocked when I discovered the Aboriginal people were suffering a form of apartheid. I remember the shock of suddenly realising that actually I hadn't found a country where everybody was equal, but one where there was a form of apartheid just as vicious as the one I'd left. I am ashamed to say that I had been here ten years before I discovered it.

'Up until 1972, I was given the job of grooming Gough Whitlam for prime minister, in an advertising sense, and one night we sat down in a hotel in Canberra and I was taking notes. He talked about the Aboriginal people and what he was going to do, how he was going to allow them certain freedoms, and my mouth fell open and I said, "What do you mean – allow them freedoms? Haven't they got these freedoms? Aren't they allowed to vote? Aren't they allowed to drink?" And he looked at me and said, "Of course not. Have you never heard of the White Australia Policy?" I hadn't and I was absolutely appalled.

'I think it had been a reaction to so much politics in my life that I had sort of expunged it and saw this as a country where politics were Mickey Mouse – they didn't matter ... Then I suddenly woke up, and realised that in my new country there was a form of injustice that was absolutely horrific. Although I must confess I haven't done a lot about it, I've written quite extensively about it and talked a lot about it.'

When Bryce visited Wilcannia in New South Wales and wrote about the town for a national newspaper, he felt he had been there before. A small Outback town north-east of Broken Hill, Wilcannia has a population of nine hundred people, 80 per cent of whom are Aboriginal. 'Wilcannia was a world I knew. I'd never been to Wilcannia but as I moved about there, I felt, "I know this town. I've been in a town like this thousands of times before." I knew all the influences that were working there. It was like going back in time for me to my childhood.'

The Power of One saw apartheid through the eyes of a five-year-old. By not taking sides as an adult would, but merely observing as a child, Bryce was able to make it look all the more terrible. It pleases him that it has been, as elsewhere, hugely successful in South Africa. 'I'm told it's been one of the most popular books in South Africa, the biggest-selling book. That's not a lot – 8000 copies in South Africa is a super bestseller and I think *The Power of One* has now sold 15 000 copies.' That is, nevertheless, outstanding in a country where most cannot afford to buy books. Bryce sees the success of *The Power of One* in South Africa as very significant to him, in helping to overcome the shame he felt at 'running away' as a young man.

As he did not himself have a happy family life he was determined above all things that he would have a family. 'I haven't had a particularly brilliant marriage,' he admits. 'It was fraught with the fact that we had a chronically ill child. But I was determined my children would have total family life and they have, and a very happy one too.'

Bryce wanted them to go forward into life, as he had, believing they could do anything. 'My philosophy of life came from my grandfather who would be called a loser, I suppose, by today's standards. He read books and grew roses; he was a scholar. I used to have to work very hard in the garden, the nursery, and he'd sometimes turn round and say, "Well lad, what will we be when we grow up?" He always talked in the plural and it was a sort of game we had. I'd come up with something outrageous and he'd give me a lecture on it.

'I used to have to dig rose holes ... It was hateful work for which I didn't get paid, but that was my job, and he did the light work, pruning the roses. I would be on my knees, digging these holes in the clay, and he'd say, "Well lad, what will we be when we grow up?" He used to have this pipe and his head was always covered in cumulus clouds of foul-smelling smoke. And I would say something like, "You know those little green caterpillars that eat your roses, well I'm going to be a scientist and grow them *that* big," and stretch out my hands. Then this highly intelligent man would give me a lecture about caterpillars and butterflies and the migratory habits of insects, until my eyes would glaze over with boredom. He used to conclude these lectures always by saying, "Well then lad, I suppose somebody has to do it. It might as well be you."

'So I went into life with a quite clear philosophy – that I could do anything. Somebody has to do everything. It might as well be me. I very clearly understood that everybody could do anything and so I just translated that into the power of one person. So that's where the Power of One comes from.'

As far as his own character is concerned, he can't comment. 'I don't think anyone can ever describe their own personality, it's actually an impossibility. You simply can't do it. I can be enormously ebullient and I can be astonishingly shy. I can be very introverted and I can be very extroverted. You could get ten people who know me intimately and you'd get ten different playbacks on me, simply because by nature human beings are chameleons, and I perhaps more so than most. I guess I do describe myself as a chameleon.'

A workaholic chameleon? 'No, I don't see what I do as work ... Work implies something that's boring ... I would never dream of doing anything that bored me – under any circumstances. I'd rather starve to death. So I've never actually worked a day in my life.'

Has the fact that he sleeps only about four hours a night enabled him to achieve more? 'I think that's all nonsense. If you sleep four hours or fourteen, it doesn't really matter. It's a question of how you use the time when you're awake. It's a cop-out when people say, "That gives you four extra hours a day, that's why you're so successful." That's bullshit. Most people muck around anyway. Just take the average life – you waste about four hours a day, just waste it. So I don't think it's a question of time or any special ability. I think it's a question of understanding, having confidence that you can do it.'

He is more than happy in Australia. 'I think countries and people become compatible. Australia gave me everything I needed and I tried to return some of the things it gave me by adding to the sum of it. I have no idea whether I have succeeded but one day, when I die, I hope somebody will say, "He gave as much as he took".'

Bryce talks of three careers – his second is to write seventeen books in twenty years, and his third is to be involved in third-world education. 'That's where I seem to be heading, and one will meld into the other. Ambition and books will carry the message and make it happen.'

It all comes back to seeing life as a journey. 'Most people seem to strive for a destination: "When I have this, I'll be happy." I don't see it like that at all. I see the idea of arriving anywhere as an absurdity. The joy is in the journey and there are two kinds of people. There are people who work very hard to arrive somewhere, quite why I don't know, and there are people who never get off their seat at the railway station. They never catch the train because they're too scared.

'Now I'm the guy who really takes the journey but makes sure it never ends. I have an open-ended ticket. One of the reasons I love being a storyteller is because I'll never write the perfect book. I'll never create the perfect story. It's an unbeatable task. It's an unbeatable journey. It's perfect.'

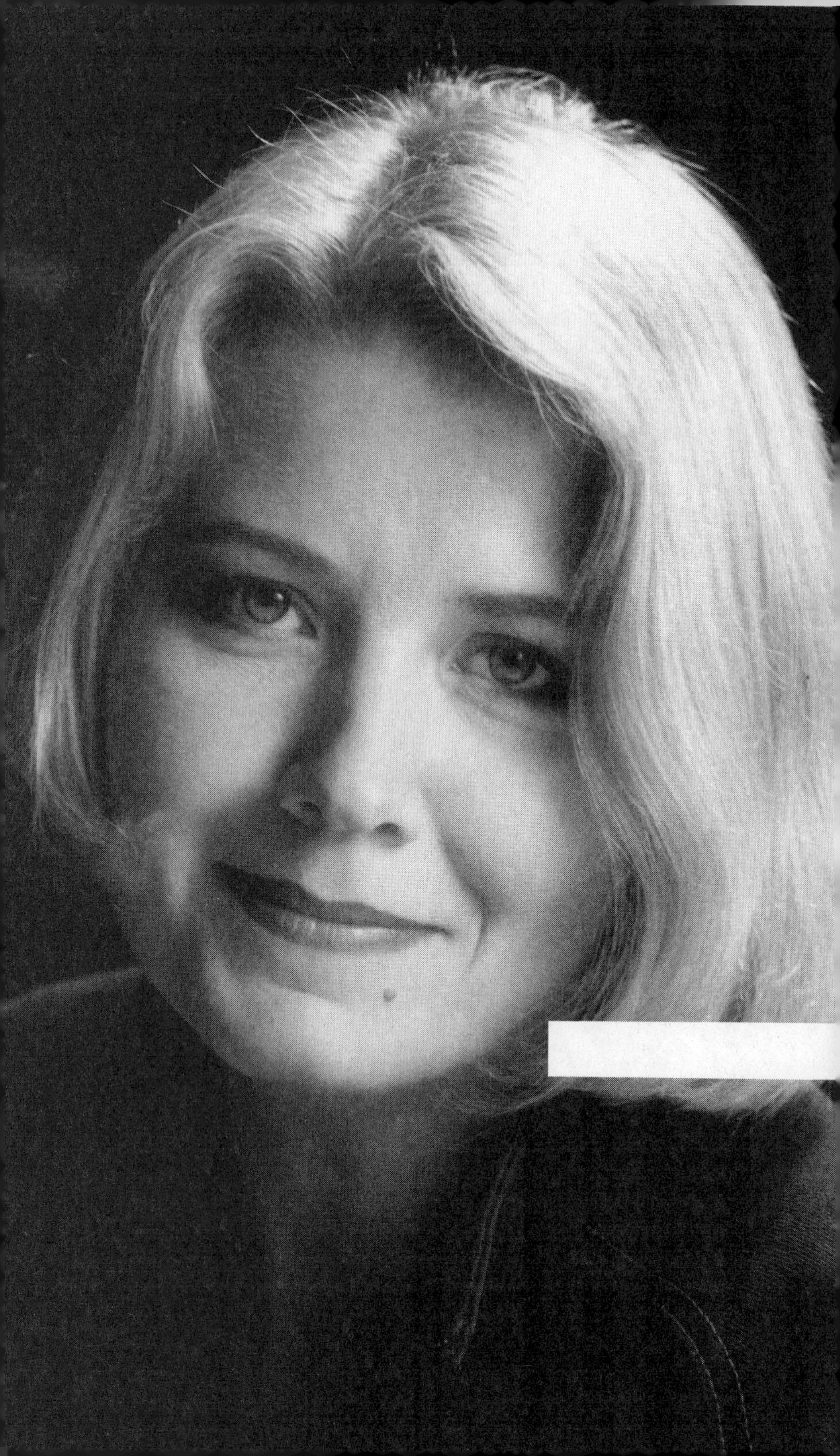

A MARVELLOUS ADVENTURE

'I think both nationalism and patriotism are very bad because we shouldn't die for our country. We should *live* for our country.'

GOSIA DOBROWOLSKA

Actress

Everything about her is soft, gentle and graceful, from her mannerisms to her voice and even her footsteps. She climbs the stairs to her agent's first-floor office in Paddington, Sydney so quietly that I am unsure whether or not I heard a sound. Then, smiling her wide smile, she shyly steps into the room and offers a warm handshake.

Her beauty is striking – from her thick golden hair cut stylishly to her shoulders, to her sparkling blue eyes, clear fair complexion and lithe figure. She is dressed simply but elegantly in a white blouse, contrasted with a dark skirt and highlighted with a piece of chic jewellery.

When Gosia (pronounced Gosha) Dobrowolska came from Poland to Australia in March 1982, she was twenty-four years old, five months pregnant and facing an uncertain future. Unable to speak a word of English, she had resigned herself to giving up her acting career for a new life in this unfamiliar country. She and her husband – actor and theatre director Bogdan Koca – knew no one here, and next to nothing about Australia.

Today she is a strong and independent woman, a successful actress with an international reputation, and the proud mother of twelve-year-old Veronica. 'I came here because of my husband,' she says. 'I had no big desire to leave Europe but he wanted to and I said, fine.' The two divorced four years ago but Gosia is philosophical about their separation. 'It's life – we just grew apart. Maybe if we were still in Poland, circumstances would have kept us together. Maybe going through this really tough thing of emigrating to another country puts you under extreme pressure.'

She speaks slowly and a little cautiously, at times almost inaudibly. It is only after we adjourn to a nearby café – Gosia driving in her blue sports car – that she starts to relax. Sipping orange juice, she laughs as she tells me of her young daughter imitating Gosia's accent and her way of saying 'somefing' rather than 'something'. Gosia retaliates by telling her she will concentrate on pronouncing 'something' correctly once Veronica learns to say her r's properly. Polish is the main language in which the two communicate – 'otherwise she has so little chance to learn' – and Gosia's speech in English is a delightful and captivating mix of an eastern-European accent with a smart Sydney overtone.

Gosia's first film role in Australia, as Nina in *Silver City*, came as a complete surprise to her; it was an eerie and fortuitous twist of fate. For not only did the part seem made for her but there were also certain parallels between the character's life and her own. Both had emigrated to Australia from Poland with no money, no language skills and doubtful employment prospects. Both had spent time in migrant hostels and were initially disconcerted with Australia's alien and bleak-looking landscape. There, however, the similarities ended. For while Nina suffered disappointments and prejudice, Gosia found happiness and acceptance.

On their arrival in Sydney, Gosia and Bogdan made an important decision – to seek out the positives in their new country and not to look back or compare. 'The first step was to say that we loved Australia and that we would accept what was here without complaining,' Gosia explains. The couple spent their first six months in a hostel at Villawood and it was there, quite by chance, that Gosia heard about a film to be made by a female director, Sophie Turkiewicz, which was to have Polish main characters. 'It seemed impossible – I had come all the way from Europe to Australia trying not to think about acting. And now here was this film with Polish characters. My first thought was, how extraordinary, and then, wouldn't it be amazing if I was to get a tiny little role in it? I certainly wasn't dreaming of a leading role.'

After making contact, she learned the film-makers had not yet decided whether to use Australians or migrants in these roles. 'So, just in case, they looked through whoever was here, anyone with an acting background. Unfortunately I couldn't understand even the audition process. They call it a reading here. I just took the script and read the words; I thought they wanted to see whether I could pronounce them. We don't have anything like that in Poland – either you do a proper screen test or you don't do anything and are cast in the role.

'After a while, I could see they were quite confused and they asked me to close the script and perform. What do you mean, perform, I thought? There I was, very pregnant, with no one else there, no actor, no cameras. How could I perform? Also the scene was about the character's daughter who had died when she was six months old – I certainly didn't want to perform that at all. So my audition was a huge failure and they went ahead and cast the whole film with Australian actors.'

Gosia thought she had lost her chance but then fate stepped in. Finance for the film was not forthcoming and the project was unable to go ahead for several months. 'It was all such an extraordinary coincidence. I was asked to play the god Dionysus in a production of *The Bacchae* by the director Philip Keir. He had worked in Germany for a number of years and knew and respected Polish theatre. Sophie Turkiewicz saw me perform in the play and asked me to do another screen test – a proper one this time. And by this stage, I knew what to do.

'I was very nervous; I wanted to do the best I could. The film people told me they didn't want to raise my hopes, that they were only thinking of me as a possible option. I remember the night I had to call the director to ask whether a decision had been made. "I really want you to come over to my house," she told me. Oh, this means bad news. She doesn't want to tell me over the phone, I thought. "I beg you, just tell me," I said. "No, I really would like to talk to you," and her voice was kind of serious and a little sad, disappointed.

'So I went there, completely prepared for her to say no. She opened the door and let me in, still with a very sour face. Then she went to the fridge and took out two chilled glasses and a bottle of champagne and said, "Congratulations." That was lovely. She had only been joking, playing a little game with me.'

Gosia was interested in the similarities between the 1949 migrant experience, as depicted in *Silver City*, and her own. 'When I spoke to early migrants they said it had been very different in their day, there was no comparison. But I think it is similar psychologically – coming to a land where you cannot speak the language and feeling separated. I really felt I had come to this island which was like a prison. I had no money to return. And I wanted to return – immediately. But it was all psychological, because there had been no one waiting to greet me at the airport. There was not a single person here that I knew, nobody with whom I could feel familiar or at home.

'I remember thinking, "Will I ever meet somebody on the street that I know or recognise?" I would look into houses where the lights were on and people were having dinner and I couldn't imagine that – a real family, with friends who would call one another or pop in for a cup of tea. I couldn't imagine that because I didn't know anybody.'

The long trip to Australia had done nothing to allay her fears. 'The plane trip goes on forever. More and more hours go by and you can't believe how far you are going from everything that is familiar to you. You are leaving behind everything you know. Then, when you land in Australia for the very first time, it smells different and it is very unfamiliar. It's the smell of different trees and of something warm. I remember it all very clearly – officials from the hostel putting us onto buses and arriving at this funny building. I remember getting off the bus being frozen, absolutely frozen. I must have had a terrible expression on my face because one of the women from the kitchen came to me and said, "Don't worry, it's going to be okay." I gesticulated with my hands, "What are they going to do with us now?" Your life is not in your hands, you think. "It's okay, it's going to be fine," she said, "you're going to have a nice room and it's going to be okay."'

Instead of the corrugated iron huts of the Silver City, where the men were separated from the women, Gosia and Bogdan found themselves together and in a pleasant unit. Yet Gosia felt isolated. 'I couldn't get over the shock and I cried non-stop for three days. "God, what is going to happen to me?" I had no idea, there was nothing I could predict. Then I sort of pulled myself together. I couldn't cry for the rest of my life, I had better do some things.'

The biggest problem was not knowing anyone. 'There was no one to ask questions of or to relate to. Life would have been easier that way, but there was no one.' Hence priorities became to make contacts, find friends and learn the language. 'Without language, you can't do anything. You are limited in every possible way.' Making contact was a matter of looking in the arts section of the *Sydney Morning Herald*, selecting a name and trying to find that person. Bogdan, while not fluent, spoke some English. 'He'd ask people where the theatres were, make an appointment and go and introduce himself. He had always wanted to establish a small theatre company and it was easy, in a sense, to go and meet people because Australians are very open. "You want to meet me? Come and meet me. You want to talk? Fine." I thought that I would not really do much. Bogdan would be progressing in that area and, from time to time, he might give me some minor non-speaking role.'

Given her background, Gosia's expectations were well justified. 'I was only interested in theatre at that time and so language was all-important. I had been born in Poland but I still had to have diction classes there, as my enunciation was not good enough to go on the stage. I couldn't have imagined anyone not speaking Polish properly or speaking with an accent being able to go ahead and act. So why should it have been any different here?'

Yet Gosia found that it was indeed very different in Australia. Although she had travelled in Europe, Australia, with its multicultural society, was quite unlike any other country she had visited. 'It was not as open as it is now, but even then people would say "My father is Greek" or "My mother is Italian". There was this first generation of children who had grown up here – Australians with another background which had given them something different. There was another side to them and I thought that was good, absolutely wonderful. It gave them opportunity as they had stories to tell and an understanding of another culture. I felt that would change Australia very much in the next few years. And I think Australia is changing and that's marvellous.

'There are so many different people living here – so many different nationalities, so many different cultures, religions and languages. Even at the hostel, they were saying there were something like one hundred different nationalities and you could mix with them in the dining room and in the English classes. It's wonderful because, like it or not, we have to learn to be tolerant. And that's a good thing to learn.

'I think both nationalism and patriotism are very bad because we shouldn't die for our country. We should *live* for our country. I don't know about marching behind a flag. I would rather we learned to be tolerant of one another, accepting one another the way we are, believing in whatever God we want to believe in. That's better than killing in the name of God or in the name of the country. Right now, it's a marvellous society we have here.'

Yet initially, Australia was a strange land. 'I was nicely surprised by lots of things – the flowers and the birds were wonderful. I come from Wroclaw in south-west Poland and, like all European cities, it has a little square in the middle where people go for walks and meet. You even meet them when you don't want to meet them! But here, there was nothing like that and I couldn't believe, living in the suburbs, that there was no footpath,' she says incredulously. 'No one is used to walking here. We used to walk to the train station to go to the city and there would be no one walking. Everybody was driving and I found that very odd. It's changed now but I found that very odd.

'I thought Australia would be more modern, as it doesn't really have an old history, not like in Europe. I found when we were travelling, on location for *Silver City*, that we'd pass houses in the country which looked like rundown wrecks to me. But the cast members would say, "No, they're wonderful." I remember this one moment when I saw how beautiful they were. "Well, yes, it's very beautiful actually," I thought, "in sync with the landscape and I like it."

'But the most beautiful surprise to me was the Special Broadcasting Service. Oh, when I heard about this channel and somebody sold us a television for $20, the amount of sweat we put into finding an antenna that would work for SBS! It was great to be able to see the world news and it was very important to us. At that stage you are still very much at home and wanting to know what is happening there.'

All in all, Australia was a very strange land. 'Everybody tried to terrify us. "You can't wear those boots because there are spiders in them. There are snakes everywhere, waiting to get you. Don't swim – there are sharks and there are crocodiles." "How do they come to the hostel?" I asked. Everything was so dangerous. What a place. How did people survive, both on land and in the water? Everywhere there was something waiting to kill you,' and she breaks into peals of laughter. 'I thought when my little baby was born, she wouldn't be able to play anywhere because there would be something waiting. It was a funny thing – how everyone tried to scare you.'

Gosia considered herself fearless. 'I'm not afraid of any creature. When we were on location, the producer would tell me not to go for a walk because there were snakes. "Really, are there snakes?" I'd ask sarcastically. "I'm going on a walk to find them." I love doing risky things like that,' she giggles.

Meanwhile language was a real problem for her. Was it hard to come to grips with? 'It still is,' she replies without hesitation. 'In any other language, there are rules. And if you learn these rules, you can read and speak and there are no mistakes. But in English there are no rules. How can you learn properly if there are no rules? You have to be a genius. The film crew on *Silver City* had fun with me. When I first arrived on the set and somebody would say, oh gosh, I would turn around and say, yes? I thought they were saying Gosia and couldn't pronounce my name.

'And the way Australians speak – that's another thing. 'Owlong-'aveyoubeen'eremate?" They drop off part of the words and run them all together. It was useless getting on a train and asking the station master how to get somewhere because he'd give me an unintelligible response ... You don't know anybody and you can't communicate. You can't even make friends because you are slowly learning the language and you feel so foolish ... You cannot express yourself. I was using my hands all the time, like an Italian, saying, "I'm telling you this word but I mean *that* word."' She felt she was a child once more, having to learn everything from scratch.

Gosia found she loved the casual attitude of the Australians. 'At that time, there was martial law in Poland and I really wanted to talk politics but nobody wanted to talk politics with me. People here were living the easy life – "don't worry, mate" and all that. I couldn't understand that, but after some time I accepted and agreed. Why should we talk politics? Why should we be constantly passionate about some other people's problems and their country's problems and politics? Why not just enjoy life?'

Australia taught Gosia to take herself less seriously. 'Poles are too serious. I lacked a sense of humour. You have to look at the light side of life too; you can't always be depressed. Life is more than just heroes – our Polish history is so strong, we always had to fight for Poland. I would look on everything as a drama. Everything had to be big and serious and, as an actress, I had to be very serious and do great and difficult theatre, so complex that no one would understand,' she laughs. 'Now I'm more relaxed.'

Despite the difficulties she encountered, Gosia never had any regrets about leaving Poland. 'I don't regret anything in my life. I'm not that kind of person. I think it was meant to happen. I was meant to come here and I learned a lot by being here. I learned about tolerance. I learned about being humble. I learned how not to be racist. I learned how to accept anybody and love. The whole process of immigration gave me maturity very quickly. I was very very immature when I left Poland and this was a big lesson for me. Within a year, I felt as if I had lived here for ten years.'

She had left Poland earlier in her life and travelled in Europe a few times, first to France at the age of sixteen. 'I couldn't believe these huge supermarkets and everything was so colourful, not so simple or drab as with us.' But this trip to Australia was to be different. 'I think it was work opportunities that attracted Bogdan ... Poland wasn't enough for him – he wanted to expand.' He chose Australia, which was acceptable to Gosia.

'I had this vague idea in my mind that I would never feel at home anywhere in Europe; it was too close to Poland. Also European cultures are very closed-in and I thought I would always feel like a foreigner. And America was terrifying to me with its commercialism and consumerism. I did not really have any expectations about Australia. This was like an open page in my life where nothing was yet written.'

Supposedly going on four weeks' holiday, Gosia and Bogdan packed, in the knowledge that this time they would not return. They had, after all, made a deal. Bogdan had wanted to leave Poland soon after they married but Gosia, still studying acting, had persuaded him to wait until she had worked for a year. That year proved to be an excellent one for her and she even landed a leading role in a major film the week they were due to leave. Was she not tempted then to stay?

'No. I believe in fate. That was the day I was going and I would not change my mind.' As it was, martial law was declared soon after the couple left, the film was not made for three years and, had they stayed, they would have been trapped in Poland. 'At that time, there was no official emigration from Poland. You had to leave and apply for a residential visa in another country,' Gosia explains.

How do you pack when you expect to be leaving forever?

'It's easy. You just leave everything behind and that's it. You pack clothes for a hot day and you pack clothes for a cold day. You take a few photographs and a couple of trinkets.'

How do you say goodbye?

'You don't. We left a fridge full of food as if we were coming back. I was rehearsing for a big new play and pretended I was returning to continue after my holidays. You don't tell anyone, because they can stop you. But foolishly *we* told a lot of people. We had a huge party – our place was crowded. I was packing while stepping over people, between one glass of vodka and another, saying, "Where is the passport? Do you want one pair of jeans or two?" We were young and irresponsible, partying like mad.'

How do you leave your parents?

'With difficulty. And what can a mother say to her child, aren't we all naughty? My mother would cry her heart out and I'd still say, I'm going. But it's the irresponsibility of a young soul and then it all seemed like a marvellous adventure. I think you have to have a huge imagination to do something like that – or no imagination at all. Because it's so large a step, an amazing change. When I left Poland it was a Communist country; it's a different story now.'

How do you say that final goodbye?

'It's very different when you are leaving for a holiday and when you are leaving for good. I couldn't see the system changing at that point. You're crossing the border and you turn back and look at those fields thinking, "Will I ever see you again? Will I ever smell that hay again or those Polish meadows?"'

Today when Veronica asks for something and Gosia refuses, explaining that she would not have been able to have that as a child, her daughter's response is, 'Yes, but you told me you could go for a walk to the forest by yourself. I can't even go to the corner shop.'

'That really struck me,' says Gosia. 'As a child, nobody drove me anywhere or held my hand to walk in the street. I was completely free – to explore, to be as a child, living and being with nature. I would find wild strawberries in the forest and sit there and eat them on the grass ... What are we doing to our children? Do we call this civilisation? They can't even breathe, they can't go and swim in the ocean – our biggest business is sunscreen.' What she treasures most is childhood. 'Childhood in everybody's life is the

GOSIA DOBROWOLSKA 91

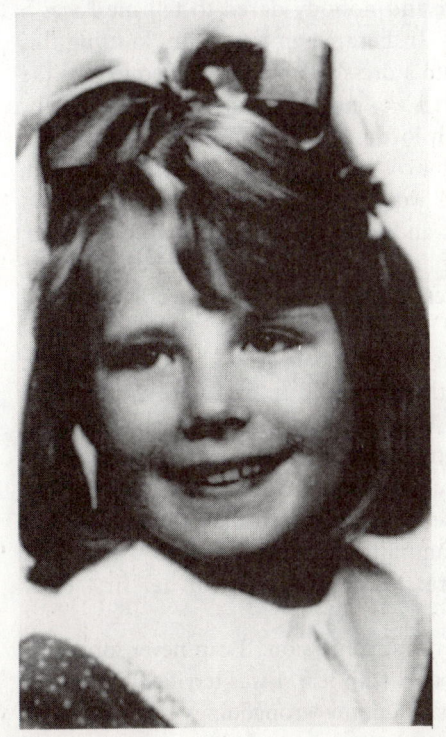

Four-year-old Gosia with her mother.

Gosia, aged eight years.

most important time. The older we get, the more we come back to childhood and the more we realise how important it is to bring up children well.'

Gosia was herself an adventurous and independent child, one of two siblings, with an older brother. With well-off parents, she may have lacked little materially but spiritual and emotional satisfaction was another matter. 'I was always looking for something,' she explains, wanting to know what lay '*za siedmioma górami, za siedmioma lasami, za siedmioma morzami*', beyond the seven hills, the seven forests and the seven seas'. These are the opening words of Polish fairy tales.

'I was a child they couldn't keep still. I always had something that I wanted to do and I always did it with extraordinary passion and no one could tell me I wasn't good at it.' These passions included being lead singer in a pop band at age eleven – 'I cried day and night to get a guitar and nobody dared to tell me I was a terrible singer'; knitting – 'it became an obsession, knitting this long thing I later made into a dress'; painting – 'I tried to pass the exams at high school but I was not good enough'; and, finally, acting – 'this is what I really love and is the only thing I have not yet dropped'. To raise money for costumes for the troupe she organised, she and her young friends would steal eggs from the farmers and sell them. 'I was the boss and would stand watch while a friend, who was the same age but half the size, would squeeze through the little hole where the chickens go, and collect the eggs.' She pursued each of her interests to the limit.

Not brought up with a religious background, Gosia seized on the Roman Catholic faith with fervour, and with exceptional commitment for a child. Unbeknown to her parents, she would regularly walk two kilometres to attend religious classes. 'I had this need. I remember I truly believed in God.' When she told her parents, they were surprised – 'children usually had to be *made* to do that sort of thing' – and although not religious themselves, bought her the white dress and gold cross for her first Holy Communion.

She also remembers her first confession. 'I can never forget the feeling. I almost wet my pants with fear. I was terrified that now I would have to tell the priest about my wrongdoings – stealing those eggs, smoking a cigarette, and drinking a beer that my father didn't finish. So I practised speaking quickly for days and days and ran the words together quickly in one breath so the priest wouldn't understand.' She liked the fat, jolly parish priest, who represented the church to her, and her faith wavered and was ultimately lost with the arrival of a new priest. 'He was mean and angry and hated everyone.'

She resolved this conflict at the age of seventeen when, passing a church, she went to the confessional and poured out her heart. 'This priest was fantastic and just listened to me express my views. "If you feel you don't believe, don't force yourself to come to Mass," he told me. My faith was restored, not in the church or in religion but in humanity.' When she left, an hour later, everyone in the church was staring at her. 'They were wondering what sort of person I was to have needed an hour for confession! I was baptised as a Catholic and I believe in God but I don't believe in religions. I think if you are a good person, that is what matters and not whether you have been to church last Sunday.' Her experiences have made her leave Veronica to make her own choice. 'She chose to be Catholic when she was eight, because the roots are there, and she was baptised then and even chose her own godparents.'

There were also other ways in which Gosia was unusual as a youngster. She asserted her independence by leaving home at fifteen – an unprecedented move in Europe in those days. But this was Gosia Dobrowolska – unlike the others, spontaneous and unstoppable. Far from leading her to reckless ways, the move from home ironically made her all the more responsible. 'We lived in the country then and I wanted to move to a big town, about two hours away. I felt restricted at home and I wanted to stretch my wings. I loved classical music and I wanted to go and listen to orchestras.'

It took much pleading and persuasion before her father eventually relented, telling Gosia he was no longer responsible for her. She rented a room in someone's apartment and fended for herself. 'I made myself go to school and do my homework.' Her incredible drive even forced her to study harder in her weaker subjects so that her parents would not be ashamed of her. 'I cooked my meals – well, I lived on sandwiches really. My parents gave me a budget for rent, clothes and food. I was the only one who lived alone.'

The challenges she thrust upon herself made her ovecome fear, endowed her with a new-found maturity and gave her status. Rather than being ostracised or rejected, she was looked up to and respected, so much so that other parents would come to her and ask for advice about their children. Some even begged Gosia to allow their daughters to stay with her for a weekend so that Gosia, seen as a positive kind of person, could make them realise that playing truant and drinking beer was not really such a good idea. Yet Gosia was no goody-goody. 'I came to this new school where everyone already knew one another and I managed to steal the best boy in the school!'

There are 800 elephants in Gosia's apartment. The various-sized figures are crammed on top of her piano, placed in glass cabinets or on wooden stands.

'I'm just an elephant freak,' she laughs. 'Who knows why? As a child at the zoo, I would stare at these wonderful huge and gentle creatures that looked like sculptures, except that they were moving. They are beautiful, faithful and very loving creatures.' Her collection includes only elephants with a raised trunk. 'That's lucky and makes it more difficult for me to find them. But I have this instinct – I can walk along the street and tell there will be an elephant in the window. I'm an elephant woman,' she giggles, as she goes to the kitchen to brew up some strong coffee, 'an elephant woman, but not in build, I hope.'

Her inner city flat has Polish rugs, tasteful furnishings and a breathtaking view of Sydney Harbour. 'I grew up in the town but because of my parents' work – my father was the manager of big agricultural farms and my mother was a zoo technician, like a vet really – we moved to various places in the country. So I had a mixture of both. That's why I live in the middle of Sydney. I want to be either very "city" or else out in the country. I don't like the suburbs; I have to be in the centre of a town or somewhere in the country to have peace. Otherwise I feel trapped. It's magnificent here. When I sit up in bed, I can see the colour of the water and the boats – what a way to wake up in the morning. Australia is beautiful, there is no question about it. Maybe it has a different beauty to Europe but it is still beautiful.'

Gosia is sitting in a comfortable black leather armchair. On one side of her is a large window with its incredible view overlooking the Harbour. As she talks, the afternoon sun streams in and falls upon her face. She looks quite exquisite, illuminated with both a radiant physical beauty and the inner beauty of passion as she speaks of her first acting role and her love of the theatre.

'When I mentioned to my father that I might try for acting school, he said that I had no chance because I was neither pretty nor ugly and you have to be one or the other – you couldn't be in between. "You're not pretty enough and you're not ugly enough to succeed," he told me. So that made me decide I would. I didn't think I was ugly but I definitely wasn't attractive. Even now, I think I am very average. Do you think I am attractive?' she asks with genuine objective interest. 'I don't feel that at all. I don't know what beauty is really – it's such a personal thing. What I find beautiful, others might not.'

Her seeming lack of ego and her views, unusual for an actress, are reflected in the roles she takes. She will act in films with no make-up – 'I know other actresses who would never do that' – and has even had her hair cropped and deliberately put on weight for other parts. Her explanation for this is simple. 'Because I don't think I am pretty, I don't mind being ugly. It's not such a big step. I want to play roles that expand me more so that people don't just look at my exterior. I would like to explore my other side.'

Gosia's interest in acting was inspired by her very first visit to the theatre at the age of nine. 'I remember that smell of make-up, the costumes and the space. I sat in the front row and the actors were so close. There were real people so close – living, crying, laughing, and I was watching. There was so much magic there and it was like I was falling for it.'

Gosia wanted to join that magic and those actors and, once at high school, she would go to the theatre regularly. 'We may have already seen one play five times, but I'd say to my boyfriend, "Come on, let's go and see it again."' Her interest grew. 'I wanted to get backstage, which was difficult, but I found someone who knew the cleaner and she introduced me to Pani Zosia, the woman in charge of the costume department. I was quite a charmer and she would let me try on the costumes left there from years and years of performing. I would put them on and look in the mirror.' To this day, Gosia recalls the particular smell of old costumes, the boots, jewellery and wigs, and her friendship of many years with Pani Zosia. 'When I came later to the theatre as an acting student, she would be really tough with the others, telling them not to mess up the costumes but with me she was different. She would let me in alone. She was a softie for me because she knew I was really into it.'

Gosia was indeed becoming more and more involved in theatre. She says she was not a child performer and did not even try to act in amateur theatre. 'I didn't want to be confronted with the fact that maybe I wasn't good. You know how you underestimate yourself all the time, but at the same time there is something telling you', and her voice drops to a whisper, 'try, try, don't give up, try. I wanted to try to reach the top. I gave myself only one chance.' She considered entering the equivalent of the state competition for poetry and prose. 'I enrolled for that and I won. I was seventeen.'

She found the courage to enter the competition after an experience that proved to be a turning point in her life. 'I got to know an actor that I really admired on stage, at that same Teatr Polski in Wroclaw. I would go and see him twenty minutes before his performance and perform for him in the corridor. He would give me a few directions and the next day I would come back and perform for him again. I remember this one love poem I was saying to him and he got really angry with me. He said, "Talk to me," and I kept on with the poem. He said, "You're not talking to me, *you're not talking to me*," and he started screaming, "Talk to *me*!"

'All of a sudden I got so angry at him. He was screaming at me, abusing me, saying, "Bullshit, this is bullshit, you are just saying words. Talk to me and tell me, tell me how you love me. I want to feel that you love me." I remember I started crying. I was so angry and so devastated and I burst out crying … "Now," he said, in a quiet, calm voice, "now I believe you."

'And then he left. He just said, "I have to run, I have to go on stage." And he left me there, all emotional while he was cool. How could he just leave me? I will never forget that. I will never forget that dark corridor and the chair he was sitting in. I was devastated. I really almost fell in love with him that night. He made me say those words, to really believe them. And then he left me. I fall in love with you and you leave me, saying you're going on the stage, what do you mean? I thought to myself. I was so shocked and I went to see the play again and I looked at him in a different way. I mean, he made me speak those words and believe them.'

Uplifted, Gosia entered the competition with the same poem, a Polish classic. She was shocked but not entirely surprised when she won. 'Because underneath, that was my dream, my goal. It was the same with acting school. At that time in Poland, you could not become an actor until you passed acting school, and there were only three acting schools and all those people. The competition was very hard and even just applying, people would say, "You're mad, you'll never get in." I did not have any connections. I didn't come from an acting background. None of my family were actors. But I knew I had to try, I knew I had to do something artistic. I couldn't see myself in an ordinary normal job, not a job where you go and sit from nine until five and then come home and cook dinner. I mean my job had to be something that I lived for, twenty-four hours a day. Nobody really believed in me except for my brother.'

His faith in her was rewarded when she did indeed make it to acting school. Yet, even then, during the three-year course, she was unsure of herself. 'I was jealous of my friends because I thought they were so good and I wasn't good enough. They considered me a good student but when I looked at some of my friends performing, I thought, God, aren't they marvellous, I would never be able to do that. I was doing it without knowing I was doing it; I always felt less of myself...'

This was proved at the end of her course. 'I was wondering what was going to happen to me when, all of a sudden, I'm asked by the dream director, the *dream* director from that same theatre in Wroclaw, to come and work for him.' Although he, Jerzy Grzegorzewski, couldn't offer Gosia a role at the time, he asked her to wait until a leading role was available. 'I asked him, "What do you mean, a leading role? As long as I am acting, the role doesn't matter." He said that there were actors who had leading roles and actors who had supporting roles or small roles and were not capable of leading roles.'

This all came as a revelation to Gosia. 'I thought that sometimes you lead and sometimes you have a small role and just walk on the stage. I didn't think I would be able to do a leading role but actually, in that theatre and in that first year, I had four leading roles.' Her first professional acting role was truly remarkable. 'I wanted to play in Shakespeare's *The Taming of the Shrew* and I really wanted to play Helena in *A Midsummer Night's Dream*. I wanted that because I felt inside me, behind this really proper nice girl, there is this girl who is so naughty.' She was rebelling against the impression she was conveying, as an Ophelia type of character. 'I hated Ophelia,' she laughs.

Gosia could not believe her luck when the theatre decided to put on *A Midsummer Night's Dream*. 'But somebody else was cast as Helena before I finished acting school, before I was even asked to join the company. It was such bad timing. I was devastated but I would go and sit through endless hours of rehearsal, endless hours. I spent so much time there I was really familiar with the play. And the actress who was playing Helena was wonderful: she really was an animal. She played this character really beautifully.'

The opening night came, soon after which there was a disagreement between the director and the actress and, early one morning, Gosia was summoned to come to the theatre immediately. 'The director asked, "Can you play Helena tonight?" and I said yes, just like that. It was just like the first time I was asked to be in a play in Australia, before I could speak English. I had no idea how I was going to do it; first of all I felt the joy and then the fear. Can I? It was a big risk. We're talking about an audience of over a thousand. All the tickets were sold out. There was no time to call all the actors together for a rehearsal – I had to perform that night. Thank God, I had been to see them rehearse so many times. I knew every move.'

She was given three hours to learn her lines and had an afternoon rehearsal with some of the actors. 'They were completely shocked. They thought I would need at least three or four days to prepare. I can't remember much about that night; it went like two minutes. I just remember those huge lights, the big stage. I couldn't see anybody in the audience, it was dark, and I was hot under the lights because I was nervous and emotional. Some of the other actors didn't even know, and I had this shocked face from some of them – a different actress is on the stage tonight! There were the lights and this thickness in the air and people clapping.'

She saw it as a huge test for her as an actress, a test that she passed with flying colours. 'When I finished, the cast was amazed and impressed.' And she was thrilled, to have stepped into her dream role, and into an imaginative interpretation of Shakespeare's play.

Acting has taken her to new heights, sometimes quite literally. When she later played Dionysus in Philip Keir's production of *The Bacchae* – her first Australian theatre appearance – she had to learn trapeze work. 'A man from the circus came to teach me and on opening night they put the trapeze right up high, with no mat underneath because it was a play. You just go through all this, you don't question it. When you start analysing, you start having fears and that's the worst thing that can happen. Fear can stop you from everything.'

She has always considered herself fearless but now 'I am conditioned to be more mature, to be more responsible. I would like to strip that off and throw it away and become what I was – to come back to do fearless things, to be a bit more dangerous. Well, now I have responsibilities. I have a child.'

Yet she still has her moments. 'I am basically an extremely crazy person. I have a great sense of fun,' she laughs uproariously. 'You don't know that but my daughter knows and that's why she can relate to me. I can inspire her. I'm not a prim and proper mother and that's why we get on so well. I'm someone who can dance on the street and talk to strangers. Veronica and I have fun together and in that way I can also get through to her to teach her about the responsibilities and hardships of life. That's very important to me – I'm old-fashioned in that respect. And she's a wonderful daughter.'

When it comes to acting, Gosia sees each of her roles as a new and different challenge, throwing herself into her research and preparation. And when it is all over, she feels absolutely drained. 'Acting is very much a burning desire in me. It's like a drug and I'm addicted to it, expressing myself through my roles. In some ways, I'm going on this marvellous journey. I am somewhere else when I'm shooting a film. I create my own world with the story and the people who work with me. The characters in the film are my world. At that point, disasters could happen in the real world and I wouldn't care. I separate myself completely from everything else.'

She would rather be on location than have to come home daily and deal with the messages on her answering machine. 'I find it frustrating to deal with people. When somebody rings me and talks on, I'm never rude but I'm not really interested. If I like the story of the film and my character, then I don't want shooting to finish. I'm going through agonising pain when there's only one more week to go, five days to go, four days ... It's sort of like dying and then you shoot the last scene and it is as if you have died. The character is not alive any more, it's finished. I go through terrible depression afterwards for a few days. I feel very unhappy and very unstable emotionally, and then I am reincarnated in another role with another group of people, another story and another world.'

Gosia's film and television credits have been wide and varied. From Nurse Cox in the comedy *Around the World in 80 Ways*, to drama in the chilling and highly acclaimed low-budget film *Phobia*, she has also appeared on the smaller screen in *GP*, *A Country Practice*, and *Fields of Fire II* and *III*. Her acting talent has not been limited, as she once thought, to the Thalia Theatre Company set up by her ex-husband, Bodgan Koca. As well as those roles, she has performed for ABC radio and her face is well known to the public from the *Woman's Day* and Oil of Ulan television commercials.

'Personally I don't care about fame,' she says. 'I may not look it but I'm quite shy and if somebody recognises me, I'm the one that's blushing. I don't know what to say; I feel hopeless. I find it very embarrassing.' Yet she is thrilled to be told someone has enjoyed a film in which she acted. 'I just calmly say, "Oh, that's good," but I am so excited inside. Maybe it's shyness, maybe it is what is expected. You are not supposed to show all that emotion. You are supposed to grow up and not be spontaneous but dress and act your age. People don't expect you to behave like a little girl when you're thirty. Why not? In a way, it would be wonderful to be able to do that, to express happiness or sadness.'

The acting profession is a precarious one, with as few as 5 per cent of those involved in the industry employed at any one time, yet Gosia is not fazed by the probability of long stretches of time between work. 'As long as there is money in the bank, it's okay. I don't want to work just for the sake of working. I want to need the work. I want to feel ready and really have this need. I don't know whether I would like to work non-stop because then it would become too automatic. I have to dream about work.' Besides, she adds, after withdrawing from the world while she is working on a film, there is catching up to do, with friends, and simply coming back to her life.

She has made several films with Paul Cox, including *Golden Braid* and *A Woman's Tale*. He describes her as a sensitive and highly talented individual with a fine screen presence – a rare commodity. 'She has an enormous ability to make things feel and look normal, a great ability just to be there,' he says. 'I find Gosia very easy to work with, totally in tune. She becomes the part without throwing tantrums, is very mature in whatever she is doing, and is totally dedicated.'

He is also impressed with her skill in being able to forge an acting career for herself. 'Once she arrived in Australia she gave away the idea of being an actress. Luck obviously helps a little – she got the part in *Silver City* – but I know that very often she didn't know what was being said in the script, her English was so poor. To have survived somehow in a very small country like Australia is in itself a remarkable achievement. There are a huge number of actors and actresses with all sorts of accents standing by – it's a very competitive business. Gosia is in a class of her own but this country is too small and it thinks small. I'm sure had she stayed in Poland or Europe she would have been much more prominent than she is now.'

After watching one of his films, Gosia knew even before meeting Paul Cox that she would be able to relate completely to the way he thought and worked. 'Film is a marvellous invention but it's abused in a lot of ways. I can understand the need for commercial films but there should also be room for people like him to express themselves.' She talks of the gentleness and compassion in his films, the fact that he has no heroes, and that the background music is beautifully composed. 'I love watching his films. Some people go to church, but I like to watch a film that gives me calmness and inspires me a little. I think Paul Cox makes movies like that and I was glad to work with him.'

In one of those films – *A Woman's Tale*, in which she appeared with Sheila Florance – Gosia learned a lot more than she had anticipated. As part of her research for the role of the district nurse Anna, she accompanied a doctor friend on patient rounds. 'It was extraordinary to step into someone's house when the person is dying and then go out onto the street where little children are playing. You see there is a beginning and an end and it is up to us what we do in the middle. That was an enriching experience for me, not a sad one.'

Sheila Florance was seriously ill while making *A Woman's Tale* and died some months afterwards. The two slowly developed a strong relationship. In the film she would call Gosia's character '*malenka*'. 'That "means little" one in Polish. Whenever I can, I try to sneak something Polish into my movies – I'll whistle a Polish song or say something in Polish. I think these are nice touches for the audience and anyone Polish watching will get a little message. I am proud of my background. I wasn't born here so it's good sometimes to remind people of that. And I don't play migrants any more – I play normal roles and instead of them justifying my accent, I am saying something in there.'

She suddenly becomes pensive. 'I heard on the news that my theatre, Teatr Polski, in Wroclaw burned down. It was a very big theatre, the biggest drama theatre in Poland. An extremely important part of my life is gone. Going back to Poland I would visit it and walk around those little corners, through those corridors and along those balconies. It was a beautiful old classical building and meant so much to me. How can a few theatre seats be so important – those seats where I and my boyfriend sat and saw the same play again and again? I cannot accept the fact that it is gone and there will be something new and modern built there.'

She says theatre is a big tradition in Poland, unlike Australia, and actors are well respected. 'They are as important as lawyers and surgeons there because they are carrying on the national tradition – speaking our poets' language from the stage and educating the crowds.' Acting schools control the number of actors graduating, so that they are all employed. 'They might not all have marvellous careers but they all have work; you will not find them in bars trying to survive or sweeping the floors. Here, because there is no restriction, it depends on how strong your elbows are. Anybody on the street can become an actor and it also depends on your luck.'

Yet despite her background, she is not altogether in favour of acting schools, saying technique can certainly be taught but talent is another matter. 'You either have talent or you don't.' Sometimes it is too easy – a young teenager becoming a soapie star – 'as long as they can read the script, they can learn the lines' – and then being dropped a few years later. 'We raise them up and then we forget them.'

She is wary, therefore, of Veronica pursuing an acting career. 'I think education is very important and I want to give her the chance of choosing what she wants to do later on. I want to protect her from too easily stepping into her mother's shoes. Maybe she'll be fantastic in science. "Do whatever you like with your life," I tell her, "later, when you are old enough to make the decision."'

Meanwhile Gosia believes the arts are the best ambassadors for a country. 'When I came to Australia, I had no idea who the prime minister was, but I knew Patrick White; everybody knows *Crocodile Dundee*, but not the opposition leader. We really should look at that more closely in Australia and invest more money in the arts … It should be a normal thing to take a child to a concert, to hear an orchestra. Let's introduce them to something else early in their lives so they will grow up different people.'

For she is concerned by the violence depicted in newspapers and magazines, films and videos and the influence it exerts on youngsters. 'Under Communism, you had your enemy and you knew what that enemy was – the system. You united yourself with your friends against that enemy and you fought it. Here the enemy is invisible, the enemy is all around us and you cannot point a finger at it. The enemy is the shop that sells guns and the newspaper that puts shooting heroes on the front page. The enemy is everywhere, the main enemy is commercialism and consumerism. Everybody needs counselling these days – before, we used to have family and friends. We used to go and talk to one another and go to the corner shop and be friends with the guy who sold the bread and newspapers.'

She is all for honesty and against commercialism and greed. She has accepted overseas film work on the basis of a one-page contract with the scantiest of details. 'I liked the producer and the director and I trusted them. So why did I need a thick contract so I could sue them or they could sue me? People told me I was crazy and that I had no protection. But it was all perfect. Fame is part of this whole system. You must be famous and so investors and distributors have more say in who plays the role than the director. The poor director used to cast you because you were talented, you were right for the part, but now they cast because "she sells" or "he sells". Everything is for sale. Luckily I'm still doing things I want to do. I love acting so much that sometimes I do compromise, perhaps in a commercial or something. But I wouldn't advertise some products.'

Of all her acting roles, the part of Nina in *Silver City* remains her favourite. 'I am terribly sentimental about that film. I love it; it is like my little baby and I cannot be very objective about it. It gave me so much.' But unlike Nina, Gosia experienced no racism in Australia. 'I can honestly say I didn't, because of the way I look. As long as I didn't open my mouth, everyone thought I was Australian.' Her blonde hair and blue eyes conveyed that impression. 'I remember once I was sitting in North Sydney Station and a very drunk Australian guy came along and started abusing the Japanese gentleman sitting next to me. "What is he doing here, bloody Jap?" he said, and turned to me, thinking I was Australian, for support. "Wrong address, mate," I said to him.'

Gosia admits she still makes some terrible mistakes herself when she does open her mouth to speak. 'I was filming in Canada – the imported star from Australia – and on the first night, the producer took me to the movies with a couple of other actors. As they were buying the tickets, I was buying the popcorn and drinks. I stood there and said very loudly, "Can I have a popcorn and a large cock?" The woman behind the counter was trying to control herself, so was everybody else in the queue, and the poor producer was thinking, "Who the hell did we bring all the way from Australia?"'

Not so funny for Gosia was the prospect of an Australian meat pie. 'I didn't want to eat one because *pies* (pronounced "pea-yes") in Poland means dog. I thought they were eating dog meat. I was sure about that, absolutely.'

The Australia she once considered a marvellous adventure is now her home. 'But I don't consider myself either Polish or Australian,' she admits. "I'm just me, with a Polish background living in Australia.'

Sometimes that Polish background calls her, but no longer as strongly as before. She is now able to return, something she did not think would be possible. 'The changes have been amazing, changes for the better. It was good to go back but a very funny feeling. Everything was so familiar, every stone, but there was no home to go to – Australia is now my home. I don't know that I miss anything, because Poland now is a different Poland. People have changed and martial law in Poland destroyed a lot. People used to visit, they used to have happier lives. Now basically it is like here – everybody is too busy to see one another.' Yet she still loves the Polish news on SBS television. 'Every time I watch, a bit of my heart shakes.'

Her family is now with her in Australia, her brother following her a year after she arrived and her parents seven years ago.

If Gosia could have one wish, it would be to return alone and anonymously to the places of her childhood, to the fields full of purple wildflowers (*fiolki*), and forget-me-nots – to smell them, lie amongst them and collect them. 'My memories are first smell and then visual. Once when I went back to Europe and was in Austria, I asked a friend to drive me to the forest, to switch off the engine and be quiet. I closed my eyes and I just smelt the air and listened to the birds.

'The bush and its smell is different in Australia and the light is different too. That's why Australian films look different to European films. They probably think we have different methods of lighting but we have different light altogether. To start with, the sun is in a different direction. When I was looking for an apartment, the advertisement said north-facing but that means dark in Europe. There the south has the light, here the north has the sun.'

While these are merely differences, there have been losses in moving to Australia. 'Christmas has lost its meaning to me. The magic of Christmas is the cold and the crispy snow. Traditionally, we start celebrating on Christmas Eve, *Wigilia*, looking for the first star at four or five in the afternoon, the family together and the table set with an extra plate, as is the custom, for a traveller. We don't eat meat, we eat only fish and vegetarian things, thirteen little dishes. So let's mix but let's keep our traditions. People can come to my home and see the way we celebrate Christmas and I love to go to the Australian lunch and eat turkey.'

When you ask whether she has contacted the Polish community and made Polish friends, Gosia becomes almost indignant. 'I don't choose my friends by nationality; I choose my friends because of personality. I have a few Polish friends as it happens, but I'm not really involved in the so-called Polish community.'

She loves Australia and her life here. 'It's very hard to pinpoint any particular thing. I like the way people are relaxed. I like the fact that we are an island and far away without any political problems. We are very lucky here.' She was pleased therefore to become an Australian citizen, and still be able to keep her Polish citizenship. 'I wanted to be able to vote and do those important things.'

She may have had extensive film experience but theatre remains Gosia's first love. 'I think actors should go back to the stage to feel the audience,' she says. 'In a film, technically it's very different. You haven't got that immediate response, things may be shot out of sequence. As an actor, you miss out on that marvellous moment of relating to an audience. The film crew never looks at you as a performer. They look at your make-up, your hair or your props. The camera looks at the framing, the sound at the way you speak. Nobody really looks at what you are doing and that hurts a lot because there is no response and just the insecurity – am I doing fine or not?

'Later on, somebody can interfere with your performance by cutting it here or there. The film editor didn't see that moment that was so important to you and it ends up on the cutting room floor. And then you get to see the film a long time after you've done it, they can do so many tricks with the performance.

'I think theatre is more satisfying for an actor. I think that's where the actor really belongs. It doesn't matter how you feel – you have to go on the stage that night and perform that part from beginning to end. And feel the audience. Nobody knows how much actors feel the audience. Sometimes there is a silence because the audience loves the performance and sometimes there is a silence because the audience is bored. You know that, you know whether you're getting through to them or not. They come to you to take them away from the reality of their lives, to take them on this little journey. And if you can speak honestly to them – because I don't believe in acting as acting, I believe in living the part – then someone lives the part with you. You can use your acting technique but they don't want to see that. They want to see the real person.

'In the theatre, you're right there and that's it. You feel and the audience responds. It's a marvellous, satisfying, beautiful feeling.'

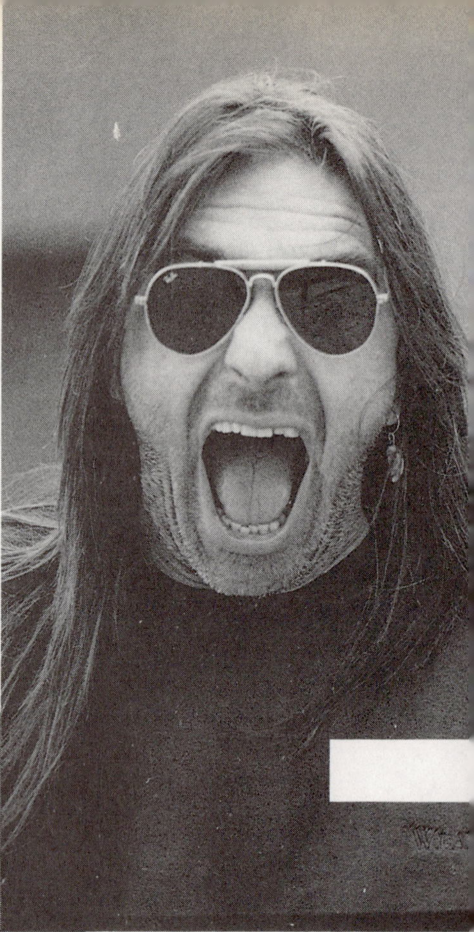

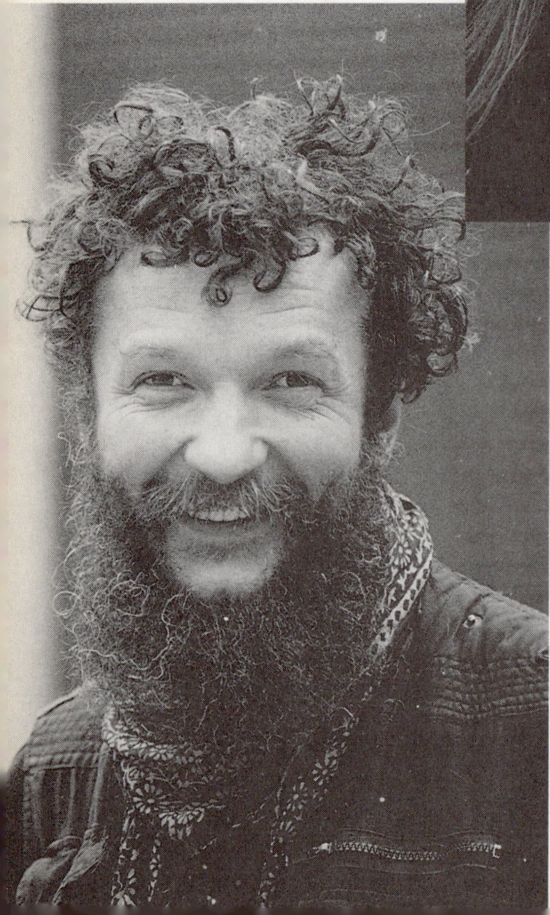

GETTING THE PICTURE

'With photography I believe that if you can combine a lot of life experience with common sense, personal sensitivity and technical knowledge, you can create whatever you want.'

ERYK

'They told me Australia was the most boring place with no social life and that it was very slow with no culture, everyone was closed in their houses. And the more I listened, the more I wanted to come here!'

TOMEK

Photographers

Sipping beer straight from the bottle, he talks through a haze of cigarette smoke and over a background of loud music. His large, muscular, 190-centimetre frame clad in a white T-shirt tucked into ripped jeans, green beads dangling around his neck and long, straight hair protruding from a tightly bound red and white scarf, he resembles a groovy partygoer. And this is a great party. It is the continuous party that is Eryk Fitkau's life. Here, in his first-floor Melbourne studio, he relaxes after another long day's work.

As one half of the photographic team known as *Tomek & Eryk*, he is loud and expansive while the other half, Tomek Sikora, presents a more serious side to the world. 'We are very different in character and I think this is part of our success,' offers Eryk.

This success has been outstanding. They are considered ten years ahead of their time by other colleagues. 'Who told you that?' Eryk laughs. 'Well, perhaps five years now,' he concedes. Whatever he admits to, Tomek and Eryk's original style and innovative techniques have certainly established them among Australia's leading photographers. Their talent and determination has brought them major advertising campaigns both here and overseas, prominent magazine spreads and notable contracts in Europe, Asia and the United States. They are unique also in that they are not limited to one area but are highly skilled in fashion, advertising, retail and commercial photography – a remarkable achievement in this tightly competitive field where, as Eryk confirms, 'You are only as good as your last job.'

Even more impressive are the facts that both started their career together from scratch in a new land, after working in a Communist country with fewer practical resources. They arrived in Australia two years apart, with minimal language skills but with a vision. For Eryk, this was to do better in each subsequent job. Photography was not even his intention when he arrived in Australia in 1980 from his native Poland.

'I had an open mind. I didn't set a goal that I would have a photographic studio. I treated everything as a challenge and as an adventure. It was like watching a film in my head – that everything was new and that this job in the factory was temporary and the next job had to be better, better conditions and better paid. I enjoyed this climbing up, this progression and I was doing very well,' Eryk explains. His first job was in a factory at Mentone. Living on the other side of the city in Brunswick, and without a car, he would rise at four in the morning to get there. 'I was working on a lathe making some carburettor parts. It was a dry lathe, throwing a lot of splinters, and I would have to spend two hours at home picking them out with tweezers.'

He says his next job, in another car factory, was paradise in comparison and so began his advancement. 'Things were good for me here. My life was pretty well set up – I had my own house, I was driving a good car and I had a pretty good cash flow.' His friend Tomek, meantime, was still back in Poland with wife Malgosia and son Mateusz. 'So I talked to him and said, "Pack up your things and come, we'll do something together," but he was pretty happy at that stage in Poland.

'Then martial law started and I managed to pass a message through to him, asking whether he wanted to get out. This was heavy-duty stuff – tanks on the streets, everything cut off, no telephones, nothing. But we managed to communicate – it was 1982 I think – and he wanted to leave.' Tomek was able to come to Australia, alone initially, and once he was established, twelve months later his family joined him. *Tomek & Eryk*, the business they set up together, went from strength to strength and they recently celebrated eleven years in partnership. 'In Poland we were basically good mates,' says Eryk. 'It was kind of 95 per cent friendship and 5 per cent business. Here the proportion is a bit different – it is more business. The friendship is still there but the business definitely dominates.' Lounging back comfortably on a chair in the room adjoining his South Yarra studio, he speaks rapidly in a strong eastern-European accent which frequently lapses into an Australian twang or American drawl.

Friends for some twenty-two years, Tomek and Eryk had met in Warsaw on opposite sides of the camera. Tomek was learning photography and Eryk was his subject, the model. Eryk had drifted into modelling by circumstance rather than by choice. 'The Communists introduced a law that young people who didn't work for the government were to be sent to work camps. So I looked for some kind of official work and came up with this modelling.'

The modelling was slightly different to that in the West. 'This was Poland and everything was government-owned. There wasn't much competition but Poland was very sensitive as far as propaganda was concerned. They were creating advertising, they were creating fashion, all for show in the West. We had fashion houses and fashion parades which were fantastic compared to Australian fashion shows. I had twenty different garments that were made for me – extravagant shows paid for with government money. Designers were going to Paris to see the latest styles, bringing back all the best fabric and creating collections that were then sold to members of government and their wives. It was all to create an image – that we too had fashion parades and advertising.'

At twenty-one he met Tomek and so began his contact with photography. 'We got talking and he asked me to come along on an assignment.' The story was on government housing and who was entitled to it and, anticipating a fiery response, Tomek invited the tall, well-built Eryk for protection. He knew from talking to him that Eryk would be well able to handle any situation they might find themselves in. 'I had a long history of street fighting,' Eryk explains. 'Anyway, Tomek put his camera down and I grabbed it and took some shots. Later on he had a conversation with me.

'"You have to be a photographer," he said. "Look, I've never taken a photograph before in my life." "Think about it," he said.

'I thought about it for two days and decided I didn't have anything to lose. Let's try. Three months later I was working for a magazine as a photojournalist.' He admits this was fast, adding that his route to photography was far from the normal one. 'People go through photography as a hobby. I was thrown into deep water and faced responsibility straight away, and the tension of thinking about whether what I shot would come out or not. There was also the danger of publication because of the Communist regime.'

His early years of rebellion and non-conformity now stood him in good stead. 'I could get into areas other photojournalists couldn't, because my contacts were everywhere. If I were to write a book about all the stages in my life, it would be a pretty entertaining book,' he adds. 'I came from a very good family, what they call blue-blooded, but when I was in my late teens I went completely to the other side and tasted a bit of – what can we call it – the underworld. Then in my twenties, my purpose in life was finding a good time and enjoying myself.

'I'm almost forty-two and still, when I go out, I always have young girlfriends. I am surrounded by a lot of young people and I can still out-rage them. I still have the energy to keep going, to drink more, to dance more. At my age, people have got families and are wearing white collars and ties. I still don't feel my age. I have to say to myself, "Look, you know you're forty-two and you should be more responsible."'

Unconventional and boisterous, offbeat and individual he may be yet Eryk declares, 'Both Tomek and I are, you know, crazy – but in a completely different way. Whatever you find in one, the other will do in another way.' That relates to all aspects of life – money, recreation and, ultimately, photographic style. They are truly poles apart.

'Tomek will save everything and I will spend everything. I enjoy the present and if I want to do something, I will not worry about spending money. If I want something, I will get it. Tomek can't spend as he has to save for old age. As for enjoying time away from photography, he will go to the cinema and sit with his Polish friends. I will sit with my Australian friends and go fishing.' This interest of Eryk's, which he describes as more of an obsession, is the one regret he has about choosing Melbourne over Sydney for an Australian base. 'When I came here there was a recession and I had information that it was much easier to get work in Melbourne than Sydney. I'm pleased here from a photography angle – we can't complain as far as the variety and amount of work we have – but I love big game fishing and to be on the ocean. And the best area for big fish is New South Wales; it is a fishing heaven.

'I need time to completely switch off from photography. When it is busy with a lot of jobs happening, you get to the stage that you become tired and you realise you can't produce good work. You have a break, take time to re-charge and then you want to start again. But Tomek takes his camera everywhere on holiday and shoots non-stop.'

As dissimilar as their characters are, so are their backgrounds – Eryk rebelling against his more conservative upbringing and cutting off contact with family, Tomek coming from an artistic environment, maintaining close family ties and learning to use a camera from his early teens. While Eryk's interest in photography came later and unexpectedly in life, his powers of observation – vital in his later career – were in tune right from childhood.

'Nature always fascinated me. I'd ride my bicycle to the water and spend the entire day by myself, lying by the edge of the river or lake watching fish and what was around me. I never was bored, like kids say they are bored. I don't know this feeling. Always, in those early days I would have just one or two friends. I never was surrounded by a big group. I believe you can have a lot of people you can spend a good time with, but you can't classify them as friends. I still believe in this philosophy.

'I was born in Warsaw and I have one sister and one stepbrother, both of them much older than me. My father was a gynaecologist and my mother a nurse. I had a good childhood. I was very shy but when I started growing up, I realised that to be shy doesn't pay.'

Shy or not, right from the start Eryk developed an inner strength and a quiet determination – qualities that were to help form his later life. 'I remember when I was about five or six, I'd go out with my nanny and I'd see these boys – strong boys, street boys – sitting on top of these tall trees. I was totally fascinated by that. I inherited a fear of heights from my mother but I was so fascinated by these guys sitting in the trees that I started climbing trees myself. Each month I'd go a little bit higher and a little bit higher. I got this drive to be tough and after a while I became too tough,' he laughs.

This type of self-motivation and persistence, cultivated in childhood, ultimately got Eryk out of Poland and ready to start a new life. 'Poland was the only country in the entire Communist bloc that allowed you, if you made a little bit of effort, to go for a holiday in the West. I went to Holland, Germany, Sweden and Denmark in 1975. I stayed away for four months and it was mind-blowing – I was amazed at people smiling, at a completely different atmosphere and reality. The opportunities were perfect for me to stay but I had to come back – I got homesick.'

But returning to Poland, he immediately felt uncomfortable. 'At the border, they gave me a razor and told me to shave because they said they couldn't recognise me. They stripped my whole car and searched it. And I remember my first day back in Warsaw. After four months I was already used to a different kind of lifestyle and now I saw these empty supermarket shelves and felt this depressing atmosphere and I thought, "What is this homesickness that made me come back?"'

At the same time, Eryk had no illusions about life outside Poland. 'I knew that when people came back to Poland and told how it was in the West, there was a bit of exaggeration. People would listen and pass on the story further and add a bit more until this story about the lifestyle grew out of proportion. The opinion was basically that you had to do nothing there – it was just heaven and even the rain falling on you was golden.

'I wanted to leave Poland because I hated the Communist system. I wanted to see how I would cope elsewhere with my life experiences based in Poland, how I would climb up from the beginning on neutral ground. I saw a lot of Polish people with the ambition to leave come back after a year or two and I did not want to do that. I made a second trip, to London, and I spent time with the Polish community there. I was looking at these miserable faces – they were not happy there and they were not happy in Poland – and I thought, no, that's not right, it's all based on this homesickness. I analysed how this homesickness was working on my second trip and then I came back to Warsaw and said to myself, right, now I start working on my mind.

'I'm pretty good when I want to implant something in my head. Eventually I will do it. I remember asking myself all the time, am I ready? No, not yet. It took me about eight months to fully prepare myself for leaving. And then one morning I said, I think I am ready. I came to Australia about fourteen years ago. It was difficult,' he comments without elaborating, 'and I haven't been back to Poland since. I think I *overdid* it a bit,' he laughs.

The technique he used was based on the way the memory works. 'Subconsciously we eliminate bad things and we emphasise good things. So we remember the good and forget the bad. When I was abroad I was analysing what I was missing, and when I came back I was facing this in a really microscopic type of approach, analysing and putting the reality into my head so I would not be fooled by the mirage I remembered.' He gives the example of looking at the empty supermarket shelves in Warsaw and saying to himself he wanted to be in a place with full shelves. 'All those sorts of things, simple everyday things,' he explains.

Little by little, day by day, he worked on his technique – and succeeded. 'Even when I had a hard time initially in Australia and considered leaving, I never thought of coming back to Poland.' Today, he says, he misses nothing about the country of his birth. He has found friendship and opportunity in Australia, choosing to come here over England and America. 'Everybody in Poland knew that life in England was hard and there was unemployment. The United States was still a promising land and you could achieve success there. But I calculated that with no money and no English, my chances of making it there were very small. Australia was then and still is a pretty good launching pad compared to a lot of other countries. If you want to do something and you've got enough energy, you can do it here. That would be much more difficult in other places. I had established myself in Poland at a young age, but I wanted to start again – to go somewhere new, somewhere unknown. I wanted to take my life experiences from Communist Poland and see how I would cope elsewhere, on neutral ground.

'After Tomek and I made it here, we could have moved to New York. He was there several times and found an agent, a star-maker for photographers just like you have star-makers in music ... This agent will take you on and you have a 100 per cent guarantee you will make it to the top. Tomek and I had a long talk and decided against it. It would be fantastic if you were twenty-five years old and single but, even if we made it to the big time now, would we enjoy it?

'I deal with a lot of American people. Australian television is mainly American and I know I would not feel right over there. I can't stand the materialism and the idealistic attitude. Coming from a Communist country, I was brought up on propaganda and am very sensitive to it. America has this idealism it tries to inject in everything – everything has to have a positive moral in the end. Australia is a kind of multicultural country and you can find whatever you want here. There is this incredible variety. I enjoy the company here and the mentality is much more down to earth.'

Eryk may have arrived in Australia with an open mind as far as photography was concerned but there was no doubt in his mind as to what was important – language. 'I knew that I had to have an Australian girlfriend – that was number one priority. And I knew that I would learn English very quickly that way. I'm as dumb as a bloody table leg at learning languages. I learned a bit of Russian at school, only because we had so many hours of it, but as far as English was concerned, my knowledge was practically zero.'

Eryk mixed with different social groups in Melbourne. 'I had one group in the factories and then another group through a girlfriend, who were kind of snobby, pretty wealthy types. Everything was new for me and then I discovered cask wine. I compared what we could buy with average wages in Poland and Australia. I was sort of underpaid in this factory but I could still afford a lot of things. I discovered this cask wine and I thought it was amazing. It was only a few dollars, what I could earn in about one-and-a-half hours.

'So I came with this cask of wine and Sally, who was studying at university, said, "Eryk, you can't drink that. It is awful." "What is awful?" I said. "It tastes good; there is nothing wrong with it." A few people came for dinner and she said, "*This* is what you have to drink." I thought the wine from the bottle tasted normal, like what was in the wine cask. So I put one bottle on its side, poured in the wine from the cask and then pretended to open it. I poured it out and she said, "Eryk, now you can see what the difference is in this wine." I laughed and told them it was the wine from the cask.

'I was curious about the Australian culture. I didn't take everything for granted. I had to observe, make up my own mind. There were a lot of funny moments – I was testing everything and comparing it to Poland. I was enjoying it – the differences, the different mentality. I came with the attitude that everybody is the same – it doesn't matter if they are Russians or whatever. The surroundings may make it a little different but I accept everybody.'

Eryk may have accepted everyone but others did not quite know what to make of him and Tomek. The pair always made an impact. 'We come across art directors today and they say, "Ah, I remember you, you came here in 1983." Why do they remember us?'

Well, how about this as a first impression?

'I looked like a cross between a builder's labourer and a gang member, my muscles were double the size they are now from playing ice hockey in Poland and from working out in the gym here. And Tomek looked as if he had escaped from a mental hospital. His favourite shop was the op shop and he'd put together very odd pieces of clothing with plastic brooches and war medals hanging off them. His hair was shaved on one side, including his moustache and eyebrow, and he had a wave on the other. What a visual impact – and a combination of one guy who doesn't speak any English at all and another speaking only broken English.'

'You make people curious. "What are they all about?" they'd ask. They'd talk about us and their curiosity would grow. In the beginning especially, we had these kamikaze-type art directors who would say, "We'll give them a job and see what they can produce." Thank God for us that most of these jobs worked out really well.'

What also worked well was the combination of the two of them as a team. 'You have to stand out, apart from the pictures you produce,' Eryk explains. 'It helps if you have a personality or something that people will remember – to get an extra edge on this competitive market. Each year photographic colleges produce a hundred or more potential photographers ready to go. How many of them make it? When it's a good year, maybe two or three. When it's a bad year, none. Well, this is the other side of success. A different style and beautiful pictures are a part of that but you need that extra edge.'

Tomek and Eryk started by working on projects together because there was insufficient work for both of them. This has now become their trademark. 'From the beginning we said that everything we did, we would sign *Tomek & Eryk*. It didn't matter whether Tomek did it or I did it. We set up a system that I think nobody has used before and we stuck to it. When people come to us for a job, they deal with *Tomek & Eryk*, not with Tomek and not with Eryk. It works and people are very curious but they accept it.'

It works because they have adopted a similar style. 'So even though we have different characters, we spend so much time together that our approach to jobs is the same. Tomek was more advanced than I was in photography but what we faced here was pretty new, in equipment and technology. We learned together and we synchronised ourselves to such an extent that even the art directors who know us very well can't pick whose job it is.' Selecting their individual job assignments is decided between themselves and it is usually an easy process. 'We decide on who the job will suit better. Then there are practical reasons – I may be busy so he takes it, he may be overseas so I will do it.'

Work content and location varies. 'We've worked in Singapore, Hong Kong, Malaysia, France, Belgium, New Zealand and the United States in recent times, and the work is all different. That is what's unique about us.

'When we presented our folio to advertising agencies nobody could pinpoint what we were good for because there were so many different pictures. What appealed to one client would be different to what appealed to another and our jobs started to cover a wide range of subjects. One day we were getting corporate work, another day we were shooting for a retail catalogue. We'd shoot high fashion one day and a beer bottle – a still-life shot – for an advertisement the next. In every field we presented our folio, clients would find what they wanted and we would get a variety of work. That's pretty unusual. It is standard for a fashion photographer to shoot only fashion and a still-life photographer to shoot only still life.'

Not only do Tomek and Eryk work in a range of areas but they use a range of styles and techniques – black and white, colour and hand-colouring. And whatever the job, the enthusiasm goes with it. 'Everything can be shot badly and everything can be shot well; it doesn't matter what the job is', says Eryk. 'A retail catalogue has some requirements and a sophisticated advertising job has other requirements. A retail catalogue is designed to sell clothes and if I can use my input to make people enjoy looking at it, as well as making extra money for the people selling the products, then I'm happy ... I'm always trying to work in this way. There is strong pressure on my side to do a job in a way which I believe is right and, if I succeed, I am satisfied. It doesn't matter if it is a catalogue, corporate work or high fashion.'

Eryk believes that, while photographic knowledge and techniques can be learned, life experience is the most important skill of all. 'Nobody can create something when he or she doesn't understand what to create. When somebody wants to do photography and spends their whole life in one house having one boyfriend or girlfriend and visiting a holiday place once a year, there is no hope.

Because there is not enough personal life experience to be able to create things. It is only when you combine a lot of life experience with common sense, some amount of personal sensitivity and technical knowledge, then this whole thing works. Then you can create whatever you want.'

He has strong views on training. 'What I say to all photographic students is that I am against photographic schools. You can't always teach people how to think, you can't teach people how to feel. Some have got it, and some haven't. You can teach them how to press buttons on the camera, how the camera works, but you can also find most things in books. You need a lot of push to break into the commercial market. If somebody doesn't have enough self-discipline to take a book and learn technical things from it, then there is no hope that he or she will make it.

'Often the people teaching in these schools have little or no commercial experience and their teaching methods are very formulaic, which immediately cuts out the possibilities of creating something new. The result is that subconsciously students will often stick to the rules or formulas that they learned in these four or five years of photographic education, and quite often they finish their photographic careers on the same level that they finished photographic school. They haven't progressed. There are, of course, exceptions – there are some teachers out there who do encourage new and exciting things, but these are few and far between.

'Technically, photography is very simple. You can compare it to driving a car. That car has got a gear stick, steering wheel, brake, clutch and so on and, after a while, you drive without really thinking about changing gear – you do it automatically. You learn how to operate a camera, how to put the film in, the whole technical side. Every camera is the same. It has the same things; the only difference is in size and shape but the principle is the same. Then we've got a few extras – filters, different films and different lights. From this number of elements, we can put this one with that one and maybe add something else – just like a Tattslotto coupon, few numbers but many combinations. Photography is the same – when you understand how the camera works, how the film is developed, how light and how filters work, then you add your sensitivity and life experience and that's what pays off in photography.'

Eryk's own life experience has provided the Fitkau family with a unique photo album. 'My mother has a whole collection of photographs of me that you can look at and it will never cross your mind that it is me. I am unrecognisable,' he laughs. His dramatic changes in appearance, however, have not been always entirely desirable. 'The pictures were taken in hospital,' he continues. 'I never missed an opportunity for a good street fight.'

Eryk's life on the wild side began at sixteen, when he left home and broke off contact with his family. 'I started living by myself. I had seven high schools. I was thrown out of one and I went to another. But I eventually managed what you call the HSC here, about four years later than I should, but I made it. At twenty-two. I survived on a kind of dark side. I'd exchange money for tourists, which was very profitable but very risky. Poland had a very big black market. Tourists would get a certain amount exchanging dollars officially at the bank but they'd get triple or quadruple on the black market. I'd bring leather jackets and jeans to Poland from England and silver fox skins from Poland to England – again very profitable but very risky, especially those fox skins. If I was caught it was probably ten years in gaol. So I went through a lot of different stages in my life. It was very rich in experiences and I think this is very important in becoming a good photographer. You can relate to different groups of people and different subjects and you can feel, you can actually understand what you want to project.'

Eryk became a photojournalist in Poland following Tomek's encouragement. 'He gave me a camera and made me walk on the street for two weeks – aiming it at people and cars and getting into the habit of quick focusing. Then he explained how the light meter worked, gave me a bag of film and told me to shoot whatever I wanted. We developed the films, talked about them and then I started giving myself subjects to shoot and building up stories.' From there, Eryk found magazine work. 'I worked for about five years on this political and social magazine. But it was only when I came to Australia that I found out what work was all about.

'In Warsaw we'd finish the working day at one or two o'clock in the afternoon and the habit was always to celebrate – anything, whatever it was possible to celebrate, we'd find some excuse to celebrate with vodka. But it's not like here, where you get just a little drink. When you ask for a drink in Poland, they give you glasses and put the bottle in between. We'd work on a story for a day or two and then rest.'

When it comes to working in advertising, he says, 'The opportunities are here in Australia – you need some amount of luck and you need to be noticed. Talent and good photography is often not enough to be able to break into the market. You require a bit of human knowledge and being able to play your cards right to really make it in this industry. I quickly learned how the set-up worked and how to press the right buttons at the right time. You need good feedback from previous jobs – when you do an important job and something goes wrong, the news will spread and this can be very bad for the photographer.

'I understand advertising a little better than Tomek as he is more isolated and quite often lives in his own dreams. I'm much more down to earth and know all the different groups in Australia. One of my part-time jobs was taking photographs in a restaurant – printing and selling them the same night. I was at a different function every night: a Jewish wedding, an Egyptian function, high society from Toorak. I did this for a number of years and it gave me a good income and taught me about who is actually living in this country.'

He has turned down work in the past. 'I don't mind doing something for no money if I believe in what I'm doing, if people believe in me and I'm the right person to do it. But if I feel they don't believe in what I'm doing, then I become a little frustrated, my enthusiasm all goes and I tell them to find another photographer. Sometimes people are a bit behind the times. So it is not that we are ahead but that they are behind. They don't realise the public is ready for new things. For me, it doesn't matter how good the advertisement is – if it doesn't stand out against other advertisements, it will not work and when it will not work, that is bad advertising.'

When I ask him to describe *Tomek & Eryk's* style, he pauses and says he has not really thought about that until now. 'On the one hand it is our own style, our personal attitude towards the job and the subject. What we have in our folio is not a copy of existing styles that are happening in Europe or wherever. A lot of photographers are influenced by that. A trend is created in fashion, for example.

Something new in Italian *Vogue* will be seen in Australia in a matter of months ... What we do is not a copy. It is ours – our own approach, our techniques and our subjective look at the subject, creating what we think is right and not being influenced by outside work. There is a lot of freedom here and everything is possible.'

The satisfaction Eryk derives from photography comes from the satisfaction of creating a good image. 'I get more satisfaction if I like it and other people like it as well. But even when people say it is bad, it doesn't matter when it is good in my mind. I will still enjoy looking at it. When I create pictures, I initially see them very generally. It will never be possible to put down 100 per cent on paper what you picture in your mind, because you are dealing with elements you can't influence. The location or the light might be different than you imagined, the model might be in a different mood than you expected. I see pictures far more in the atmosphere I want to get rather than in the exact details.

'To produce good images, you need to charge yourself up before shooting and that also includes your physical condition. When I have an important job, I make sure I have two nights' good sleep before, I eat good food and I play the right music. I put myself in the frame of mind that I know will give me the best performance.' For him, music is all-important. 'A lot of people complain about that,' he laughs. 'I'm famous for it. I'll drive my car to a location blasting music – black music, 1960s soul and blues. It puts me in a good frame of mind and then I can create the right impact and reaction from the models, even if they don't like what I'm playing.'

Now looking back on the times he spent aloft trees in his childhood, he says he gained a sense of space and perspective he can use in photography. 'Your environment definitely has an influence in creating images. Things from your past have an impact that will come out sooner or later.' Such as his rebellion in his youth.

He hands me a business card. I look down at an image of two heavily-bearded faces, each with half a hard-boiled egg in its mouth. Eryk looks menacing with wild eyes while Tomek stares out with a placid gaze. 'This was a serious assignment by a professional photographic magazine and we made a bit of a joke out of it. They wanted photographers' pictures of themselves and they approached a number of photographers to do an assignment including an egg.

This was my idea but Tomek also hates this sort of hype. A lot of people have this image of photographers as these serious, deep sort of people. We decided to take this opportunity to do something totally different. So we sent them this picture and another one of ourselves, sticking out tongues.

'I went for a holiday and when I came back Tomek said, "I've had a great idea. I've made a business card with this photograph." "That's very good, Tomek," I told him, "but have you heard of the expression 'suck eggs'?" He hadn't and we were stuck with this card, a very controversial card. It does the job but a lot of people are offended.'

There is an image that Tomek Sikora returns to often. It is a picture that for him sums up a very important message about where he is and about what he left. It is the memory of 1 October 1982, his first day in Australia, and the drive from the airport into the city. 'I was on the way to Eryk's house and I saw a few people crossing the street, smiling. They were each on their own, not together. A young girl was crossing and she was smiling to herself and there were people just walking along the street very slowly. It was such a big difference, such a shocking difference, in the way they were walking and in the expression on their faces, compared to people in Europe. I had come to Australia from Belgium, which is quite a slow country compared to France or Germany, but even Belgium seemed to be much faster and the people much more stressed-out.'

For Tomek, Australia was a refreshing and welcome change. Even better was the acceptance. 'I didn't speak even one word of English but, after a few days, when I went to a shop or somewhere else, I realised people were not shocked at that. They just treated me normally. I noticed a few people around me at the Victoria Market, mostly old people, who could speak only Greek or Italian, so it seemed to be an absolutely normal situation – many foreigners speaking little or no English but being part of society. They weren't excluded from society because of language or culture, which happens very often in Europe. So I quickly realised that this country is open to everybody.

'I know people might have had other experiences but I never had a bad one because I am a foreigner, quite the opposite. I'm surrounded mostly by artists or people from advertising agencies and, when I pick up an award, they tell me it is good to have foreigners coming to this country, to share a mixture of different cultures and to build up something completely new together. I've always had a very good response but I guess this is very personal, because I've talked to many foreigners and of course some complain. It makes a difference if you are accepted professionally; it means you are one of the people, and if you are creative, they like the fact that that creativity comes from outside and that you are giving them something.'

Tomek came to Australia with an already well-established reputation, having worked in Poland as a staff photographer on the magazine *Perspektywy*. He had also produced film and theatre posters, book illustrations and record covers in collaboration with major graphic designers. His work had appeared in exhibitions in France, Finland, Holland, England and America as well as in his native country. He came to Australia on a three-month contract to teach photography at the Victorian College of the Arts and later applied for permanent residency. After being initially rejected, he successfully re-applied and his wife and son were able to join him in 1983.

'My creative input comes from eastern Europe, where I spent thirty-four years growing up in a certain culture. So I came here as a photographer with an independent approach to many problems in advertising. I don't think that happened because I am a completely different person but rather because I am from a completely different culture. That's all. And I was able to open up people's eyes to another point of view and they really appreciated it.'

When Tomek showed Australian advertising agencies some of his work, they were amazed. People couldn't believe that he had managed to produce international promotional calendars for major companies *without ever showing the product*. 'The government was trying to export Fiat cars but, if you have produced exactly the same car for twenty-five years, you don't want to show it because it looks really bad. It was the same Polish Fiat 125 as in the early 1970s with only a few small changes, while Fiat in Italy have produced, I don't know, about one hundred and fifty completely different models over that time. They asked me to produce this calendar and the first thing they said was, "Don't show the car. If you can find some idea that would relate Poland to the car, it would be fantastic."

'It was the same with the Polish airline, Lot. "We have to produce this calendar for our clients around the world but we can't show those old Russian aircraft", which they had to buy because we were basically under Russian occupation. "We can't show what our airport looks like; it is all old and bad technology. Please see if you can do something that is attractive visually but don't show the product."'

Australian advertising agencies were captivated with the calendars and the concept. 'Everybody shows the car and it's so boring,' they told Tomek. Those original calendars, he says, were quite abstract for the time, fifteen years ago. 'Usually people showed reality but, for the car, I shot through the windscreen with a horizontal camera, and you could see some side windows, the windscreen, and some people in front of it. In one case it was people from a wedding, in another the car was surrounded by children from their first Holy Communion. It was more like how Poland was looking, Polish tradition.'

For Lot Airlines, Tomek used a few small models of aircraft. 'But they didn't dominate the pictures. One was of a girl in colourful clothes leaning up against a green wall which had the shadow of a palm tree and the shadow of an aircraft, so you could realise that Lot could take you to different countries quite far away. When I showed people these calendars, they wanted to use these ideas because their dream was always to be more independent of the product.'

Tomek was able to do this himself just a few years back, offering to shoot pictures of ordinary young people in the street, not models, for the clothing company Le Shirt, while he was in Europe and the United States. 'They didn't want to kill the character of the people or the atmosphere, they wanted to show potential clients who like to wear their stuff. Sometimes you could see a little bit of logo somewhere but that was it. It was a very successful campaign. Young people started to approach the shops and they bought the posters as well – they really liked the posters.'

Quietly spoken in comparison to Eryk, Tomek is a more earnest and serious character. We are talking in his inner Melbourne house, spacious yet unimposing from the outside, set on a main road not too distant from the city centre. The pleasant green front garden provides a shaded walk from the white picket fence with its peeling paint to the front door. A grey van is parked in the driveway, 'Tomek' on its numberplate.

Entering the house is like stepping into many other worlds. There are traditional Polish tapestries and Balinese batiks on the walls and bronze medallions the size of dinner plates, crafted by Tomek's father, on the mantelpiece in the front room. Colourful abstract paintings and cartoons from Poland adorn other walls and every bit of space seems to be filled with wooden carvings, small sculptures or other objects either collected by Tomek and Malgosia on their travels or created by family members. The rambling rooms lead into an equally large and rambling back garden where, in one corner, sits a cherubic figure furiously pedalling a tricycle. Trapped in time, this metal sculpture was made by Mateusz, the twenty-three-year-old son of Tomek and Malgosia.

It is an exciting, intriguing and stimulating environment, full of a myriad of ideas and notions, just like Tomek's own upbringing. His father was a sculptor and his mother a painter, and he comments on his artistic background saying, 'It was absolutely normal, as normal as having breakfast daily, to create something. Instead of my parents going to a factory every day, sitting in front of a machine for eight hours, being paid and then buying goods to survive, they used to make sculptures and paintings. It was their life as well as their hobby and they were able to earn a good living.

'One of the good things about the Communists was that they always wanted to show the outside world how good Communism was and one of the best ways of showing that was to support art.' Writers, he says, were supported less than artists and theatre because 'Writers sometimes wrote about things the Communists didn't like and the same with photography, but visual art was all right because it was quite abstract, you couldn't show reality. Many art galleries, government art galleries and museums used to buy the best sculptures for their collections and there were a lot of exhibitions. My parents would take me to these exhibitions and to coffee shops full of artists. Everyone used to have a special sense of humour, always laughing, a little drunk, more open, more crazy than others and, if you grow up in such a situation, you need such a lifestyle. You can't just go to an average home, where people are less active or active only certain hours of the day, when they need to make money.'

Tomek has one brother and one sister, both several years older. His sister is a landscape designer and lives in France with her family while his brother, an astronomer specialising in black holes, spends much of his time in the United States but is based in Poland.

Like Eryk, Tomek was involved in an advertising culture in Poland that was unknown in the West. 'The advertising was very artificial. We didn't have to sell any products in Poland because there wasn't any competition. Posters and brochures were produced but they never sold the product. That was already sold before it was produced. There was never enough product on the market. So advertising accumulated a lot of artists – real artists – who would expose their talent and they didn't have to compromise. Film posters became more like street art – usually very symbolic, very intellectual, very strong visually.'

When Tomek decided to leave Poland, his parents were not pleased. 'They told me I would lose many years in order to be able to do what I was doing in Poland – to be independent, to work in art – and they were right. It took me three years or more to really break into the market and I had to do really terrible work in the beginning because nobody wanted to accept my style then.' By 'terrible' he means commercial, 'very commercial – it could have been done by anyone. *Now* if you look at my pictures, you would know they were mine; nobody else could do them.'

He demonstrates by producing a selection of magazines. Haunting figures dressed in the latest fashions look out from surreal landscapes of half-tones interspersed with splashes of colour. They are complex pictures – movement conveyed by a dramatic blur, impact intensified by the unexpected hue and pose or stance of the model.

In *Melbourne Bride Magazine, Tomek & Eryk's* twelve-page spread 'turns the tables on tradition and blends the old with the new' as the bride acts shocked, surprised and gleeful as characters dressed in Arab garb, Polish highlander costume or peasant dress pass by. Eryk too had shown me striking portraits. Flicking on the studio light box, he revealed outstanding celluloid images trapped in cardboard frames: a Porsche on the sea front, a Monaro with its owner by his workshed for a car oil advertisement; contented sleeping cats – 'We had to wait until three in the morning for them to fall asleep and I was covered with scratches and blood' – for a pet food ad; and other shots for Singapore Airlines, Intercontinental Hotels, Honda and Harley-Davidson, Australia Post and Telecom, British Petroleum, Elders IXL and the State Bank of Victoria. The list and the images go on and on.

❋

As original and memorable as their advertising work may be, Tomek and Eryk feel that their creativity is not totally expressed in this way and, for this reason, each year they work on a project of their own. 'I think that people should be outstanding in advertising,' Tomek asserts, 'but clients find this a dangerous way to be. Everything which is acceptable is always in the middle, always mediocre. It's just like playing on evens or odds at the casino – you don't lose a lot but you don't win a lot. You play it safe.' Their projects may take the form of a book or a calendar. Not only does this satisfy their inventiveness but it also acts as a form of self-promotion. The item is produced for nothing – the printer, graphic designer and others involved donate their services in return for their own copies to distribute to their clients. The concept has resulted in major international contracts for *Tomek & Eryk*, with clients such as Singapore Airlines and Intercontinental Hotels.

These annual projects were triggered by an early experience in Australia. 'I had exhibited at the Paris Biennale de Jeunesse in the Museum of Modern Art, the biggest cultural event in Europe, one year before I came here,' says Tomek. 'This was for the top artists of each country and I was one of three from Poland, so it was a great honour. Works were bought for the museum; it was something new in photography at that time, and I was in the first *World Encyclopedia of Photographers*. I came here with the documentation and the pictures and I went to a government gallery in Sydney specialising in photography, with Eryk because I didn't speak English yet. They said my work was wonderful and fantastic but a panel, planning the exhibitions for the following year, would need to look at them in three weeks' time and decide.

'They still hadn't contacted us after two months so Eryk called them, said we needed the pictures to show to agencies and asked what was happening. They said that the people sitting on the panel had decided not to show my work because it was too advanced, and if I could contact them again in four years' time, they would really appreciate it.' Tomek was confused, taken aback, and angry. 'I realised that I would have to do everything for myself, push more of my personal work in advertising and self-promotion, and not rely on art galleries. I did not feel restricted, just the opposite. I thought it was a very good indication that if you are a gallery photographer, then your work is shown only to a very limited market.'

While he and Eryk can now work in their own unique and highly sought-after style in advertising, it was not always this way and compromises had to be made. 'I had a lot of problems with this,' Tomek confesses, 'and then I met an art director and we got drunk one day and I told her, "We shouldn't be in this profession, it's really against my views. I'm not so materialistic and I don't think we are doing the right thing selling products to people."

'She looked at me and said, "Look Tomek, it's your choice, but you have to understand one thing. If you are not going to do it, somebody else will – so it will be done by somebody. The second aspect is that as a photographer you produce images and people look at your images. You can have terrible images in advertising, ones which don't help people in normal life, which don't give them anything extra emotionally, only this terrible information. But it can be photography like yours, very imaginative, which can sell the product but also teach people about good images."'

Her advice had a big impact on Tomek and his future career direction. 'I changed my attitude and told myself that this is what I wanted to do all my life, to create images and give these images to people. As an artist I can have my photography in an art gallery but how many people go to an art gallery? One or two hundred, maybe three hundred will look at my picture which is behind glass. They can't touch it or enjoy it every day. But if I produce a good advertising image, it will appear in *Vogue* magazine, for example, and let's say 300 000 people can cut it out, put it on the wall and enjoy this image.' It gives him great pleasure therefore to walk into a local coffee shop and see one of his images stuck on the wall there. He smiles with delight yet is too shy to tell the owner he is the photographer.

His parents may have been against Tomek leaving Poland, fearing for his career, but others too warned him against Australia. 'I spoke to several people – ones who had lived here for twenty-five years and other young French photojournalists. They told me going to Australia would be the biggest mistake of my life. They told me it was the most boring place, with no social life, and that it was very slow, with no culture; everyone was shut in their houses. And the more I listened to this, the more I wanted to come here! Because I was tired of living in the middle of Warsaw with lots of people coming in every day, with heavy discussions about politics and art, and a lot of vodka of course. For some, Australia was boring compared to Poland, but it depends on your expectations.' Tomek had left Poland during martial law, at a time when, he says, 'Everyone was psychologically down. I wanted to forget about everything and this was an absolutely beautiful place. I spent the first week here walking around Camberwell where Eryk lived, just walking and looking at the gardens, the flowers and houses, and having the best relaxation in my life. I was in heaven, I was really happy, the place put no pressure on me. Then I discovered a few things – the National Gallery, cinemas, libraries; everything was here. Whatever you are interested in, you can find here.'

As for nightclubs, 'People say you can't be inspired by a decadent lifestyle here but I disagree. If you want to get lost, drunk and surrounded by unknown people and just fly for a few days, Melbourne is a fantastic place for that, there are so many nightclubs. And you are safe. Do that in New York and you can end up in a cemetery because someone can kill you for a few dollars if you are a little weak and can't walk straight. Here you can do whatever you want to do and nobody will touch you.' He also disagrees about the boring and slow lifestyle. 'Here I have a choice. I can be absolutely alone in the garden, enjoying the fresh air, or I can make a few phone calls and have a house full of people drinking and dancing and talking. It was a more decadent atmosphere in Warsaw.

Everybody was drunk every day and really wanted to create something and talked about it. It was less creating and more heavy discussion. I think that was the age as well as the place and I went through that too. But I wanted more contact with nature and I couldn't have that in Warsaw, which is a noisy place. I would have to get into the car and drive 150 kilometres to find a quiet, enjoyable place. Here it's just three minutes and I've got it.'

Australia also gave Tomek a choice of company. 'I would just walk to a coffee shop in Acland Street and meet someone from a different country each time – from Albania, from Cyprus, from Brazil. I would talk to them as much as I could, because of the language barrier, but my eyes were opened and I was happy to be surrounded by people who had had different experiences – in culture, in religion. Poland is a hermetically closed culture. There are a lot of people there who have never met a foreigner – maybe somebody from East Germany or Russia, but not very often.'

Each time Tomek would meet these new people, these new immigrants, he would see the reflection of his own face one, two or three years ago; he noted the same excitement and exhilaration. 'I remember the first time I travelled to Sydney, I used to stop the car every few kilometres and look at the sky. I couldn't believe how the sky was so different to a European sky. Now I hardly compare it. Then my friends used to come over and tell me exactly the same. One painter friend said, "This sky looks much lower and the clouds are so completely different." After ten years, I couldn't see the difference. Everything struck me then, when I first arrived – the impact of nature and the different shape and colour of the landscapes – it's a shame people get used to things so quickly. I will never forget seeing a red parrot on white snow at Mount Buller with eucalyptus trees. In Europe you have pine trees and so this was completely shocking, but in a positive way. Every day for at least a year I would go to the seaside and sit there for half an hour or an hour, looking at the water and the sky and the ships on the horizon. That was very important to me.'

He would often think of his wife Malgosia and their eleven-year-old son Mateusz and how they didn't yet have the papers to leave Poland. But he would mostly think about how wonderful it was to be absolutely free, even if he was not able to see his family for at least a year. 'The best way to dissolve this problem was to go straight to nature and realise how tremendously big nature was and how small your problem was. That was the best therapy. So often we get upset by stupid unimportant things and we get very stressed out and nervous. Just go out and look at the ocean, or the stars at night, and you will see that your problem is nothing compared to the universe and then you can relax and start again.'

Just like Eryk, Tomek believes in experiencing life to the fullest. And, for him, that experience is gained through travel. 'If you just sit in front of the television, you end up just receiving something. You can't give anything, you can't think, you can't produce anything because you are constantly bombarded with information ... It's very passive; activity is completely killed ... because they show you everything that's already been done and you start to think that there's nothing else to do in this world. I think this is the problem of the young generation, growing up in front of the television.'

Tomek, however, obtains his enjoyment and stimulation from travel. 'If you stay in one place ... your obsession becomes the dust on the window sill or a dirty window pane. Closed in one room, you just concentrate on that, things that are not important.' Travel is vital to his work and well-being. 'Most photographers look through magazines, analyse the pictures and say, "This is good but we can add a few more elements." This is not very personal photography. Whenever I looked through magazines or photographic books, it was a problem for me – I was stuck to something. I couldn't get away from the images. So I decided not to look at anything but just to be inspired by normal life and what I saw with my own eyes.

'Photography is a language – a communication between a photographer and people. That means that a good photographer gives you the best feeling about the situation he or she was in. There are many photographers who do well, who are well known after college and very professional. They are called professional because they know everything about techniques – they are spot-on and they are sharp but very often there's no heart behind it, it's very technical. There are only a few people about whom you can say, "This person has got a lot of feeling and the feeling is in the photography."

'It doesn't matter if it is in advertising or in a gallery, if you can see behind the photograph and see the emotion, then it shows the power of this picture. This is the way the photographer is talking to you.'

Tomek first picked up a camera at the age of fifteen. 'My sister's boyfriend, Marek, was a magazine photographer and I found this camera on the table and clicked into it straight away. It was a good-quality East German camera, a Practisix, a six-by-six camera for photoreportage. He showed it to me and then lent me a different camera and I started to take some pictures. It was slow, very slow. It wasn't like an explosion of interest in photography. It went slowly because the conditions for progress were terrible – I didn't have good equipment or access to a darkroom and this guy wasn't keen to help me a lot – he wanted me to discover everything by myself.'

So Tomek did – processing his film on a plate in the darkroom he set up in the family bathroom. Today he looks back and says, 'You are more proud of yourself when you feel everything you have achieved is yours. Marek and I are still friends to this day.'

Did Tomek ever, in his wildest dreams, imagine that he would be able to escape from the first-floor two-roomed apartment he shared with seven others – his parents, siblings, cousin and grandmother – for a new life travelling the world? He first had a taste of that life at twenty-two when he worked for a year in France.

'Actually my family's living conditions were excellent compared to other people who lived in basements or much smaller rooms,' he explains. 'Warsaw was completely devastated by the Germans during the war and we felt really privileged to be living in such a place. I had a lovely life; my childhood was very long. There was warmth in the house, we were always together and I couldn't imagine living somewhere else without my parents. In Poland children stay at home until their twenties or even later because of accommodation problems.

'When I went to Paris, I was completely lost. It was a really big effort to survive because up until then everything had been arranged by my parents – I didn't have to work to make money or look for a job. So I missed them terribly and wrote them letters and we established a new quality of communication. I wrote things we had never talked about before – and it was the same with Malgosia when I was in Australia and she was in Poland. When you talk with someone directly, it's often about unimportant things, but now, by letter, we talked more about the philosophy of life.'

Tomek was not alone in Paris for that year. Malgosia, his girlfriend then and now his wife, went with him, having persuaded her family to let her go to study French. She joins us now to talk of their experiences together. Tall and slim, with short hair and fine delicate features, her English is impeccable.

The year they spent in Paris together was a difficult yet profitable one, living in cramped and basic conditions and existing on a meagre income. 'The West was always worshipped,' says Malgosia. 'It was a symbol of something better but it was over-idealised,' as they discovered. While Malgosia worked as a waitress, Tomek spent long hours in a photographic colour laboratory. The work, while tedious and repetitive, meant he was able to get colour film. The photographs he took as a result found him excellent work in Poland.

At home, Tomek was employed by *Perspectywy*, 'the best magazine for photojournalism without doubt. But I immediately made a lot of enemies. People were angry because I was very young, only twenty-three years old, and there were people in their forties who had been waiting for this position for ages because it was the best place to show your skills. After a couple of years, I started to work on my own photography – creative work. I did illustrations for the book *Alice in Wonderland* and Malgosia and I dreamed up fashion pictures.'

This type of imaginative work did not exist in Poland and Tomek was breaking new ground in between his magazine assignments, which he also experienced to the full. 'They would send me to do some pictures for a day or two but I would pay for myself and spend four or five days to do it properly.' He would, for example, live with miners for a week, rising with them at four in the morning and going down the mine, so as to produce a totally authentic and well-researched set of photographs.

Eryk, meantime, was going one step further. 'He wanted to show the guts of it all. Other people would take pictures of just the horse-racing but he wanted to show everything – the drunks, the people making love in the car. It was much too controversial.' But things were changing. 'At the end of the 1970s, the Communists would have a big party meeting each Thursday and they would tell a press representative what we could talk about for the next two or three months. For the first five years, the subject of alcoholism was totally forbidden and then, under the new government, this was relaxed a little bit.'

By the time Eryk went to Australia, the situation in Poland had deteriorated. 'It was really depressing and we were just about to leave,' says Malgosia. 'We already had three invitations to leave, organised by friends in France,' adds Tomek. 'Everybody suspected something was going to happen – martial law – and, three or four weeks before, twenty of us resigned from the magazine. We realised that if martial law did come in, we could be in a very tricky situation. A few people did stay and they had to do propaganda, taking pictures of soldiers on the streets and having their names under the pictures. The comments were terrible.'

Ironically, Tomek and Malgosia – who had studied linguistics at university – were in a better financial position after martial law. 'A lot of my pictures were published in the West for good money. They showed what it was like, with the soldiers and the tanks, and Malgosia had work with a Japanese film crew.'

'All these journalists moved into Poland straight away and so paradoxically this was the best time for people like me,' Malgosia says. 'Martial law helped us to make the decision we had been thinking about. We were both thirty-five years old, Tomek was pretty well established and we thought what's going to happen next? Not much. Maybe it's time to make a move, a change. We were keen to go to Australia because we already knew France and Europe, and it wasn't fantastic to live there. Being a foreigner was not a great feeling, you were never accepted, so we thought, "Let's try Australia." She says their fourteen-month separation was probably harder on Tomek. 'I was busy with work and at home. He was alone and at Eryk's mercy,' she laughs. 'But he loved the country immediately and that helped him live through it.'

Today Tomek and Malgosia work together, for both practical and emotional reasons. 'I felt depressed and insecure here and that lasted for a year,' says Malgosia. 'I had to prove I was worth something and so I looked for a job, which was difficult. Finally I found a researcher's position at the Special Broadcasting Service and that was enough – I could have quit the following day as I had just proved something to myself and I didn't need the job any more.' She had several contract jobs with SBS and later worked on independent film and script-writing projects.

Tomek was working on overseas assignments for several weeks or months at a time. 'Each trip was so exciting and exhausting and by the time I had settled down and come back to reality, I was away again,' he says. 'I remember once standing for an hour in one spot in Hong Kong, a city of seven million, with people just rushing by me. It was amazing. I couldn't believe what was happening and I couldn't explain it to Malgosia. You can't understand unless you are in the same spot experiencing it.'

A gap developed between them. 'You just see so many things that you change. You change much faster than the person who is settled in one spot with a normal everyday life without any excitement. It's dangerous for a marriage – if you want to be together, you have to be really together.' Malgosia agrees. 'When he came back he was all vibrant, he couldn't sit in one place because there was so much going on in his head. It was like a revelation to him, the world he hadn't seen, and he couldn't calm down.' Now she works as his assistant and stylist and, after each assignment, they are able to explore and discover the world together. 'All I need is a pair of good shoes and a camera,' says Tomek. 'I am a very active person, a walking person.' 'He's still a very adventurous man,' adds Malgosia.

Tomek sees the future as more of the same. 'I'm going to leave my studio in a few months, cut all my expenses, and just travel, taking some pictures to sell. Presently 95 per cent of the work I am doing gives me a lot of pleasure; only 5 per cent doesn't. I want to leave the studio to avoid this 5 per cent. Life is short and there are so many things to see and experience so why should I lose this time?'

He misses nothing physical about Poland. 'I am missing youth rather than a place. It doesn't matter whether we are in Poland or Australia. I miss the place where I used to play soccer and was absolutely happy, my childhood.' When he and Malgosia visited Poland a few years after leaving, they found nothing had improved. 'There was economic stagnation and things were even worse.' The risk for Tomek of returning and not being able to leave was a large one. 'This is the typical immigrant's dream – that you go home and you can't leave again.' The trip alleviated that fear and they now visit Poland every year, unlike Eryk who has never returned.

Tomek and Eryk enjoy a good and open working relationship. Eryk laughed at the advantage they had in being able to argue in Polish without anyone else understanding. 'Of course there is some competition between us, such as when one wins an award. But nobody knows about that except us,' Tomek reveals.

Their best-known images are 'Happy Nuns' and 'The Promised Land'. The first, of nuns roller-skating along Chapel Street in Prahran one morning, was a scene spotted quite by chance and the photograph was made into posters and cards. Neither Tomek nor Eryk knows who these nuns were or, indeed, if they were nuns at all, and they are not particularly interested. The second image, 'The Promised Land', shows two individuals with their backs to the camera – one in a stockman's oilskin coat, a symbol of Australia, and the other in a Polish mountain hat – holding hands and looking across at the Sydney Opera House and Harbour Bridge – 'two people amazed by the miracle of where they want to live', say Tomek and Eryk.

Australia has indeed been the Promised Land for Tomek and Eryk.

'Happy Nuns' by *Tomek & Eryk. Courtesy of Edition Habit Press.*

Photo by Ernie McLintock. Courtesy of News Limited.

A DIFFERENT LIGHT

'The point is that whether or not you move around, the world around you changes.'

ELIZABETH JOLLEY

Writer

Sometimes Christmas, in spite of Christmas card pictures, was mild and grey and wet. Sometimes there was a frost, very cold and with bright sunshine. The iron tips on the fast running heels and toes of boots and shoes struck sparks on the pavements. There were frost flowers on the bedroom window panes, and a robin, perched on a winter-bare twig in the garden would sing and sing as if its little heart was bursting with joy.

And there would be the silent night of snowfall, that strange stillness the next morning and the bedroom ceiling lighter than usual with reflections from the snow covered world outside.

We had a sledge with heavy iron runners. We sledged down the street where we lived, using wooden pegs, one in each hand, to push down first one side and then the other in order to steer the clumsy conveyance. Then, of course, there was the dreadful long haul on the rope to drag the heavy thing up the hill so that there could be another ride down. Christmas then was a time of wet coats and gloves and socks and boots arranged at the kitchen fire in the evening to be baked dry ready for the next morning.

I was not very old when a visitor to the house explained that the robin singing in the garden, so fresh and happy, on Christmas day was not singing with joy as I imagined. Robins if they sing like this the visitor, persisting with his doctrine of disillusionment, explained, robins sang in their distress, usually because they were bereaved or, like now in the snow, they were starving. Robins, he went on, were territorial and their song reached orphean excellence, in our hearing, when their territory was threatened, invaded by another robin, an intruder.

In a family, my mother said then, there is always something the matter. There is always something wrong for someone. And it simply is not possible to close a door on trouble or unhappiness. The same is probably true with animals, she said, and that goes for fishes and birds as well, especially, she said, robins.

So recalls Elizabeth Jolley, one of Australia's most distinguished writers, looking back to a childhood Christmas in the 1930s in the English Midlands. The author of ten novels, three collections of fiction and one of essays, Elizabeth Jolley has had her poetry and plays published in anthologies and broadcast on Australian and British radio. She has twice won the *Age* Book of the Year Award – with *Mr Scobie's Riddle* and *The Georges' Wife* – and has been the recipient of other eminent literary awards including the New South Wales Premier's Award and the Miles Franklin Award.

She left the cold and damp English climate for the heat and sunshine of Western Australia in 1959, together with her husband Leonard and their three children – Sarah, Richard and Ruth, then aged thirteen, six and four years old. The move was not seen as an opportunity.

'Oh no, we came out with great trepidation really. Leonard was invited to be librarian at the University of Western Australia and to see about new library buildings. The library wasn't built then. I had no idea what we were coming to but I'm very glad we did come. Leonard was given a three-year contract with the option to stay on afterwards. The university could say, we don't want you, at the end of that time. It was a three-year thing to start with, just to leave a bit of freedom. But of course we did like it very much and the university seemed to like Leonard all right.

'I didn't see coming to Australia as an opportunity as I simply had no idea. And it never crossed my mind to *not* come, you know. If Leonard wanted to come, then I would just follow – devotedly, like Ruth. My name isn't Ruth, but it never occurred to me that I could say, well I'm not going, you see. Economically I wouldn't have managed if I'd stayed behind.'

Elizabeth is seated in her Sydney hotel room, conversing between her appearances at the Writers' Festival. A slim and slight figure, her short grey hair brushed back neatly, she talks with humour and enthusiasm. She is dressed simply, in a long flowing skirt and a T-shirt which bears the slogan *Avoid clichés like the plague*. It is difficult sometimes – in her public talks and interviews – to know whether she is joking or not. Sometimes she is earnest or intense, at other times quite light-hearted. Just like her books – some dark and mysterious, others black and macabre, but all full of unexpected humour and ironies.

Elizabeth had no expectations of her new life in Australia. 'None whatsoever, because I knew nothing about the country. That sounds awful. We did look up the rainfall in Western Australia and found it was about the same in Glasgow, where we were living then, but it all fell at once, of course! And we realised it was a warm country, which was nice after the freezing fogs of Glasgow. We looked forward to that. But I hadn't thought about the bright light and all our clothes looked very dirty when we came.'

Prior to leaving for Australia, the Jolley household had already made three moves – from Birmingham to Edinburgh and finally to Glasgow. 'I was very fond of my house in Glasgow. I never thought of leaving it. But there again, I suppose a destiny is made for one and that's it. But my mother was very upset at our leaving and, now that I'm a grandmother, I understand that. I didn't then. I never gave her a thought; I was very selfish. My father said of course they would be getting older and that we mustn't at all think of dashing back if they were old or ill. He gave quite a little talk on that which was very reassuring. Well, he was run over in 1977 and my mother died in her eighties in 1979, very quickly. She just didn't feel well, felt cold, and she died before the doctor came. I suppose it must have been a heart attack. So I was really very fortunate in that they didn't have a long illness in hospital. But I think my mother was very lonely in the two years after my father's death.

'I suppose that if I lived near her, I could have done her shopping and housework and the children could have visited her. But when we went back on study leave, it was not very successful. She didn't like the way the children were developing. She didn't like anything. It was very very difficult.

'But I had to realise that whatever I would do for my mother wouldn't be right. I have written that several times in my diary to remind myself. I don't feel guilty, because in family life there is a certain amount of destiny. There is destiny in everybody's lives and the destiny of one person may cause a hurt to somebody else. But you can't alter your destiny. You may make a decision but you make the decision that is taking you along the way that you're meant to be going, I think.'

Once Leonard had made the decision to take the job offered him in Australia, the family had a year of preparation in which to get used to the idea. 'That year meant that Leonard could finish at the University of Glasgow and we also managed to sell our house in that time,' says Elizabeth. 'Everything was arranged by the University of Western Australia. We were allowed to bring our furniture and they gave us a certain allowance of money. Since I didn't have a great deal of furniture, we were able to bring everything and the children's toys.

'A funny little man with a very Scottish accent came to give us a quote as to how much we could take for the money. When he came up the garden path, he helped himself to a rose and put it in his buttonhole. Then he went round the house hitting things with his walking stick, saying, this isn't worth taking and that isn't worth taking. So then I thought I'd get a quote from another firm. But the same man came and said it was no good getting a different firm as he did all the quotes! We were warned not to make all our arrangements immediately as we wouldn't get a sailing for about a year. So that gave us a year really to get used to the idea.'

Elizabeth packed fifteen crates of books to bring with her to Australia. 'I gave lots of things away, things I regretted later, like my hymn book from school, *Songs of Praise*. There was also a very big old *Times Atlas* which really I should have kept because historically the world has changed so much. I left it at somebody's house just on the morning we left. It was huge, a very thick book and the mind just boggled about packing it up.'

She remembers clearly the trip to Australia and the family's last night in England. 'We had a night in London on the way. The children stayed with my parents for the last bit and my mother brought them down to London. She was very upset and my father was very white-faced. We stayed in a dreadful hotel because the motor show was on, the whole five of the family crammed into one room with a very low ceiling. There was a double bed and a single bed and somehow we were all to sleep the night in that.

'The next morning we went on a boat-train to the ship and it was a tremendous experience because it was an ocean liner, a P & O liner the *Orion*. It was a one-class ship at that stage but we were rather special: we were paid for by the university, and we were treated like first-class passengers. The children even had their own steward, a man called Green, to run their baths, make their beds and look after them. At that stage Ruth was still wetting her bed and I put a rubber sheet on the bed. Mr Green said, "She'll get prickly heat with that, you can't have that on," and I told him she'd wet the mattress. "Well, if she wets the mattress, I'll just throw it overboard and put another one on," he said. And I had a vision of mattresses bobbing along behind us the whole way! But actually she didn't wet the bed. It cured her.'

Elizabeth remembers others on the ship also emigrating to Australia. 'There were a lot of British people from Kenya, with their babies. Their prams were fastened on deck so they wouldn't move. I felt so ashamed of these women who'd been used to black servants, and spoke to the stewards as though they were scum. Later on, some Indian people boarded the ship and I can't help wondering how they got on because they were coloured and it was still the White Australia Policy then. There was a schoolteacher, a British subject. He brought his old mother with his family. I had a very miserable letter from him later on. He'd been sent out to the country where there was no sanitation and no water laid on; they had to carry water to their house.'

The three-week ship voyage included several ports of call. 'We had a lovely day in Naples, a day in Gibraltar, a day at the beginning and the end of the Suez Canal. We stopped at the Great Bitter Lake, where you couldn't get off but little boats came all around, and then Port Said, Aden and Ceylon. There was a trip to the pyramids but I didn't go because Ruth wasn't well. The children were ill on the ship; they got sore throats. Apparently this is very common – or was. There would usually be an infection on a ship – measles, chickenpox or scarlet fever.'

Finally the ship approached the new continent where they would make their home. 'My first view of Australia was the flat land; it was so flat as though there was nothing there. It was the bright light that struck me most, the really bright light and the clean air.'

Fremantle, where the ship docked, was not a welcoming place in the late 1950s. 'There were tin sheds, really shabby, with things like "Poms go home" written on them. At customs, they just opened one of our boxes and kept it because there was a book in it called *What Katy Did Next*, along with Leonard's books. So they kept the whole box just in case there was some pornography in there. They didn't know it was a children's book even though we said it was.' She pauses.

'*What Katy Did Next* does sound a bit pornographic, doesn't it?' she smiles.

The Jolley family were met and welcomed by university staff. 'The state librarian took Leonard and Sarah and the professor of history took me and two of the children for a short drive before we went for morning tea. Both my children threw up in his car. I knew they would. They weren't used to going about in cars.'

Settling in required some useful advice. 'The professor of history was such a kind man and took me to buy a fridge that day, saying that if English people bought a fridge themselves, they bought something tiny. So he took me to a shop where we bought a simply *enormous* refrigerator and that was the first thing to be put in the university house.'

Her first impressions of Australia were vivid ones. 'We arrived in November. The jacarandas were in flower and it was absolutely beautiful but scalding hot. The other thing that struck me was that Perth was full of what I thought were little sugar buildings with sugar balconies, all in different colours, like a little Swiss or Bavarian town. I thought it was all very pretty but, after Glasgow, it looked like a camp. There were some solid buildings but I thought the flimsy, temporary-type buildings with verandahs and verandah posts looked as if they were just set up for a Western film. So when somebody asked me, "Where did you get your fridge?" I said, "Oh, there was this temporary shed in Milligan Street." They said, "That's not a temporary shed!"'

Elizabeth was soon to find that lifestyle and attitudes were different from those she had experienced up until then. 'I was completely out of tune with fashion. I'd been sort of buried in Glasgow with a large family. Women in Western Australia were far more emancipated. After a week of being in our little house on campus, another university wife rang me up and asked, "Will you come to the beach this morning?" Two of my children were at school and the other one was at kindergarten, you see. I said, "Oh no, I never go anywhere in the morning, I do my housework." It went all around the wives,' she laughs.

'They played tennis and went to the beach, because it was that sort of climate. And if it was a very hot day, dinner wasn't prepared and you all went down to the beach or river and took a salad with you. I had to really make an effort to change an attitude in living and adjust to the hot climate.'

She describes the family's new place of living, (near Crawley Bay on the river), as idyllic, like 'a magical enjoyment park after coming from Glasgow. I found the Australians were very open, friendly and helpful. It always seemed to me, when I heard Australians speak, that there couldn't be a deceitful or wicked one among them. That was because their speech seemed honest, and countryish in a way.'

Her new existence proved to be community-style living. 'All the university couples and their children had come from somewhere else and they all needed kind of relatives, you see. The greengrocer that came along in his van would say that whichever house he knocked at, the same woman would come to the door, meaning they were all in each other's houses. People would drop in on us at all hours. Children would come rushing through the house before eight o'clock in the morning. And when you went down to the river with your children, a wife would come running out and say, "Oh, you're going down to the Crawley, let so-and-so come," and you'd find you'd get about ten or eleven children coming with you.

'I liked that to a certain extent but you had no privacy. I was already wanting to write and I found, after a bit, that it was quite frustrating to always have someone sitting in my house wanting to chat. But they were very very friendly people, from different parts of Australia and from America, Germany, Hungary, Holland and India. The whole street was a wealth of cultures and every house had their own background as you all were able to bring your own things from overseas. When we first came here, the streets – the main highways as it were – were very narrow and there were hardly any traffic lights. Perth was like a small country town, but of course it has changed enormously.'

As have attitudes. 'I opened an account and bought some things in a department store in Perth. They actually rang up Leonard at his university library to ask if his wife could have an account. That has changed completely; no shop would do that now. I had all these things they were going to deliver – an armchair, cutlery and a few things I didn't have enough of – and I said "Jolley with an e". Everything came delivered to Mrs Jelly.

'On that same shopping spree, I had been told that a particular Houghton's wine, 1957, was an especially good one. I went to the Palace Hotel in Perth where two very kind barmaids said they would send some out for me. When it came,' she laughs, 'all the labels had been altered. The date had been changed from 1959 to 1957 with a sort of scratchy pencil. They were so obliging, they had changed the date on the wine. Wasn't that lovely? I was really touched by that. They just wanted to please me.'

This incident demonstrated to Elizabeth the kindness of Australians, in complete contrast to her experiences in Glasgow. 'When I asked for some English tomatoes I nearly got blown out of the shop because they should have been *Scotch* tomatoes. All I meant was that I wanted fresh tomatoes, not ones that had been grown in straw in the Canary Islands.'

After two-and-a-half years on the university campus, the Jolley family bought a house in Claremont, half-way between Fremantle and Perth, and moved there. Elizabeth lives in that house to this day.

Before coming to Australia, her writing had been purely for herself. 'I kept a journal and looked forward to writing in it. I wrote all the way across on the ship. The first story that I wrote was to do with an outing, a group of university people going out with their children and having a kind of picnic. The whole world seemed to spend Christmas on the banks of the Swan River with little tables. They don't do that now because they all have their own backyard pools. It was an extraordinary experience to meet university people for the first time in their bathing things, so that you just didn't recognise them when you met them again. I wasn't used to that kind of communal life and my children weren't used to being thrust among other children and expected to get on with them. My first story was a bit sinister – one of the children gets lost and is never found again.

'I think that story was probably an outlet for the kind of sinister feeling of the bush that is quite close to Perth. You only have to go a little way out from Perth and you are in the bush and that can still occur apart from the various ribbons of development.

'The next story was "The Hedge of Rosemary" and again, without consciously meaning to, I united the Black Country of England with the feelings of oriental appearance and the flowers and the trees. You see, all the things like oleanders and hibiscuses were foreign to me. I didn't know them and I didn't know the birds. "The Hedge of Rosemary" is a sort of migration story but I didn't know that at the time. It's only looking back that I realised I was linking my childhood with this new environment.'

This was to be the start of her writing career. She sent 'The

Hedge of Rosemary', together with a few other stories which she now considers 'very naive and almost child-like, about uneasy picnics on the beach with unsettled children, irritable fathers and careworn mothers', to competitions and to the Fellowship of Writers in Melbourne. 'In 1965 or 1966, "The Hedge of Rosemary" won a prize in the Moomba short story competition, so that was very nice. At that time I was writing what I called *George's Wife and The Feast*. I had several notebooks and I was writing a manuscript from which I have since taken material for the trilogy. I would just write away at that, no re-writing, just continuing because I wanted to write it.'

Elizabeth describes her writing as a compulsion going right back to her childhood. 'Not writing would make me feel angry – if I didn't have the time for it, or was weary, tired. You see, life is kind of wounding. Husbands' and wives' words are wounding, people that you meet casually ... these secret wounds get sort of buried and then they come out in fiction whereby you turn a pain into art.

'Leonard once said something about Wordsworth being able to take the pain of life, as it were, and create a poem, a work of art, from it, and I didn't understand that about writing. There will be a moment of awareness or truth that makes you want to write something but it isn't enough just to describe something. As well as observation, you've got to have thought and feeling. I think it's Goethe who says that the writer takes all of this from himself, the thought and feeling. But of course you do listen to other people's thoughts and you are aware of other people's feelings if you're going to write well, I think.'

Early influences shaped Elizabeth's writing career. Notepads and books were welcome gifts. A paintbox showed her the disparity between light and shade, and art lessons at boarding school reinforced that contrast, now demonstrated so powerfully in her writings. 'Books were always my main wish at Christmas. I liked to have an old Boots [pharmacy] diary given to me. I always had one, even before I could write, and I filled any empty pages left in it with loops and dots.'

She vividly recalls the pleasure of receiving a new paintbox at nine years of age. 'The names of the little squares of colour excited me – ultramarine, cobalt blue, yellow ochre, vermilion, burnt sienna. I think painting and drawing in childhood is very important, for children to paint and make pictures, to like the colours and the names of the colours. We did a lot in my school and before we went to school. I've still got the paintbox. It's a Reeve's paintbox, only a very small one, but it's lovely.

'Colour, light and shade are all very important in writing.' As they are in a landscape. 'You can see the light and shade on our property at Wooroloo where we have the orchard. People coming there might think, "Oh, what a boring place," but if you're there all day, you have this subtle shift in the light as the sun moves over. It's the same in Claremont too, which is a very leafy suburb. The sombre light can affect you and then the early morning light, which is so full of hope. I think it's all very important.'

Elizabeth may have physically left the country of her childhood, but she brought it with her in her mind. 'It doesn't take much for me to recall the landscape of my childhood and coming to another country sharpens that. So it is not a loss. In fact I think it would be very painful to go back and find it changed. I did go back to my school; we went in 1966. I wanted to take my children to the field paths along the streams, but they were all overgrown because the farmers were now using tractor and motor truck transport instead of walking through the field paths. The labourers no longer walked, so there weren't any paths that we could follow.'

She has written of migration, commenting that we do not have to leave our place of birth to find ourselves in a strange new world. She quotes the German poet Maria Luise Kauschnitz who says, 'We do not leave the world: the world leaves us.'

'The point is that whether or not you move around, the world around you changes. Britain has changed enormously. At one time, people didn't leave their villages and then somehow the villages seemed to move or amalgamate themselves. Towns would spread with suburbs so that you might be living in a small town and then find that your town is actually joined to the next town with suburban development. And, of course, wars change places.' There are also other factors that promote change. These are, according to Elizabeth, the results of advancement – supermarkets and their wares. 'A supermarket alters a town completely,' she says, and smiling, adds, 'How did I ever manage without plastic wrap?'

Yet whatever changes progress or technology has brought and however many major moves she has made, Elizabeth considers her home in England to have been the Black Country of her childhood. 'I cut out the other places, you see. I think this is what happens as you get older. More and more things come to mind from your childhood and I find, as I get older, I remember things with great clarity – my father and mother, our first house and so on. I remember more German than I used to – I suddenly think of certain phrases or a song. Maybe it's a kind of defence to lift you a little bit away from the difficulties of the present and perhaps a bit of enrichment.'

Elizabeth's mother came from Vienna and Elizabeth sees German as a comforting language, describing it as 'the childhood language spoken to you in the night when you have a pain, or if something upsets you'. That, and the tone of her mother's voice accompanying the soothing words, created 'the language of cherishing' for Elizabeth. She explains how in later life she muddled up the two languages of her background, often writing nouns with capital letters as in German. An early rejection slip returned with her manuscript stated, 'I do not understand your notion of capital letters.' 'I've always remembered that,' she says. 'I do still see nouns – a house or a rose – with capital letters.'

Elizabeth and her younger sister, Madelaine, were brought up speaking both English and German and with a musical background. Their father came from an English farming family and was jailed during the First World War for refusing to fight. He met his future wife, who came from an aristocratic background, in Vienna, while he was distributing food supplies with the Quakers. They returned to England together and were married. 'My father had been turned out of the house by his father, with just a shilling, for being a conscientious objector. So when he returned with my mother as a bride, the reception was not good. But on the whole the family did accept her.

'My mother spoke her Viennese German and my father learned

High German, which we were taught, but with a soft s instead of a z so that our pronouncation would be more like our mother's. I spoke German when I was little but when I started school at six, I stopped immediately. My mother was upset because my sister and I rebelled against the German and against the piano lessons. I had piano lessons until I left school at seventeen. My mother would scream while you were playing that you were not right – that the rhythm was wrong, that it was the wrong note. "Mistake!" she would yell from wherever she was and it was the same with pronunciation, with German and with French, so that it made us both very self-conscious. We both turned our backs on it … I did French and German for the school leaving certificate but speaking it was another matter.'

Elizabeth's education was a mixture of governesses, short spells at school and then boarding school. 'My father thought that school spoiled children's innocence. We were living in the Black Country and – this sounds awful, but it was a rather poverty-stricken area, heavily industrial and fairly rough. In fact we were a bit frightened of going to one school because of gangs of boys.' This environment is reflected in her writing – the slaty backyard, among the slag heaps, where nothing except thin carrots and a few sunflowers would grow, in her short story 'Pear Tree Dance'. It is a background of which she often makes mention yet not all are happy with her

Elizabeth (right) and her sister Madelaine in June 1929.

choice of subject matter. 'My sister gets very annoyed when I write about the Midlands in that way, the industrial Midlands. She gets very upset and says people will think we grew up in the slums. Which we did,' she laughs. 'There was a coal mine behind our house, a brickworks across the road and a bone and glue factory with a terrible smell nearby.'

From an early age, Elizabeth regarded her father with pride. 'He was a science and mathematics teacher and insisted on staying in a school in a very poor district. The boys were very rough, very poor and not properly fed. They would fall asleep in class because they were so tired. My father started free school dinners before the war and he never moved from there.

'He thought that was God's work. He was … how can I put it … a noble person … Often he wouldn't come home straight from school; he might take his boys to a playing field or a trip down a mine, and he always took them to the swimming baths, things they wouldn't have in their education or home lives. And every year he took a group of boys to the Tyrol, to the mountains in Switzerland. The school at which he taught was just called the Central School, Bilston Central School, but then it became a grammar school after the war. And of course after the war, there were automatically school dinners. But before that, he paid two women to come and cook. He also bought vegetables and meat and different shops tended to give him food.

'My father thought he would educate us at home. Maybe he wanted to protect us from school, I don't know. My parents were upset about the German, you see, and they wanted a different kind of education for us. So they obtained permission from the Education Department to have us at home and we had governesses and radio, wireless lessons.' Far from feeling lonely or restricted, Elizabeth loved those days. 'I had a very wild time and in fact I didn't turn up for many of my lessons.' Instead she would run away into the surrounding fields – 'little bits of leftover farms' – and hide there for the entire day. 'I think ultimately that's why I was sent away to boarding school.'

Her previous experience of school had been at primary school between the ages of six and eight. 'I was a tall girl at this infant school and so, when any small girl or boy wanted to leave the room to go to the lavatory, I would always be asked to go with them as I could reach the doorknob. My sister was in a different room and the teacher would come and ask me to go with my sister. So I think I grew up to be terribly responsible.' This sense of duty was reinforced by her early Quaker upbringing. 'It made you think you were your brother's keeper, so you always took on more responsibility than you could manage.'

She enjoyed school. 'Of course I learned to read there and I loved reading. We had reading cards and were allowed to choose which card we would read aloud from and I just adored that. Then I missed the lesson on how to tell the time and it took me ages to catch up.

'The second school was bigger and rougher; that's when we moved house. I remember getting into trouble when it was my turn to read in class. I'd already finished the story and was onto another story in the book. We were reading *The Little Fir Tree* and I was on a different page and I got slapped for that. I also got a slap in my first school for opening my exercise book and bringing my pencil down on every page. I couldn't resist it.

'I remember having what was called a Pound Day at both schools. Every child took a pound of something – sugar, rice, flour, that kind of thing – and it was then sent to poor children. My mother always put in a pound packet of rice and my rice packet burst once. Yes, Pound Day was a very important occasion, and in a way, it wouldn't hurt to do it now, would it? The public hospitals used to have a Pound Day and there was also an Egg Day. People went along the streets in Birmingham with long sticks which they passed up to houses and offices, and eggs were put in these nets and other foods, which then went to the hospitals. You see, in those days very little food was provided by hospitals. A cup of tea and bread and butter might be a meal.'

Elizabeth says she had a few friends at school – 'I had my own little gang' – but she wasn't used to being with a lot of children. Apart from two years at primary school, she and her sister spent just a short time at Bilston Girls High School. 'My father thought it would be a bit better than the other schools but it was very difficult for him.' He would take the two girls to school in his motorbike sidecar and then go on to his own school. 'But there was the worry about coming back, because his school went on longer in the afternoon and we had to play somewhere. I think he found it a great strain so probably that's why we didn't go on.'

Right from childhood, Elizabeth was outstanding at writing. 'I wasn't very good at maths. My father was ambitious and taught me algebra and geometry and plotting graphs but I never mastered the decimal point, pounds, shillings and pence and long division – all the things that I needed for school. Maths was a horror subject for me. I sat for a scholarship to boarding school in the Quaker meeting in Wolverhampton and I didn't pass the maths. But apparently my English was so good and my composition excellent so I was taken on a scholarship. I think that was for two years and then that was extended to six. So I was there for the whole time on something like eleven pounds a term.'

Elizabeth was eleven when she left for boarding school. 'That was quite a shock and the first year was very difficult. I went by myself and my sister didn't come till the first year of the war, 1939.' Here again her sense of responsibility led her to care for others. 'When I became Senior I looked after the new children, the smaller children when they were ill, put the little ones to bed and that kind of thing.' In adult life, she cared for students. 'I belonged to the East West Friendship and always had Chinese and African students staying. They had a few weeks to get acclimatised and find lodgings.' And in Australia, on the university campus, she looked after wives and members of staff who weren't well or who were homesick for the country they'd left.

Boarding school was an unhappy time for Elizabeth. 'I had to manage an extraordinary amount of teasing because boarding school can be very cruel. They teased me about everything: the fact that I wore glasses – I couldn't stand being called Four Eyes – and then, because I had no bosom, I was called a plank. Many of the girls were very podgy and fat but I never had to wear a bra at school and I felt self-consious about that.'

She thinks her sense of humour came from those days. 'Maybe I cultivated it at school without meaning to, because I was very shy. I hadn't been to school for all those years. You make a joke about something and then somebody laughs and everything's all right. My father also had a very quick humour and so did my aunt, so I think it's probably inherited, that ability to say a silly thing that will disarm people.' Later on in life, she used this same humour in her nursing and teaching in order to break down hostility. 'When you're nursing, you have to disarm and yet at the same time not reduce people but just break down hostility. The same applies to teaching.'

On leaving school, Elizabeth trained to become a nurse. 'It would have been unheard of to leave school and do writing. Everybody who left my school went into some training or job. I would have liked to have been a doctor but I would have had to go to another school to learn Latin. Also I was no good at maths. So I did just an ordinary school certificate, which was fine for nursing but not medicine. I never regretted it. I enjoyed my nursing. I don't think I was really cut out for medicine.' It was while nursing that she met her future husband, Leonard, who was a patient in her hospital, suffering from arthritis. They exchanged books and records and met again some time later in Birmingham, where he was a college librarian.

Elizabeth sees a connection between nursing and writing, describing them both as occupations that 'require a gaze which is searching and undisturbingly compassionate and yet detached'. 'That may sound harsh,' she admits, 'yet it's true. As I got older, I realised I couldn't be in the presence of a small baby crying – it fills my eyes with tears. Whereas when I was young, I could be in a whole nursery of babies bawling their heads off, newly born, and it didn't do a thing to me.'

Her early education has also shaped her writings and occasionally teachings from those early years come back to haunt her. When, on the first page of *Miss Peabody's Inheritance*, she put a misprint in Miss Edgely's writing as a joke, a reviewer commented it was in bad taste – to have a joke on the first page. Elizabeth smiles. 'That's what my English teacher said at school, about not playing to the gallery, when we gave a talk or wrote something. You don't do something silly at the beginning. On the other hand, that's how I operate because I'm shy. So when I get up to speak, I usually say something silly first.'

Her sense of humour can be in complete contrast to the painful content of her writing. 'Yes, I do see family life as extremely painful and difficult. Family life … neighbours even more difficult, workplace problems, so you've got to be able to see the ridiculous side as well.' While Elizabeth uses much material from her background in her fiction, it is just that, she stresses – fiction. 'In fiction you heighten everything, so you're not really expressing yourself at all. You're creating characters and situations. I wrote a number of stories with road accidents in them. "The Shepherd on the Roof" was one. A woman rang me up and said, "Oh, Elizabeth, I didn't know you had been in such a serious accident," and that alerted me. It made me realise people were actually seeing me in all the things that I was writing about.'

But that incident even rubbed off on Elizabeth herself. 'It alarmed me. When my father was run over and killed on the road in 1977, I said to Leonard, "I've got five road accidents in my stories. I feel almost responsible for my father's death." But he told me not to be silly. "Road accidents are happening all the time and not because you're writing about them. You haven't caused them." But my paternal grandfather used to put his head round the door when we were children – we'd be in our nighties by the fire – and he'd tell us how many children were run over each week at the end of the farm road by the tram. So it was ironic that his own son should be killed on the road, wasn't it?'

While Elizabeth is now aware that people take what she has written as fiction to be true, it does not unduly concern her. 'No, I'm rather touched that people read the books. I really don't mind what they think. People should be free to think about writing.' And society attitudes have changed. 'Of course I make no secret of the fact that I lived with Leonard for many years without being married to him, that I had a baby, that I worked in a school. You see, those things are autobiographical. They were all things that I had to keep hidden at that stage, because of the climate of opinion, but now one can talk about those things and has been able to for some years. It is no longer the kind of disgrace that it was. Leonard read my books as long as he could. He managed to read *Cabin Fever* but he didn't read *The Georges' Wife* as he had a deterioration in health.'

Leonard died in July 1994. In the past, though, he had read Elizabeth's books when they were finished and commented on them. 'He helped me with *Mr Scobie's Riddle* because, of course, it was just such a terrible lament. He didn't know what to do but he just said that it needed lifting from the lament. The people that rejected it said that too. I couldn't bear to read it myself and Leonard said, "If you can't read it yourself, then you can't expect anyone else to." I rewrote it and introduced black comedy.'

Following on from this theme, she stresses it is important not to become too involved with your writing. 'If you cry while you're writing or if you laugh at your own funny characters, I think that's suspect. You often have writers, especially men, who read their work aloud and they nearly die of laughing. Have you ever seen that in performance? They laugh so much at their own work and no one else is laughing. People like to say, "It's wonderful, your characters take over", but they don't. You're in control of them the whole time. The thing is, you've got to be in control. You're writing the book and you're using the craft of writing. Your characters aren't doing the things, you're making them do them; it's your brain that's thinking. I shouldn't generalise but I do feel the quality of your writing is suspect if you laugh or cry when writing it.'

Of which of her works is she the proudest? 'I don't know that I'm proudest of any of them. They've all been hard to write and it's always been a great relief when each one is finished. You see, I'm not proudest of any of my three children, not that your writing is like your children.'

Not a favourite amongst them? 'No, I had them all in the drawer under my underclothes, nighties and things. This drawer got a bit heavy to pull open and Leonard said, "Why do you have them in there? Put them on the shelf in the living room." And so I did. I think I feel a bit pleased when I see them. It kind of gives me a little lift to see the little row of books. I don't know why I put them in the drawer – I've never told anyone this before – and especially that drawer. I could have put them where the jumpers and things were!'

Elizabeth never talks about the current book she is working on. 'It's impossible. Once you try to explain what something is about, it sounds so lame and stupid. There again, Leonard advised me about that. He said, "When people say, 'What are you writing now?' just say, 'Oh, some writing.'" He said it's a bit like when people would ask, "When are you going to stop growing?" when you were young, or "When do you go back to school?" It's just a social grace to ask. I'm really secretive when I'm writing. That's why I can't work on a film script because you have to talk about everything, talk for three hours and write three words. I want to work on my own.'

Elizabeth finds she is unsettled when she is writing. 'It's a very restless occupation because you're never really able to rest from it. You see, I don't pay someone to do things to give me a morning or an afternoon to write because I write all the time.' All the time includes when she is on the phone and preparing the vegetables for dinner. 'Yes, and those little pile of notes and observations are the most important part really. I couldn't work without them.' She cannot work for hours at a stretch. 'I have to get up and mess around somewhere and do something and then go back to it. Early morning is good, because if I want to stop I can go and put the washing machine on and then come back again.'

She rises at 4.30 in the morning to write, a habit she cultivated when working as a nurse and raising three children. It was the only peaceful time she had to herself. 'I used to have to stop at about seven o'clock because I would take Leonard his morning tea then.' By this stage she was also looking after him, as he was crippled with arthritis.

'I would have my breakfast then and after that I wouldn't have any time till I'd done his shower and everything. That would take me up to about ten or half past ten. Then he was in the nursing home after 1990 and I could go on writing in the morning. But I tended to do household things and get him in the afternoon, because once he was home, I couldn't do much other than pull a few weeds out of the garden. I'd put the wheelchair where I was working or sweep the verandahs and so on.'

When writing, Elizabeth feels as if she is in another world. 'I feel better. It gives me a lift. I like to leave off where I know I can go on. I always scribble a few pencil notes down in the manuscript and arrange my little bits of notes. I often read through the notes and, as I use everything, I put a line through them and put them in a folder of used pages. I don't throw them away in case I want them back again, you see. Because I write by hand.' She says she would never use a typewriter or computer. 'No, no, I couldn't. The actual mechanical effort would knock everything else out of me.

'I have students who hand in work from computer or word processor and the work that comes in handwritten is *much* better. It's facile on the word processor and they're taken with it and do ornamental titles. Actually, some of them don't manage it very well and you get repeated paragraphs,' she laughs. 'I know people who write poems on the computer but the poems have no feeling in them really. Some people may be different of course, but I feel what is being done with pen first is better. And I sometimes ask them for working pages to go with the finished pages.' Elizabeth herself writes with a pen in black ink on old, good-quality paper and has her work typed.

She is both happy and bemused to be approached in public. 'Sometimes people rush up and tell me how they hated my last novel and when they describe it I notice it isn't one of my books at all.'

Her own skills of observation coupled with her imagination have led to some equally unexpected encounters. She describes how, in a coffee shop, she once watched as an elderly man and a woman at a nearby table drank their cups of coffee in absolute silence. 'How sad,' she thought, 'to have been married for all these years and to be left with nothing to say, no communication at all.' While Elizabeth was musing further, the man stood up, went to pay for his coffee and walked out. The couple were not a couple at all.

Elizabeth has never thought of herself as a migrant but rather, because of migration and travel, as someone who inhabits several worlds. Yet it took her time to feel at home in this one. 'It was two years before I picked any flowers to put in the house,' she says. And some time later, the discovery of an old Birmingham road map among her belongings at Claremont, unsettled her. 'A migrant feels for a time that life is temporary in the new country,' she explains.

When asked whether she considers herself Australian and what that means to her, she replies, 'I don't really think about it except if I'm being described by somebody as "an English writer". That gives me a shock. I don't consider myself an English writer and certainly not just Australian, but West Australian.' And that for Elizabeth is someone who writes from a Western Australian environment, an environment comprising physical, political and emotional elements – 'everything which has helped form and mould the writer, including people'.

Living and working in Western Australia has changed Elizabeth's attitude and awareness. In this country's vastness, she has acquired a new sense of distance and learned of isolation. She has also learned of the importance of water and its effect on the land – knowledge which has shaped and been reflected in her writing. 'People often ask what I would have written had I stayed in England,' she says, 'I have no idea. But I would have missed these observations had I stayed there. When you come to a new country you make an effort to succeed, perhaps to justify making the change. People attempt to overcome the feelings of strangeness by making a tremendous effort to belong – working towards owning land and having a house on it.'

She ponders on the multicultural nature of Australia today. 'It's all a matter of respecting other cultures and liking different things rather than separating and having ghettos.'

For migration to be successful, Elizabeth believes that the emphasis must be rather on creating the future together than preserving the past. 'I think people do want to preserve their past but if you dwell too much on the past, you don't look ahead to see what would make a good future.' In agreeing that it is important for children to learn about their past, she believes this should not be at the expense of ignoring the present and the future. 'If you do dwell on the unhappiness of the past that tends to lead to bitterness, and nothing is achieved really.'

She sees the moves she has made in her life as significant. 'Any move is of course a turning point. We moved about four times in the British Isles before we came here. And you can't travel all across the world and remain unchanged. Coming by ship you really do travel across the world; you see the world on the way. It's so different for people coming by air: they only see the inside of airports when the plane touches down.'

Landscape has without doubt, Elizabeth says, influenced her writing while the process of migration has refined it. 'I think region matters enormously for writing.' Her view is that 'a dramatic change of landscape and country can make a powerful impact on a writer'. She uses the beauty or harshness of that landscape to portray the feelings of her characters.

Times and places have changed but for Elizabeth, one of the

positive aspects of migration has been that the memory of her previous country, far from being erased, has been sharpened, by the contrast with her new environment. She expands on this in her writing, as demonstrated by the following extract from her first, and previously unpublished short story, 'At the River', set in Western Australia.

> Denis read and Isobel relaxed and peered about, she wore spectacles for short sight. After a while she said 'How about if I go home and bring some lunch down for us all!'
>
> 'What could you bring' said Denis doubtfully.
>
> 'Oh salad and cold meat. I could put lettuce and things in my big pastry bowl, that is what people seem to do here.' Isobel was enthusiastic.
>
> 'That would be very nice,' Denis was agreeable. Isobel hastened to the car and in a few minutes she was at home.
>
> Christmas had collapsed in the heat. The little house was not big enough for them and for Christmas and the heat. The small sitting room was burdened with coloured streamers and lanterns, balloons and greetings cards. The children had hammered up festoons of paper and had pasted gold paper angels on the doors and windows. And the tree, laden with memories from previous Christmases, leaned heavily to one side. As they had unpacked the little carved decorations, the coloured balls and faded tinsel, Isobel and the children had experienced the bitter sweet nostalgia for another place where they had known Christmas, and for the people they had been with, and for all the things that go with Christmas in a cold winter climate. They had made dozens of mince pies; they ate a few of them and the rest were wrapped in newspaper in the dustbin. Silently they were all longing to clear up the sitting room.
>
> Isobel paid no attention to the mess. She let the fly screen door bang and went swiftly through the sitting room to the kitchen. She sang softly as she washed a lettuce and peeled and cut up a magnificent carrot and an even more magnificent cucumber. She had radishes and tomatoes and spring onions in the refrigerator and fresh butter and cold meat. She ate a bit while she prepared it. The pickled beef, or corned beef as they called it here, was delicious. She wrapped up two bottles of iced water in sheets of newspaper and filled a big bag with ripe peaches, plums and apricots. The kitchen was fragrant with the fruit. She must remember to write home about the fruit and the smell of it. Finally she cut up a loaf and wrapped it in a cloth. Hurriedly she took everything to the car and very soon was walking carefully over the crowded grass, the pastry bowl nearly slipping from the crook of her arm and the string bag cutting her fingers cruelly, to where Denis lay reading.

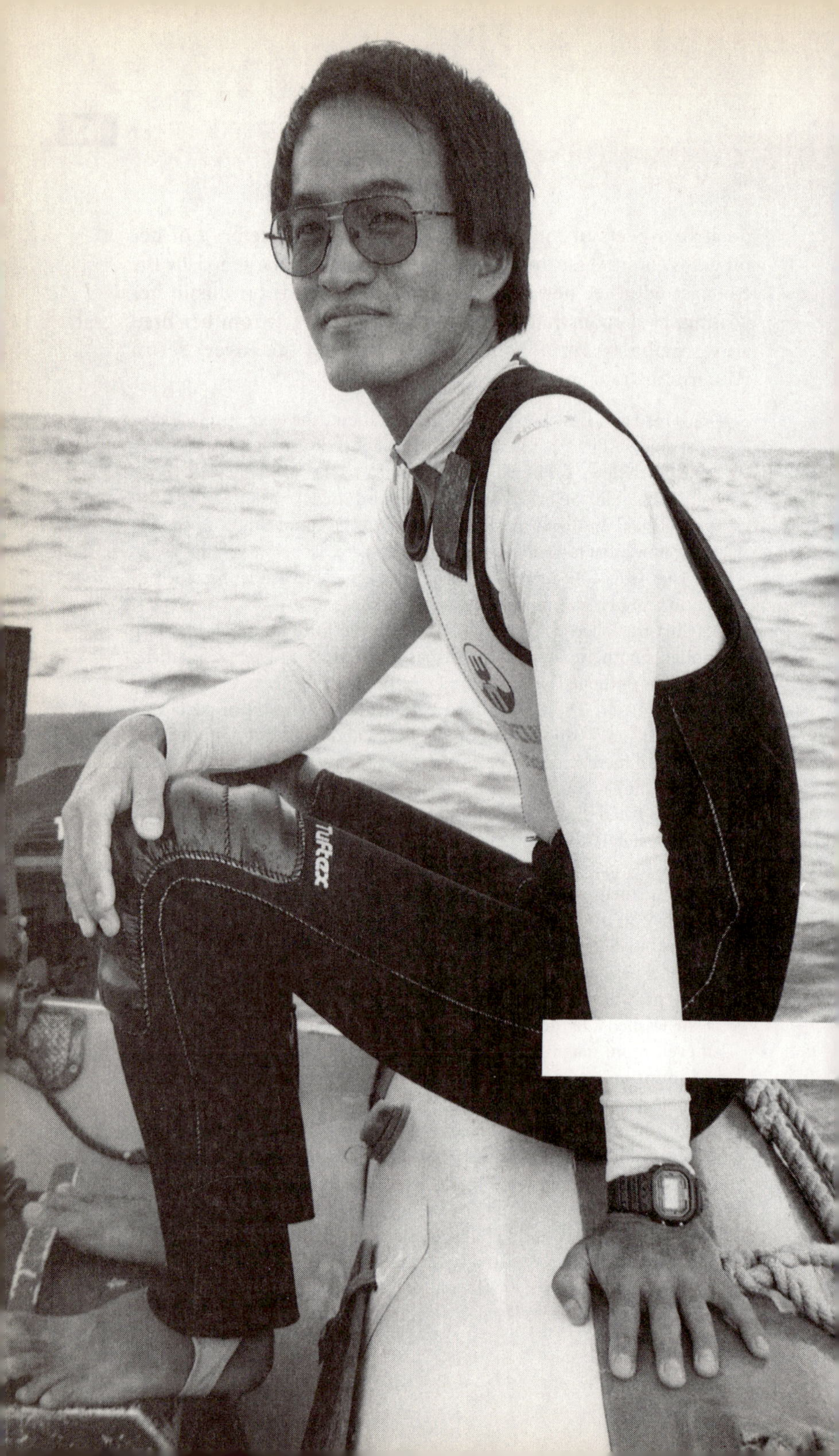

ALL AT SEA

'If I wanted a big salary, I might have stayed in Japan. Money does not make people happy. You may be able to buy some things with it but you cannot buy other meaningful things like friendship.'

TENSHI AYUKAI

Oceanographer

'Just keep your eye on the horizon and get your balance,' oceanographer Dr Tenshi Ayukai urges as we stand on the stern of the swaying ship. It is sound advice, not only for the present moment but also for life in general. Fix your gaze, set your sights and keep your balance. We are some ten kilometres off the Queensland coast and heading south. After leaving Cairns at dawn, our destination is Townsville, a two-day voyage away.

The *Harry Messel* motors on noisily. It is one of three main research vessels used by the Australian Institute of Marine Science (AIMS), which is based at Townsville. Those on board the ship include seasoned sailors – the hardy crew of four, Tenshi Ayukai, research scientist from AIMS, with his three volunteers – and myself, a landlubber. This description was to be well and truly confirmed over the next forty-eight hours.

Tenshi, as he is known by friends and colleagues, has been in Australia since 1988; initially he came from Japan to take up a postdoctoral fellowship position at AIMS. Three years later he joined its staff. This is one of his regular field trips.

The work day had started just after seven when the ship's motor was suddenly cut and Tenshi and his team of volunteers assembled on the stern. The silence and stillness is welcoming after the continuous noise of the engine and the movement of the ship. It is an overcast day, so humid that my camera lens instantly mists and refuses to clear, and the sky is completely white. The view in every direction is of endless sea – a deep azure blue and slightly choppy. Tenshi picks up one of the four Niskin bottles (grey, cylindrical objects about forty-five centimetres long), attaches it to a steel cable and sends it plummeting down to a depth of ten metres where the sea water will be forced inside it. In this region, the sea can be up to fifty metres deep.

Once the container is winched up, the volunteers take over. Everyone knows his or her role well. James – a British marine zoology graduate presently doing research for his master's degree at the National University of Singapore – hands Tenshi the Niskin bottle each time, together with the heavy brass 'messenger' that fits on top to weigh it down. Janet – a zoology graduate from Sheffield, here on a year's working holiday – removes the sea water samples from the bottles while Carolyn – a marine biology student from

Townsville's James Cook University – filters this sea water using the equipment in the small laboratory on board. On deck, the team work quietly. There is no room for error. Tenshi is a perfectionist and the gear is expensive. Each Niskin bottle is worth $1 400 and the current price of the brass messenger – to be paid for by the volunteer, if accidentally lost overboard – is $120.

The whole operation moves along smoothly, like clockwork, despite some bleary eyes and tired bodies. Breakfast has been soon after six this morning – a sumptuous feast of piping hot croissants, fresh tropical fruit juices, toast with exotic spreads, home-made muesli or cereal, tea and coffee. Large meals are needed to replace the kilojoules burnt up with the daily physical effort.

On this morning, there are three sets of water samples to be taken, at spots forty-five minutes of travel apart. Some analyses will be done on these samples here at sea, the rest at the AIMS laboratory. There will be two dives – down to as deep as fifteen metres – morning and afternoon, and Tenshi will still be working at eleven tonight, entering data on his lap-top computer. He has set a tight and demanding schedule. Each volunteer has received a detailed itinerary, which Tenshi expects to be kept. He was disappointed therefore, on the previous evening, to have picked me up at Marlin Jetty in Cairns a few minutes after the pre-arranged time.

He apologised profusely. 'But you've been at sea for ten days,' I said, as we powered to the *Harry Messel* in a Zodiac dinghy equipped with outboard motor. 'What's a few minutes?'

'We pride ourselves on being punctual,' Tenshi explained. It was a sentiment echoed by Peter, the skipper, whose first words to me on board were also by way of apology. 'We needed to take some extra sea water samples and that delayed us.'

Of medium height, very slim, with jet-black hair and wearing light wire-framed glasses, Tenshi is softly spoken. Yet his gentle manner commands respect and authority. He is widely admired – by crew and volunteers, by AIMS staff and colleagues – for his excellent work, his precise and thorough manner, and his sensitive and caring personality. On my guided tour of the twenty-two-metre vessel with its compact living quarters, he pointed out the fishing reel he has brought – 'for fun, everyone must be comfortable and happy'. This is his philosophy. 'We have to enjoy life; it is very short.' But he puts in a hard day's work to earn that enjoyment.

The early morning shift completed, the volunteers retire below deck to their cabins, for a rest or a short sleep before the next water samples are to be taken. The main purpose of this trip is to measure the chlorophyll content, temperature, salinity and turbidity of the sea water at thirty-four designated points along the Great Barrier Reef from Lizard Island in the north to Townsville in the south. At the same time, Tenshi is taking the opportunity of checking up on reported sightings by recreational divers of the crown-of-thorns starfish. These starfish have caused extensive damage to the Great Barrier Reef over the last thirty years in two separate outbreaks – in the 1960s and 1980s – and now it seems their numbers are increasing once more. 'The outbreaks have occurred every sixteen or seventeen years and we are concerned about whether or not there is a link between outbreaks and human activities,' Tenshi says. While I joined the ship at Cairns, the others – after ten days at sea – are on their return trip to Townsville. Janet and Carolyn are adding to their knowledge in helping Tenshi, while James has his own additional project. He is studying the clownfish, which is able to live amongst the stinging tentacles of the sea anemone.

A couple of hours, and two more sampling stations later, it is diving time. Again, everyone knows the procedure. The dinghy has been lowered alongside the ship and is loaded with weight belts, scuba tanks, masks, fins and other diving paraphernalia. The outboard motor has been checked and lifejackets, flares and drinking water are in place. It is an exhilarating feeling as we zoom off, cool seaspray splashing in our faces as we leave the *Harry Messel* in our wake. We travel about a kilometre before Tenshi stops, putting the engine into neutral. He stands up and surveys the sea, moving the dinghy in this direction a little and then that, before he is satisfied. Finally he asks for the anchor to be lowered and cuts the motor.

Tenshi and James are to dive first and they attach the heavy weight belts and scuba tanks, and then put on masks and fins. Mouthpieces in place, they sit on the edge of the dinghy and then gently drop backwards into the sea, leaving a trail of bubbles as they descend and disappear from view. Above, on the dinghy, the blue vastness of that world is still and peaceful while below, an even more beautiful universe beckons.

The water is clear, the visibility excellent and the fish life varied and plentiful. Fish dart around the divers, in colours of iridescent blue and green, in shades of yellow and orange, in gleaming black and white. Among them is the Moorish idol with its long pennant-like dorsal fin, brilliantly coloured angelfish and yellow-green wrasse. Some fish are less than a centimetre in length while others extend to half a metre. As the divers swim on, they are surrounded by corals of stunning and remarkable beauty, in all manner of colours and patterns, sizes and shapes.

Tenshi has already informed me that there are about four hundred species of hard coral on the Great Barrier Reef. Coral polyps – tiny animals – secrete limestone skeletons to construct the reef, while the algae living in the coral tissues are also important reef architects. Pieces of dead coral and debris add to the structure, which becomes a home for fish and worms, starfish and molluscs. The plate corals are most spectacular, extending for a few metres across, like enormous flat plates set for a giant's dinner party. They look and are delicate, and the divers take care not to touch or damage the coral with their fins. They swim over enormous round and solitary boulder-like corals. They linger by staghorn-shaped corals, their bumpy polyps a shade of pink, and look closely at a mushroom coral, which resembles an overturned fungus. Soft white coral polyps wave in the current. Others are blue, purple and bright yellow.

This is Tenshi's world – magical, enchanting and almost silent, punctuated only by the sound of the divers' breathing and that of the sea, the tap-tapping of the parrot fish as they scrape algae from the coral with their front teeth, which form a parrot-like beak. It is a world that is difficult to leave.

Tenshi first discovered this kingdom in his childhood, off the island of Okinawa. He recalls his first snorkelling experience at the age of ten. 'It made a vivid impression on a child's eyes. I saw all sorts of colours; it was just paradise,' he says, explaining how the coral reef around Okinawa was once unique, with a vast number of different species, similar to the Great Barrier Reef.

Born in northern Japan, Tenshi and his family moved a lot because of his father's occupation as a teacher. They lived, however, for several years in a small fishing village in the province of Yamaguchi. There Tenshi enjoyed snorkelling and fishing. 'The beach was fine yellow sand, and I'd collect shells and catch very reasonable fish, like the flounder, with my home-made bamboo fishing rod. My friend and I would snorkel in the summer. The sea was green, not blue, and all you could see was sand and seagrass. It was a very productive area with very high fish stocks. Fishermen used nets or lines to catch all sorts of fish, yellowtail being one of the main ones.'

Then the factories came and everything changed. 'There was sludge everywhere. The beach became smelly, the sea was brown and the fish disappeared. The fishermen couldn't catch anything and the seaweed "nori" culture died off. It was simply terrible.' All this happened in the early 1970s when Tenshi was sixteen years of age. He saw the destruction of an environment and a people. The impact of that changed his life. Pulp mills and chemical factories caused the massive pollution of the beach and the bay, discharging foul-smelling hydrogen sulphide and other processing by-products, with no regard for the consequences.

Unable to make a living, some fishermen turned to these same factories that had ruined them and sought work. Some moved elsewhere but a few, devastated by what had occurred, suicided. Tenshi was deeply affected by the tragedy he had witnessed. 'I had seen something beautiful and now the sea was dying. I wanted to help, to do something about the marine environment.' He decided to study oceanography.

Today, the coral reef around Okinawa is all but gone. 'Most of it is dead: all you can see is the coral skeleton. In some places, there is no coral reef, just rock. When I last dived there, several years ago, all I saw were small pieces of coral,' says Tenshi sadly. The reef was destroyed over a ten-year period by the sediment flowing from agricultural fields, by the effluent resulting from urbanisation, and by the action of a creature also found in Australian waters.

As Tenshi emerges from the tropical Queensland waters, he carries that same ferocious-looking creature with a pair of metal tongs. This is the scourge of the Great Barrier Reef – the crown-of-thorns

TENSHI AYUKAI 171

Tenshi with a crown-of-thorns starfish several kilometres off the Queensland coast.
Photo by Helen Chryssides.

starfish, with a myriad of long, orange, venomous spikes covering its numerous arms.

'We counted twelve starfish,' says Tenshi with concern. His anxiety is due to the fact that for each crown-of-thorns starfish seen, there will be a lot more hidden from view. 'Counting is only a measure of maybe less than half the population,' he explains. 'It is a very time-consuming process and some people doubt its efficiency, but we are desperate. These starfish are cryptic. They can hide in the spaces between the rock or corals and often you cannot see them in the daytime.' The spines of the specimen he is holding bristle with movement. 'You must not touch the spines,' he continues. 'They are poisonous and can break off and lodge in your skin.'

Tenshi knows from personal experience. Careful though he was, while measuring the size of one of these starfish a couple of days ago he touched one of its spines. His right index finger is now swollen and extremely painful. Grasping the crown-of-thorns starfish tightly between the metal prongs, he turns it over to show me its mouth. It is a large specimen, a good forty-five centimetres across, and there – in the centre of its fourteen or more arms – I see the mouth opening.

Then Tenshi produces a piece of staghorn coral. While the bottom half is a deep brown, the top half is in stark contrast – a bleached white colour. This white part is dead coral, eaten by the crown-of-thorns starfish. 'In the early stages, the juvenile crown-of-thorns starfish eat algae, not the coral. About six months later, their food habits change. They attach themselves to the coral and force the stomach out through the mouth. Enzymes are secreted to break down the coral tissue.' Digestion takes several hours, after which the stomach is retracted and the crown-of-thorns starfish moves on. Left behind is the white coral skeleton Tenshi has shown me.

It has been estimated that one crown-of-thorns starfish can consume up to ten square metres of coral a year. Multiply that area by many many thousand, as occur in an outbreak, and the potential damage to a reef system is enormous. In the second series of crown-of-thorns starfish outbreaks – from 1980 to 1993 – about 17 per cent of the 2900 coral reefs in the Great Barrier Reef were affected, half of these being heavily damaged. The coral reef can recover to some extent but never fully so in the case of slow-growing corals if there are regular crown-of-thorns starfish outbreaks. Faster-growing corals, such as staghorns and plate corals, however, can recover in twelve to fifteen years.

Tenshi is monitoring a section of the reef over a three-year period. The water samples he has taken on this trip will also be analysed for chlorophyll content which, he explains, is a good measure of phytoplankton – a food source for crown-of-thorns larvae. The plankton (floating organic matter), over two microns in size, can be eaten by the larvae. A high level of chlorophyll in certain areas would therefore indicate the possibility of more crown-of-thorns starfish larvae being able to survive and recruit successfully.

'The Great Barrier Reef is the last pristine coral ecosystem in the world,' says Tenshi. It is also the largest and most complex living reef system. With an area of 350 000 square kilometres, it extends over a distance of 2300 kilometres from Lady Elliot Island near Bundaberg, northwards along the Queensland coast. 'The public have told us they have seen quite a few crown-of-thorns starfish in different locations in the last year or so and we need to know whether this could be the start of another outbreak. We know very little about the very initial stage ... So far, it seems the crown-of-thorns starfish population is building up. We saw some increases around Lizard Island and now here, around Flora Reef.'

This work aptly demonstrates one of the points Tenshi wants to emphasise. 'It is wonderful to do research for the sake of science but it is also important, as in this case, to do research for the sake of management.' In this respect, he regards himself as perhaps 'not quite a scientist'. 'I mean a scientist does research for philosophical reasons and maybe we should be doing more science for management.' The exact cause of crown-of-thorns outbreaks is unknown. 'It's still a mystery. One argument is that they may be a natural phenomenon ... The problem is complex and the present management policy is one of non-intervention. That's very sound if this is a natural phenomenon. But if the outbreaks are human-caused or exacerbated by human activities, then we have to take decisive action to stop them.'

Later in Townsville I spoke with Dr Peter Moran, recognised authority on the crown-of-thorns starfish, principal research scientist, and then Acting Director of AIMS. He considers Tenshi's work to be vitally important. 'This is the first time we have been in a position to identify what may be the beginning of outbreaks and therefore to look at the conditions that give rise to them,' he says. 'What impresses me about Tenshi is not only his background but also his wide-ranging skills in technology, applying these to a very important question – namely, the future of the Great Barrier Reef.'

According to Dr Moran, Tenshi was a quiet individual when he first came to AIMS to join the team of thirty scientists. 'He was so quiet you almost never heard from him, but now he's taking a leading role in a very important project; in fact he replaced me as project co-ordinator for crown-of-thorns research at the Institute. It's a problem that's Indo-Pacific-wide, not just on the Great Barrier Reef … We're presently negotiating with a number of different organisations over joint collaborative research and it has been beneficial having Tenshi act as our Japanese liaison person.

'The Japanese are world-renowned in terms of their technological capabilities, while Australia leads the world in its understanding of biological and environmental issues relating to the marine environment. So I suppose what the Japanese lack we have, and vice versa.'

❂

Once Carolyn and Janet have completed a dive with Tenshi, we return to the *Harry Messel*. The coral that Tenshi has shown me looks a dull brown colour in the sunlight, quite different to its underwater hue. I learn how each coral has three colours – the colour seen underwater, the colour seen on the surface, and that captured in a photograph. Sea water acts as a selective light filter, a fact that can be clearly demonstrated by picking a piece of blue coral at a depth of ten or more metres and watching it gradually change colour to a shade of pink as it is brought to the surface.

Back on board, Dave the cook serves up another feast – a smorgasbord of cold meats and salads, fresh fruits and cheeses. Feeling a little queasy after our morning at sea, I decide wisely, though not without some difficulty, to pass on the delicious-looking array. The others tuck in eagerly and Tenshi eats with gusto as he laughs and jokes with the crew and volunteers. His language skills, he tells me, have improved vastly in the last few years. Although fluent in the reading and writing of English – indeed he wrote all his theses and scientific papers in English – he did not feel confident in conversation. That was a top priority for him on arrival at AIMS.

'I could have stayed in my office all day and not spoken to anyone at all. But my English would never have improved. So I started going to every morning and afternoon tea break – and I still do – and attempted to talk as much as possible with other staff members. I used these tea breaks as my English lessons.' More formal classes were out of the question due to his busy workload. He admits the Japanese reputation for being hard-working is justified, and describes his university days. 'In my case, I was working for a water supply company during the day, checking on water quality, and studying in the evenings. I'd start work at nine in the morning and often stay at the university until eleven or midnight.'

To some extent, these long hours were forced on him by circumstance. 'I had no financial support from my family. My wife also had to work – everything in Japan is so expensive; the cost of living is very high.' Consequently Tenshi had many part-time and casual jobs. He studied for his Bachelor of Science at Japan's Tohoku University in the city of Sendai and followed this with a master's degree and then a PhD.

Writing his theses in English taught him to be concise. 'Our professor recommended this, which is not done by everyone in Japan, as he himself had worked in the United States for several years, liked their system and thought this would make us avoid the use of unnecessary words. Another benefit of writing in English, of course, was that our work could then reach more people. In his day, my professor wrote his own thesis in Latin. Again the basic idea was the same. Writing in another language, and in this case a dead one, would ensure that only the necessary and vital information would be included.' Tenshi also improved his English by reading newspapers, equipped with a dictionary.

He applied to come to AIMS after seeing an advertisement in the English scientific journal, *Nature*. 'I had applied for about thirty jobs in a year, over sixty in two years. Most were in the United States, some in Europe – France and Greece. The reason was that my real interest lay in the area of marine environmental science and protection of the ecosystem, and there's not much wilderness in Japan. The ecosystems there are all inhabited and I wanted to work somewhere like the Great Barrier Reef.'

At the same time that he was accepted by AIMS, Tenshi was also offered a post at Fairbanks, Alaska, to work in the Arctic sea. 'That's a pristine system too,' he says, 'but quite opposite to the Great Barrier Reef. It's too cold,' he laughs. And he far prefers the tropical climate to the winter cold of his homeland. 'In Japan, we'd have two metres of snow each winter. I don't miss the freezing weather.'

Although he knew nothing of Australia before he arrived, Tenshi found it a very special place with gracious, welcoming people. 'We lived in a small apartment at first and simply everyone was so kind and looked after us.' Friendships forged then, six years ago, have been kept to this day. But the family found living in the two-bedroom apartment difficult initially. Too small for him, his wife and their two children? 'No – too big!' he pronounces. Their accommodation in Japan had consisted of thirty square metres of living space, located on the third floor of an apartment building. Their new home was at least three times that size. And three years ago, the family moved to a house. 'That would not have been possible in Japan, something I could never have achieved. Perhaps in the countryside you could still take out a mortgage and pay it off in twenty or thirty years but in Tokyo it would take three generations, one hundred years, for ordinary people to pay off a house.'

The Australian lifestyle was attractive to Tenshi in other ways also. 'Here the people are friendly – that's the most important thing. If you're living in a city in Japan, you would never talk to your neighbours or know what sort of work they are doing. People work different hours and long hours so you don't get a chance to see them. There are so many people in the city, yet we live in isolation in Japan and that's simply terrible.' So Queensland came as a complete contrast. 'Townsville was simply fantastic – we had never been to such a place before – with big palm trees and a beautiful beach. We arrived in August, in winter, so it wasn't very hot but very dry. I would have liked to have had a holiday then.'

But following the six-and-a-half hour flight from Tokyo to Cairns, and then to Townsville, Tenshi went to work the very next day. Why? 'Maybe because I was still like a typical Japanese person, a workaholic,' he laughs. 'I thought I should start work immediately and so I left my wife Rumiko, my three-year-old daughter Misaki, and my four-year-old son Keishi, and went to work. I felt very sorry for them but I couldn't stop working.' He still can't.

In a rare free moment, Tenshi is on deck late that afternoon, gazing out to sea. Before him are several shades of blue – from a light colour with the shallow sandy sea bottom visible, to the ever-darkening layers of the depths. 'It's beautiful, isn't it?' he remarks.

A sensitive man, he is concerned with the well-being of each individual on board. 'One person that is unhappy or dissatisfied on such a small vessel can drag the others down,' he explains.

One of the disadvantages of his work is that it regularly takes him away from his family for a few weeks at a time. The family has grown with a third child – three-year-old daughter Mio – and Tenshi thinks his three children will have a better childhood here than in Japan. 'There it has become more difficult. It's tough, too tough for children, and that's one of the reasons I want to stay in Australia. Children grow up too fast in Japan. They look and talk like adults and their future is not bright.' This is not because of lack of jobs – far from it. 'There are many jobs but, in that society, each job has a rank. There you decide on the value of people by the kind of work they do. There are many unhappy people in Japan and life is stressful.' Australia, on the other hand, may be too easy-going in Tenshi's opinion. 'Sometimes I think people need to be a little more disciplined in the workplace,' he chuckles.

Tenshi is bringing up his children to learn Japanese and admits he is probably a little too hard on them. Ask him whether he was a good student at school and he'll burst out laughing. 'I was very cheeky,' he admits unexpectedly, 'cheeky to my teachers and to my friends. I liked playing sport and almost became a professional tennis player. But I had to stop at twenty-one as I developed bad tennis elbow.'

He says he was a different type of youngster. 'I tended to say no when other people said yes; I've no idea why.' This got him into frequent trouble. 'Sometimes even my friends got sick of me. I enjoyed school but I was naughty. What sort of things did I get up to? Should I be telling you this?' he chuckles. 'Once I collected the powder from fireworks, put it in the top of a pencil and placed the pencil cap on top of the door. When the teacher came in and shut the door – bang! an explosion and smoke.' Tenshi spent the rest of the day standing in the corridor as punishment. How did the teacher know it had been him? 'Not many children would do such a thing,' he laughs.

He combined sport and school – playing tennis from late afternoon well into the evening and then studying until midnight. University entrance was very difficult but he did well in his exams. 'My parents were so excited when I was accepted – my mother even cried.' His father, still working, is a high school teacher of Chinese literature while his mother, who died three years ago, taught disabled children at a special school. Tenshi has one sister, eight years his junior.

Buddhism is the main religion in Japan. 'My father was a temple master for several years. It is not an easy life, you only see a limited number of people. I think he probably quit because he liked being with people and wanted to be in society. Being a teacher was one of the best opportunities ... He then married.'

Tenshi is the sole breadwinner in his family. While his wife is a trained nurse and midwife, she has to undertake further study and sit exams for her qualifications to be recognised in Australia. But for both of them, money is not the most important factor in life. 'Naturally I would like to have a reasonable house, a reasonable car for my children, but do we need more than that?' asks Tenshi. 'If I wanted a big salary, I might have stayed in Japan. Money does not make people happy. You may be able to buy some things with it but you cannot buy other meaningful things like friendship. Family and to make them happy is the most important. I have to work hard and, because of this, sometimes I do not have much time to talk to them.'

There are other significant priorities in his life. Tenshi holds strong – and perhaps unexpected – views on development. 'I think tourism in general is a very important industry for Australia but it is also essential to develop only in areas in which it is safe to do so. I'm opposed to random development in order to obtain tourist money.'

To illustrate his point, he talks of a large freehold area in Queensland put on the market for a tourist resort development.

'This spot contains a very big mangrove area and has a large dugong – sea cow – population. It would be a great pity to lose the natural beauty and, in addition, it would be harmful. Mangroves act as a buffer zone, efficiently retaining nutrients from the soil, preventing erosion, and stopping sediment from entering the ocean. The coral reef is very close to the coast in this area. Once the mangroves are removed, there would be nothing to stop sediments and nutrients from the land entering the sea. Nutrients may increase phytoplankton concentrations which, in turn, would decrease the light penetration into the sea. While coral is animal, it also contains algae and these would die without adequate light reaching the coral. The coral would then also die or else some type would become dominant.'

The fragile and unique ecosystem would be destroyed. 'As a scientist, I have to prove these possibilities by monitoring the area – so that's part of my job.'

What would make Tenshi happy is for the Great Barrier Reef to remain in its present state, untouched as far as possible. 'I think there is a simple theory in ecology – if people suffer, then the environment suffers. If people are suffering, generally the government supports the developer and, in some cases, this development is not planned very well. A typical example of this is in the Amazon, where people are so poor they *have* to log. They cannot stop logging. That is the only way they can survive. As long as the people in Brazil continue to suffer poverty, that problem will continue. That may be an extreme example but it applies to any country, in any system, anywhere in the world.

'People have to be reasonably wealthy so that the environment also can survive. That is the concept for sustainable development and that's where scientists can help most – that's our contribution. It *must* be our contribution.'

Ecotourism is, in his opinion, a very interesting concept. 'That's probably the best way to develop. People and the environment will get long-term and maximum benefit.'

It is our last evening at sea. Tenshi, indefatigable as always, works at his lap-top computer while I try to cope with my ever-increasing nausea.

'Have a sleep now,' Peter advised me late in the afternoon. 'You won't get much sleep tonight.' As I carefully made my way back to my cabin, grasping each solid object along the way in order to keep my balance as the ship pitched and rolled, I envied Tenshi's solid constitution. From day one at sea, he had never suffered any such problems.

It is a tricky night. I feel as if I am on a roller coaster, lurching up and down as the vessel ploughs on southwards to Townsville. Every so often, I am lifted off my narrow bed a few centimetres into the air only to be flung straight back down again several seconds later. This time, however, I am not the only one affected. There are a few pale faces at breakfast the next morning.

'The interest may be there but I'm just not cut out to be a marine scientist,' I complain to Peter as the others leave for a final dive. 'Don't worry,' he says reassuringly. 'You're not the worst I've seen. Some scientists are so anxious they start throwing up two days *before* they get on board. And once at sea, they'll wear a bucket around their neck on deck.'

When Tenshi returns, I summon up my remaining strength to ask him how difficult it was to settle in Australia.

Starting afresh in a new country is not difficult at all, he tells me, provided there are good people around you. 'It was a very quick process and I was able to pick up the habits, culture and way of thinking. I like the personalities of Australian people. These days, the Japanese people are more like a uniform society. People tend to look and be the same and that's not fun.

'When Japanese people visit Australia, they tend to congregate in certain places such as Sydney. It may be convenient, and welcoming, to have signs in Japanese for them but I think this should be done in a limited way. I want Japanese people to understand the real Australians, and to do so they must try to speak English. There are also big Japanese communities living in certain suburbs of Australian cities. Again, I do not think this is a good idea. You cannot understand Australian people if you live in that way.'

As for multiculturalism, Tenshi enjoys the mix of our population

– 'it's far more interesting to see many different people' – but he believes Australia is still in the process of forming its own culture and identity. 'It takes generations to make a new culture. You cannot change a person's way of thinking. You pick up your way of thinking as you grow up and so it will take time for these new generations. I, for example, was brought up as a Buddhist and so I cannot think like a Christian. But the next generation, my children, will probably be able to think like Christians. So it takes time, it's a slow process, and we shouldn't look for a quick change.'

Tenshi's Buddhist philosophies include 'doing things for other people – that's most important'. He believes hard work should be rewarded but, in modern society, he says hard work does not necessarily translate to wealth. If he has any disappointments about Australia, it is the tendency he has noticed here to 'criticise each other unnecessarily. People need to be more generous and listen to others.'

There is nothing he misses about Japan, not even the food. 'Japanese society is already Westernised. We eat Western food at home but we always have rice every night. It's healthy and I like it. And I still cannot eat meat pies! But otherwise I probably can have any Australian food.'

Peter Moran can vouch for Tenshi's Western food tastes. 'It's quite funny actually,' he says. 'When the previous director, Tenshi and I went to Tokyo last year for a scientific meeting, we did everything Japanese, eating Japanese food and so on. We thought that because Tenshi was back in his homeland he would have been very happy. When the director and I left – Tenshi was staying on for a few days – we were saying goodbye at the airport and we asked him what he was going to do next. He said, "Well, I'm going off to McDonald's to have a good feed." It turned out he wasn't that keen on Japanese food at all! In some ways, Tenshi is probably more Westernised than I am.'

But there are some differences. 'Japanese society may be more formal and not favour individual differences as here,' says Tenshi.

While he and his family have been welcomed in Australia, he has experienced some racism. He is reluctant to talk about it, saying only, 'Some children point at us as we look Japanese – that's not quite racism. What is more serious is some old people who still remember the Second World War and the Japanese as enemies. But I don't think that is racism either – that's just something you can never forget.'

He finishes talking as we come in to Townsville. It's been a successful trip. Tenshi has collected all his water samples as planned. He's counted the number of crown-of-thorns starfish: fifty around Lizard Island and forty around Flora Reef; relatively high numbers. 'We cannot say whether this could indicate the start of an outbreak but we'll come back in six months and check again.' Before that six months is up, Tenshi will have been on an oceanographic trip to Western Australia. 'I spend about half my time on the crown-of-thorns starfish project and the other half on microbial ecology and biological oceanography.' He is at sea for seventy days a year.

After unloading all the gear, Tenshi drives the volunteers and me to the Institute, located a short distance from the wharf. There, in his office, he points to a map on the wall and says, 'The Great Barrier Reef is the last untouched coral reef in the world. Tourism would be better if used more for public education. Thousands visit the Great Barrier Reef every day and there are basic rules to follow. If every one of them picks up a shell, for example, naturally that shell will disappear. Tourists can enjoy more than the diving. They should also have the opportunity to learn about the coral reef system itself.' Here in Townsville, AIMS encourages visits by the public and gives guided tours.

This field trip of Tenshi's has found the coral to be quite healthy. 'It has almost recovered from the previous crown-of-thorns starfish outbreak but there is something happening at the moment. More research is necessary.' And that requires more funding. 'Unfortunately government funding tends to decrease as the number of crown-of-thorns starfish decreases. That is what has happened in the past and we are saying to the government that we need more funding now, before it is too late, before there is another outbreak.'

It may only be a matter of several hours' flight from Tokyo to Townsville but the journey from the winter snows of Tenshi's childhood to the tropical climes of Queensland is far greater. It has been a journey that has seen him develop new opinions, expectations and priorities. 'If the Great Barrier Reef is healthy, then I'll be happy,' he laughs. 'It's as simple as that.'

Back on solid ground, two days later and three kilograms lighter, my world is still swaying. It takes me a day to feel stable. In the meantime I know what I have to do. 'Just keep your eye on the horizon and get your balance.'

Courtesy of Victoria State Opera.

SCALING OPERATIC HEIGHTS

'Two Italian chefs were working with me and they used to sing all the time. One day I turned to them and said, "I can sing Italian better than you." They got a shock because they could not imagine that Asian people could sing — and certainly not a little Asian dishwasher singing Italian!'

HAO ZHOU

'I looked down out of the plane and said, "Wow, what a country". Everything was red. The soil was red. There was no grass and there were no trees. How could I live there?'

WEI LI XING

'I believe people have many choices for their lives but only one opportunity, one thing which can best represent the value of that life.'

XIE KUN

The Three Tenors

All three come from China. All had early musical backgrounds. All left prestigious careers to come to Australia, and all now work on a freelance basis for the Victoria State Opera. They've been dubbed Australia's Three Tenors by a media anxious to promote them and create a common identity. And that's where the similarities between the three opera singers end.

Hao Zhou was a child prodigy, who began performing at the age of three and went on to tour the United States while a member of a Chinese opera company. Xie Kun was a notable singing teacher and distinguished soloist, and Wei li Xing a wealthy pop star, who gave up the fame and adulation, the riches and luxurious lifestyle, to come and iron shirts at ten cents apiece in downtown Melbourne, in order to follow his chosen career. What they do all have in common is a love of opera – a love that has taken them across the world and far away from their country of origin, a love that has separated them from family and friends. It is a love for which they are prepared to work long and hard hours for low pay, and to exist in frugal conditions.

On a warm balmy Melbourne evening, Hao, Wei li and Xie are sitting on the grass on a hill overlooking the Sidney Myer Music Bowl. They are here to rehearse for the following night's concert, *Viva Italia*! As the State Orchestra of Victoria plays in the background they speak, against a backdrop of fine classical music. There is much joy and laughter as they recall their early experiences in Australia and later pose together for photographs.

Xie appears to be the most serious of the three while Hao is the extrovert, most confident in English and the most outgoing in character. Wei li, who now calls himself William, shows his sense of humour in his choice of outfit – a white T-shirt the front of which is emblazoned with the words 'G'day Mate!', while the back features a myriad of black dots depicting flies.

The three men have been friends since they first met in 1993, when they performed together at the Chinatown Food Festival, an event organised by the Victoria State Opera. Since then they have delighted audiences all over the country. They have sung to 250 000 at Darling Harbour on Australia Day, proved so popular they ran out of prepared encores at a concert in Launceston's Cataract Gorge and had to sing unaccompanied, and have even been asked to lead an audience in a rendition of the national anthem. As long as they are performing and pleasing audiences, they are happy.

For Hao, that performing began before he could even walk properly. 'People told me I had to stand leaning against a table when I was singing – I was about three.' He smiles at the memory of his home town of Chang Sha, the capital city of Hunan province, which is located in the central part of China. Small in stature, Hao is big on voice and personality. Like William and Xie, he is dressed casually – in brightly coloured shorts and a T-shirt. A gold earring in one ear, Hao's long flowing hair is held back neatly in a ponytail. He is good-humoured and easy-going, eager to talk but even more eager to sing. He constantly listens to the orchestra rehearsing as he tells his story.

'My mother used to be a dancer and my grandmother was a music teacher so I think they always wanted me to do something with music. When my mother went to perform, they would let me sing songs about China – revolutionary songs, songs about Chairman Mao. At school they also made me perform. I enjoyed singing and so it was great to be taken out of school to do another performance. I remember when I was about seven, there were two songs, "A Little Singer" and "A Little Driver", which were very popular because of me.' He recalls singing on radio stations for big celebrations. 'We used to have a station in China that broadcast to Taiwan and they always asked me to sing for them.' He sang when the Japanese prime minister visited and on national television in 1976 as a twelve-year-old.

Hao came from a poor family. An only child, his parents divorced when he was four years old. He does not remember his father and has had very little contact with him. 'Yes, we were poor, but a lot of people are poor,' he says, 'and I enjoyed my childhood.' He admits, though, that it was hard to grow up without a father. 'My mother used to ask me to call her Daddy, just to make me feel better about family, because everybody had a father.

'My grandfather was a Nationalist and when the Communists

Three-year-old Hao Zhou with his mother at his first performance.

came to power in 1949, he was killed. My grandmother had three children and she suffered a lot. My mother worked really hard. She worked in a plastic factory, where they made shoes and plastic for farms, that sort of thing. My father worked for the government and was a member of the Communist party but my mother's side of the family is completely different.

'I spent a lot of time on the stage as a child as I was singing all the time – and I didn't even finish my high school. I went to opera school and then to the state opera company.' He states this information matter-of-factly, neglecting to add that he was a mere twelve years old when he began vocal studies at the Hunan School of Arts, China's leading opera school, from which he graduated with distinction in the specialist art techniques including acrobatics, kung-fu, and dance. He then became, at the age of seventeen, one of the youngest singers ever to be admitted to the Hunan State Opera Company, and toured the United States with them in 1983, performing in New York and Washington.

'There are two types of actors in Chinese opera,' he explains. 'One just sings and the other does movements – backflips, gymnastics, that sort of stuff. I had a great interest in backflips and might have become a gymnast but I had a strong mother who wanted me to be a singer,' he laughs, adding that he can still do those backflips and has found the opportunity to put them to good use in his performances. 'In Western opera, you have to act and do a little movement but it is mainly singing, and musically it is quite different. Both operas have their own kind of difficulty.'

Hao always wanted to be a Western-style opera singer. 'I always wanted to sing in Italian.' Looking back on his ambition, he recalls only ever having seen and heard one such complete opera while in China. But the sound immediately attracted him. 'That was always the kind of voice I wanted to have. I liked the European music style just as a lot of people here are probably interested in oriental, in Asian music. It's just a different feeling, a challenge, and you can feel that different life and that different culture. For me, I realise or recognise the world through music and through singing.'

He was greatly impressed by Dame Joan Sutherland's singing, knew of the Sydney Opera House, and dreamed of coming to Australia for 'good training in European opera. I wanted to find the best people for training.' He came but he was to be confronted with a different system, one that was not so straightforward as he had anticipated. 'In China, if you adore somebody, if you want to learn with them, all you have to do is go and see them and ask whether they can take you on. I wanted to go and study in Australia and sing at the Sydney Opera House.'

In order to be able to achieve his dream – of studying and performing in Western opera – he had to make sacrifices. Leaving his mother and his girlfriend caused him much pain. He arrived in Melbourne on 13 December 1987. 'I thought the country was lovely but on the second day I felt I wanted to go home. I felt it was going to be incredibly hard for me, as I didn't speak the language and I didn't know anyone at all. I couldn't see any future for myself.' His first impressions on arrival had reinforced this attitude.

Hao had applied to study English at a Melbourne college 'but they didn't come to pick me up at the airport'. Fortunately he met someone at the airport who spoke a little Mandarin. She called the college and then a taxi for him. 'I had paid $150 for the pick-up but the college didn't care. They said I couldn't have my money back and to find my own way there. So I was a bit upset.' Once in the taxi, he started to wonder at what else lay in store for him.

'It was a hot drive from the airport to the city. I felt the sky was different – the colour was brighter, a bright blue, and the air smelt a little different. I had absolutely no idea what Australia would be like.'

Arriving at the college, he found himself amongst many other new students. 'I had to wait for hours. They gave me a person's address for accommodation and expected me to get another taxi there. Luckily a Vietnamese man kindly gave me a lift. I'd really like to meet him and thank him again because he had to drive me miles and miles, further than the last tram stop.' The college had organised accommodation for Hao with an Australian family. 'I had to pay $120 a week and stay in a caravan with another Asian student. I did not feel welcome and moved out after a week.'

Hao had signed up for a twenty-week English course but he found he didn't learn much. 'I only picked up the language when I was working with people.' It was only a sense of shame that prevented him from returning home. 'We used to have a saying, "You must have face to see the people in the village". In the old days in China, if you are going away to make a career or do something, you have to do it gloriously, so that people can be proud of you. In old China you could come back as a mandarin, after an enormous amount of study, and you could then be very important in the dynasty. I would have been incredibly embarrassed if I had come home straight away without learning any English or doing anything. I wouldn't be able to face people, to see everybody, just like that saying.'

The greatest difficulty for him in Australia was the language and, according to him, still is. 'I would like to speak much better English,' he laughs. 'If I was a European-language speaker it would be different, because the languages all have a Latin background. But because I know an Asian language, it is difficult. There is no relationship between the languages. Even now I speak funny English. I just try to make people understand.'

Hao could not speak English at all when he worked at his first job in a factory. 'They didn't treat me well because they thought here's just another Asian guy who can't speak English, we can pay him less, and stuff like that.' He found a job as a dishwasher in the Victorian Arts Centre, learning of the vacancy through a friend. 'Two Italian chefs were working with me and they used to sing all the time. One day, I turned to them and said, "I can sing Italian better than you."'

To their astonishment, Hao suddenly gave them a wonderful rendition of 'O Sole Mio' and 'Come Back to Sorrento'. 'They got a shock because they could not imagine that Asian people could sing – and certainly not a little Asian dishwasher singing Italian!'

Hao's boss at the arts centre got to hear of his talents and Hao sang also for him. An interview was arranged with the *Age*, and many other newspaper and television interviews followed. Suddenly Hao was big news, even if he himself could not communicate personally. 'They had to have somebody translating for me. It was lucky I was working in the kitchen at the arts centre. It was a good image, a good story for the people upstairs going to the opera and theatre, with me singing in the kitchen. It would not have been the same thing if I had been working in a sports centre,' he chuckles.

The Victoria State Opera came to hear of this new talent and offered Hao some coaching. His career started to take off, with performances in the children's opera *The Snow Queen* with the Opera Melbourne company. He took part in a country tour for schools, worked for the Melbourne Theatre Company and in 1989 was accepted as a guest singer for the Victorian College of the Arts which enabled him to study while performing. By now Hao was feeling more settled in Australia. 'I had a singing teacher in Melbourne and good friends, people who loved me. When people like me I feel good about life; that's very important to me.'

Then came an opportunity to travel to Sydney and be in the Australian production of Andrew Lloyd Webber's *Chess*. 'They wanted me to sign a contract for fourteen months. I'd have to face another city and leave the people I knew. I didn't know what to do – because I might have difficulty in a new place again.' And his singing teacher in Melbourne did not want to lose him. But his decision was made when he remembered his early dreams of the Sydney Opera House and Dame Joan Sutherland. 'I thought I had to go to that place. It was a big decision but I went.

'I met Jim Sharman and we became friends. I had a good time in the musical – different small parts – dancing, singing and doing backflips.' While he enjoyed his time in Sydney, *Chess* closed after six months. 'They didn't have enough audiences,' says Hao. So he made contact with the Australian Opera and worked in the chorus. When they moved to Melbourne, Hao returned with them. Today Hao performs for the Victoria State Opera, often with Xie and William. But he is not keen on the label often used by the media to decribe them: the Three Tenors or even the Three Chinese Tenors.

'I felt a bit funny the first time we were called the Three Tenors because I don't like doing things that somebody has already done – it's like copying them. Also I don't want us to pretend to be three European tenors, just because they are famous.' As for making mention of the fact that Hao, Xie and William are Chinese, 'I suppose people think it is more interesting than just calling us the Three Tenors. But there are different nationalities everywhere – why should we be called the Three *Chinese* Tenors?'

Associated publicity has sometimes offended him. A radio advertisement for a school fundraiser in which the three were performing had actors speaking with Chinese accents. 'They pretended to be us and one said he was an opera singer who worked in a laundry and liked Peking Duck. They were trying to be funny but I thought this was very racist, especially for a public radio station.'

Hao has learned to be patient. 'People would look at me differently or treat me differently, or I'd be walking and someone would yell something rude to me from a car because I'm Asian. I used to get upset and angry.'

His experiences have also taught him tolerance. 'If I was in China now and there was someone who didn't speak Chinese, I would be much more polite. I would welcome them and show them more love because they don't speak my language. Here sometimes people get incredibly impatient if you don't speak good English.' He believes there is no need for this response. 'I feel all places belong to human beings. The world belongs to everybody – it's not people who own the place. I mean I would never say I want to take over Australia. People should have the choice to live wherever they want to live. You might not agree with me but I think it all belongs to the world, to human beings.

'And there is no need to be racist – different cultures just make things more interesting. They don't make more trouble as some people think. I think it is absolutely fascinating in Australia with all these different cultures and I feel sorry for people in China because they don't have that.'

Hao has made many Australian friends. 'I like a lot about Australians – they are very honest about things. If they don't like what you are talking about, they might say, shut up,' he laughs, and proceeds with an example that illustrates the difference between the Australian and the Chinese personality. 'In China, someone might come to my place for dinner and I would say, "Please, have some more." "No, I think I've had enough," they would reply, but they are just being polite. Here people are much more straightforward and ask for more! I like that.

'I also like the trams here in Melbourne and the gardens. There are gardens in the streets and in the middle of the city. I like the countryside and my favourite place is the Great Ocean Road.'

When possible, he would like to become an Australian citizen. 'I would still be Australian–Chinese because I experience two different cultures and two different lives.'

Reflecting on his career to date, he considers the last two years as the most important. In that time he has worked for the Victoria State Opera in various roles (including their schools program and performing in *La Bohème* and *My Fair Lady*), understudied two major roles for the Australian Opera, and been a Young Artist of the Victoria State Opera in 1993.

Rather than nervousness, the feeling he experiences when he performs is a strong desire for everything to be exact, correct. 'I want the Italian, French, German, whatever, to be perfect. Personally I don't think you should completely relax as a performer when you are on stage. You need to have a certain level of concentration and you need to be prepared for anything happening, like people not coming in on time or forgetting their words.' Hao studied the Stanislavski method of acting in China. 'I would feel the character first and then add the traditional Chinese movements. Now I do the same – I always try to be the character. Of course wonderful music makes it easier to feel the drama and the character.'

It has, nevertheless, been a hard and demanding road to his

achievements and he has been prepared to take on any work to follow his career choice. 'I ironed clothes and I baked cakes. I worked in a factory and a kitchen. I didn't stop washing dishes until I started working full-time with the Victoria State Opera.

'What keeps me going? Before, I used to think I wanted to be like such-and-such an opera singer. I don't feel that any more. I enjoy the music, I enjoy the singing and I enjoy performing for people in the audience. I try to do my best every time I perform – to get the language and the music right and to please the audience, even if that audience is only one person. How far my career goes is another matter and depends on so many things. All I can do is always work hard and try my best.'

And he is not yet out of the kitchen. 'I think I'm still going to wash some pots, just to remind myself that if I want to be something good, I have to work hard.'

With that, he joins Xie and William on stage as they rehearse 'Come Back to Sorrento'. Their clear, strong and melodious voices project far into the dusk and the fortunate few that are present applaud vigorously.

As the city lights sparkle in the darkness, rehearsal now over, William ponders on how different this Australia is to the one he had expected. He recalls his journey here.

'I looked down out of the plane and said, "Wow, what a country." Everything was red. The soil was red. There was no grass and there were no trees. How could I live there?' He was therefore somewhat relieved to land in Melbourne and discover a city. 'There was nice air, and green trees but I saw no people walking on the streets. Where were they all, I wondered. They were in cars and at first I thought what a wasteful country this was – one person driving one car. They must use a lot of petrol. In China, cars are always overcrowded. If a car can take five people, you will find seven people inside it.'

He came to see that this 'wastefulness' extended also to other areas. 'When I worked in a canteen, they would make lots of food and throw it into the rubbish bin at the end of the day if they couldn't sell it. In China, we don't do that – we keep it in the fridge and sell it the day after.'

William had been led to believe that Australia was a country of wealth and opportunity. 'People told me that if you come here for three years, work hard and save money very carefully, you can make 100 000 Chinese yuan [then about A$25 000] after three years.' This may have been a considerable amount for a factory worker, who could only earn up to 100 yuan [A$25] a month, but to William, who was used to a lucrative income as a pop singer, the sum was unimpressive. Like his introduction to the Australian workforce: at one stage, he held down two jobs – cleaning supermarkets and working in a factory – to be able to survive.

'I made $27 on my first day, ironing long-sleeved shirts in a factory in Brunswick.' The hard-earned $27 represented 270 shirts. 'When I told people I was paid ten cents per shirt, they did not believe me. They said it was much too low and should be fifty cents a shirt. At first it was hard but then I got better, faster and faster until after a week I could iron 700 shirts a day. I was the fastest but I had to work long hours, from seven in the morning until nine at night. Maybe the Chinese people who owned the factory had a hard life when they came here and they thought others had to start the same way,' he laughs. 'I felt I had to try everything here, to feel how hard it was.'

That work, however, was irregular and after a couple of months William found a job in a Chinese restaurant. He was disappointed that even though he told them he was a singer, they employed him as a kitchen hand. 'I started to clean the dishes and got very fast. They thought I was good and made me a cook after a month. I still got paid the same money but I learned to cook!' Occasionally he was asked to sing to a small restaurant audience, for a nominal fee, but it was a far cry from the screaming fans of up to 20 000 per performance in China and his massive salary, which had made him wealthy. 'I had everything – a colour television and air-conditioning, the best food, the best clothes; and I had not just one but *three* motorbikes,' he says, explaining that in China, with poor roads and considerable traffic, cars are not as popular.

He started work in China as a factory worker earning just 18 yuan a month – 4 or 5 yuan were then equivalent to the Australian dollar – and made a small fortune in his first month as a pop singer. Yet he was prepared to give up all of this to come to Australia. Why?

His story begins on the island of Gu Lang Yu, off the south-east China coast, where he was born. 'It was a very beautiful little island, a dream for foreigners, and every country had its embassy on that island. They called it the Island of Music because people said everyone had a piano at home. That's not quite true, but almost. It was very Western-style there. People played the violin and piano and sang.'

His father was a navy engineer who designed harbours and lighthouses and his mother a doctor at the public hospital. He says his talent comes from his mother, who had a good singing voice. While interested in singing, William preferred initially to play music and chose to study the violin. Yet his ability was quickly spotted and he recalls being told, at the age of nine, 'Your music is quite good and when you sing, you never get out of tune.'

It was not until high school that he considered singing. 'During that time, all the school students had to march for exercise. I was in charge of them and had to shout out,' he recalls. 'One of my teachers said my voice was very big, very powerful, and he asked me to sing in the choir and then as a soloist.' By the time William finished school, he was already well known as a singer on his island.

After graduating from the Teachers' University of Fu Jian with a Bachelor of Arts, he joined the music theatre company of his home province. 'There were 400 people in my troupe and I was a solo singer for about eight years.' For six months of the year, he would work at a factory – which manufactured car parts – on the mainland, just 800 metres away, and for the rest of the year he would rehearse and perform with the troupe. He was able to survive on the low wages by living at home. 'Parents make more money and buy for us. Everyone stays with their parents if they are not married.'

He later studied singing, piano and opera for two years at the Shanghai Conservatory and, in 1986, entered a competition which was to dramatically change his life. 'I won the top prize of the whole country, the Centre Television Young Singers' Competition. I never imagined I would win a prize.

'I became part of a team of ten pop stars and we travelled the whole country for three years. It was a happy life and good fun – big audiences and more money to make than as an opera singer. We performed in big stadiums for 20 000 people and most of the songs were Chinese – new ones, love songs and rock-and-roll.' He became a star of stage and television. 'The fans were mainly young people. In China, the pop music style is still growing up, still a baby, but it's growing up very quickly. Now that China has opened the door to the West, the music gets in very quickly, people like it and we have lots.'

He rapidly became a millionaire. 'I made 6000 yuan in the first month, which is huge money. At that time the biggest note was only 10 yuan and so 6000 yuan was very heavy. I could feel it in my shirt. I was very rich but I still performed with my troupe and let them have the wages.'

The events at Tiananmen Square led William to Australia. 'I was at Shanghai Conservatory with my classmate and we heard what happened over the radio. They said over 3000 people were killed and Tiananmen Square was just covered with blood and the army hosed it with water. We got angry and very sad. One of my friends knew someone studying in Melbourne and he sent some information about an English course. I decided very suddenly to leave for Australia. It cost a lot of money – 35 000 yuan – but that was all right for me. So I came out very suddenly, in January 1990.' He made the decision quickly and it took six months to achieve.

Leaving was a traumatic experience in many ways. 'I went to my little island to say goodbye to my family. I can remember that last night. I was asleep and my mother was shaking me, saying, "Son, please don't go." She was crying. "You have a happy life here, don't go, please." I just felt awful. I said, "There is no freedom now. I have to go."'

For William's pop singing contracts had stopped. 'I don't know why, but the whole country became very quiet. Also I felt I had been singing the same songs again and again and I got bored. I wanted to sing opera.' In addition he had a serious argument with his girlfriend. 'I was very sad during that time.'

William's father, unlike his mother, encouraged him to leave. 'He stood by me and said I had to go. He was very clear. My father had worked for the Chinese Communist Party for his whole life but he seemed to have something on his mind. "You have to go; don't stay here," he said. And my two brothers, they had all joined the army before and worked in a factory, normal jobs, nothing to show for it.' William wanted another life.

Having the opportunity, and the money, he applied to study English in Australia. It was not an easy process. His application was carefully screened by both China and Australia and, even at the Hong Kong–China border, he was unsure of his future. 'They held my passport for about three hours at customs, putting it in the light and checking it. I was very worried. I went with one of my friends and she got through very quickly, very easily. I had to stay there for three hours. I was in a tunnel and I sat on the floor and I thought, "If I get through these customs, I will never come back again. I just hate it."'

As he waited, he watched some English people, working in China, going to Hong Kong to shop. 'What lucky people they were. They could go through easily and come back and we just stayed here like prisoners.' Yet William was soon able to join them. Finally cleared through customs, he rejoiced in his new-found freedom, spending a week in Hong Kong. 'It was very crowded, very busy and very fast. I could feel Hong Kong was making huge money, which was going very fast, everywhere, not like China where people have few dollars and they spend very slowly – everything goes very slowly.'

Arriving in Melbourne, he could speak only a few words of English and it was a painful transition from wealthy celebrity to impoverished cleaner and factory worker. At one stage he became so despondent he wanted to return to China but Hao and Xie, whom he had met by then, persuaded him to stay. He is pleased he has remained here, for his operatic career in Australia is now well established. After auditioning for and being accepted by the Victoria State Opera he has had roles in *The Barber of Seville* and *Otello* as well as making many concert appearances both in Melbourne and interstate.

'I miss my family but I do not miss the money,' he concludes. 'Here I feel that even if I am very poor, it doesn't matter. I had a lot of money in the bank in China but I was not free. The leader of my troupe chose the songs they wanted us to sing but here you can choose everything. Freedom is more important than money. In

China you had to be careful, especially if you were a well-known person, that everything you said and did – even your marriage – was perfect. You couldn't say anything that hurt the government.

'Here you can feel the freedom. You can do anything you want. You don't need to be careful. People look on you as they feel, they discuss you and they discuss everything.'

※

The following morning I meet again with William and Xie, at Xie's apartment on the outskirts of Melbourne. Inside the neat but sparsely furnished unit, I find my eyes drawn to a large and beautiful fan adorned with oriental flowers, which is hanging on the wall.

Xie sits on the couch below the fan, listening to some music. He asks whether I would like to listen with him and, as I do so, I watch his lips form a smile and his eyes glaze over as he appears to be transported to another world, a wonderful world he was introduced to as a youngster in Nanjing, the old capital city of Jiang Su province in south-east China. Like Hao, he too loved singing as a child and was greatly influenced in his formative years by his parents and five siblings. While none of them was a professional musician, they all loved music. 'My family used to have a piano, which my father played a little, while my brothers played other Chinese instruments. My sisters and I would sing.'

The youngest of the six children, Xie – now thirty-seven – says that growing up during the Cultural Revolution, he was only able to sing revolutionary propaganda and traditional opera. He showed talent and aptitude as a singer while at high school, and was chosen to be a member of the performing group for his area, Jiang Su province which is now, coincidentally, a sister state of Victoria. 'I performed quite a lot while at school,' says Xie, 'but my [political] background was not very good and caused problems for me later on. All the universities and colleges were shut to the public. Those chosen to be students had to have a Red background and their fathers had to be leaders in the Communist Party, for example.' As this was not Xie's situation, he was assigned to work in a factory where he made plastic light switches for two-and-a-half years.

'I kept singing and my first singing teacher, who had graduated from Shanghai Conservatorium, told me I had potential and I had to be serious about my career. He made me promise not to join the small performing troupe but to do more than that.' Following his advice, Xie waited until the universities were opened to the public – in 1977 – and studied hard for the required entrance exams. 'They had strict rules for someone with my type of background, but I got the highest score and was accepted to study at the Nanjing Academy of Arts.'

Graduating four years later as the top student, he was employed by the academy as a singing teacher. Xie later studied for a postgraduate diploma at the Beijing Conservatorium, where he furthered his knowledge of opera and performance. Continuing in his position as a music teacher at Nanjing, Xie regularly performed leading roles in Western-style Chinese operas and also recorded many Chinese and Western songs. While in Nanjing, he came to know an Australian teacher of English. 'She was an opera lover and we'd cook Chinese meals together and talk music. At the time I could not speak English so a friend had to translate,' Xie explains. 'When her son and daughter-in-law visited, they spoke a lot about Australia and so I had an image of the country.' This contact was later to prove critical for Xie.

Drawn to Western opera, like Hao and William, Xie has a strong and clear philosophy on life. 'I believe people have many choices for their lives but only one opportunity, one thing which can best represent the value of that life. Some people are lucky – the first job they grab is the right thing; but this is not true for the majority. I could be a good teacher, I was a good singing teacher at my college, and I was a good worker too, but there is another way I can present my life.

'The direction of life and its aim is very important, to prove your potential as much as possible. I've tried many things – a factory worker, a teacher, I was an accountant for a year in China and a land surveyor. Here I have worked as a kitchen hand and in a factory. I did a great job but I am an opera singer. That doesn't mean I can't do other things – I do, and I do them well – but I believe as an opera singer, I can present my life better and prove my potential.' And he has no time for regrets. 'When I decide to do something, I never regret it. Even if I fail, I never regret anything. I just change that regret and do something.'

Xie greatly admires the opera singers of old such as Caruso – 'the greatest singer in the world' – and those of today: Pavarotti, Domingo and Carreras. He vividly remembers the first time he heard Placido Domingo's voice. He was watching Domingo's performance in a film of the opera *La Traviata*. 'I was twenty-two – I studied late in life – and I was watching this at the college library. It was very moving and I just cried and cried. People just stared at me – "What's wrong with that guy?" But I couldn't help it, I was touched so deeply.'

Xie later saw Luciano Pavarotti perform in person in Beijing. 'There were probably more than five concerts and I went to every one. The tickets were cheap, about five yuan each, and as I worked at the Nanjing Academy of Arts, I could get all the money back from the college plus the train fare. The concerts were packed out and there was also a recital in the Chinese People's Great Hall, just beside Tiananmen Square, which is huge and has more than 10 000 seats.'

Xie's overwhelming love of Western opera made him plan to come to Australia to pursue his career, and he obtained a passport in 1987. But, with the Chinese economy then progressing rapidly, a friend persuaded him to stay and establish a recording company together. 'So I was delayed and then the events happened in Tiananmen Square. After that the students and academics lost confidence in the future of China. It was very depressing and a lot of people wanted to leave. I was one of them.'

Fortunately for Xie, his Australian teacher friend, now living in Darwin, came to his aid. Thinking, mistakenly as it turned out, that she spotted him being beaten in television coverage of riots following the Tiananmen Square massacre, and fearing for his safety, she quickly arranged to sponsor him to come to Australia to study English. Xie was keen to take up the opportunity. 'I told my family I would be back but I was not sure when. My old father was in bad health at the time and he just cried. He was so upset when I left, thinking he would not see me again. Fortunately he is still alive, and healthy.'

Xie arrived in Darwin in January 1990, in the humidity of the wet season. As he had watched movies on television and read many novels about the West, Xie was aware of the differences to expect. Yet there were some surprises. 'The appearance of the city was very impressive but there were so many banks and churches. It is very rare to see that in Chinese cities.'

William has now joined us and, serving Chinese tea, he enters the conversation. When he arrived in Australia, he was taken with the fact that no one seemed to live in the city. 'It is just a working area, but in China people live everywhere; the city is crowded. Here people live in the suburbs, which are beautiful and quiet. In China, there is a lot of noise. And everything is mixed up – the office, the restaurant, the bank. People sometimes live in the kitchen and even on the roof – they use every inch of space.'

Xie studied English and, like Hao and William, worked in menial jobs. His main goal, however, was not just his own survival. He was determined to repay his sponsor. 'I don't like to owe people money,' he explains, and five months later he was able to pay her back the full amount. 'I had three part-time jobs – as cleaner, kitchen hand and shop assistant. I stayed with a lady who was very kind. She was a widow and had a big three-bedroomed house. She allowed two Chinese students to stay with her.'

His big career break came in the form of a singing competition. He was not yet able to read English, but a friend told him of the contest advertised in the local newspaper. 'You're a singer, why don't you enter?' 'So I sang Italian opera and passed the first round. For the final, someone suggested I sing in English to impress the judges and that my voice probably suited "The Music of the Night" from *The Phantom of the Opera*. So I learned that song and won first prize – two bus tickets for one month's travel around Australia.'

He used his prize to move down to Melbourne, where he had some friends, and where the Victoria State Opera was based. 'Darwin had no professional performing group, so I knew I had to come to Melbourne or Sydney to develop my singing skills and performing experience.' He is presently studying voice performance at the Victorian College of the Arts, writing his thesis – a comparative study of Western and modern Chinese opera – and is employed, like William and Hao, on a casual basis by the Victoria State Opera.

Like Hao, both Xie and William have been made to feel welcome in Australia. 'Only once when I first arrived in Melbourne, some people yelled "Get out, Chinese" but that was okay,' concedes William. 'There are a lot of Chinese people here and maybe they think we take their jobs or money. You just ignore them, that's all; they have no idea about this land, this country. Actually most of them come from England or Europe – they are not the original people here. The original people here are the Aborigines. All human beings should be treated equally here. But most people are friendly. I lost my wallet and it was returned two days later with my driving licence and money still in it. What a country!'

He considers it a country that has only a couple of problems. 'Too many flies,' he laughs, and, on a more serious note, 'Sometimes people are too undisciplined. They paint on the trams and on the walls.' Such defacement of public property in China, he says, would result in a gaol sentence. Xie nods in agreement.

William, Hao and Xie met as members of the chorus for the Victoria State Opera. While Hao was brought along, complete with television crew, to audition for conductor Richard Divall after he had been 'discovered' in the Victorian Arts Centre kitchens, William and Xie made more formal applications. Yet while Xie indicated his willingness to participate in chorus, understudy or solo roles, William demonstrated his ambition by ticking only 'soloist' on his application form. When reminded of this today by Xie, he laughs at his nerve and at the response he received. 'They told me if I only wanted to work as a soloist, it would take five or six years. So then I said I would do anything.'

All three were initially accepted into the chorus, overcoming stiff competition, and have gone on to understudy and have both minor and major solo roles. Fully committed to Western opera, they practise daily for anything up to four hours. 'It depends on your mood and your energy,' William explains. 'And that's just for voice practice,' adds Xie. 'You can spend an entire day listening to and preparing music.'

While he practises in another location, William plays his piano at home and sings, which is not to everyone's delight. 'I really sing out very loud and fortunately my neighbours are good friends. But one person upstairs will turn on his television louder than me when I sing. A house would be much better than a flat but we don't have enough money to rent one.' William was married four years ago; his future wife came out to Australia from China a year before he did. He likes to joke that Hao's command of English is much better as he has an Australian girlfriend, but admits that all three of them have found singing in European languages to be a challenge.

'The diction, the pronunciation, is not very hard,' says Xie, 'but it is hard to present the fluency like a native speaker. Italian is a little easier than French or German.' Perhaps he is too demanding of himself for he continues, 'Sometimes when we sing a concert in Italian, Italian people will come to us and ask us to speak Italian. "You sang perfectly so you should be able to speak Italian," they say.'

'We were in China for our whole life before coming here,' adds William, 'and Chinese writing and pronunciation is very different. We use different muscles when we speak Chinese – the position of the tongue is different.' They have had to learn to adjust to that and to speaking in English. 'If we were talking in Chinese now, I could talk very well and you would be able to understand everything,' William says. Assuring him that I do, he shakes his head. 'No – I would be able to choose every word to describe my feelings but I still can't and I am very sorry for that. I'm trying to tell you more but the problem is the words, I just don't have the right words.'

In China, too, there are communication problems. 'We speak different dialects,' William explains. 'In my province, just my province, people speak seven different dialects. You can drive a car for two hours and you won't be able to understand people. The writing is the same but the speech is different. When Hao speaks his dialect, I can't understand him but with Xie it's all right. His dialect is similar to Mandarin and everyone in China understands Mandarin.'

Ask whether they left China in search of a better life or in order to pursue a career in Western opera, and they will answer that the two are connected. Xie, like William, greatly appreciates the freedom in Australia. 'There is the freedom to do anything you want to do and I also love the atmosphere of classical music and the appreciation of the audience. The audience response is just wonderful. When we sing in concert and get a standing ovation, you never forget the feeling.'

It is a feeling that they all experience that very same evening. On the same hill where we first spoke, there is not a patch of grass left visible as hundreds upon hundreds of opera lovers gather in the Sidney Myer Music Bowl for the *Viva Italia!* concert. As the sun slowly sets and the surrounding Melbourne skyscrapers are bathed in an orange glow, the State Orchestra of Victoria accompanies artists from the Australian Opera and the Australian Ballet in an outstanding program of voice, music and dance, all with an Italian theme.

The Three Tenors, conducted by Richard Divall, are the final act and, resplendent in tails, they delight the audience with a selection of Neapolitan songs. Italian grandparents proudly hold up their bambini to listen. The applause and the encores go on and on.

'The Three Tenors' during rehearsal for the *Viva Italia!* concert in Melbourne.
Photo by Helen Chryssides.

'Sometimes we feel a little strange,' William had said. 'We sang recently in Sydney at Parliament House and the Governor of New South Wales, Mr Sinclair, said he never would have imagined Chinese people singing Italian opera in Australia. He was very impressed. They call us Australia's answer to Pavarotti, Domingo and Carreras but we are not Australian. We are Chinese. We hope to become Australian citizens.

'Last year we were at a function in Melbourne where there were more than a thousand people, including Prime Minister Paul Keating. We were asked to lead the audience in the national anthem and it was a very strange feeling – we were overseas students leading the national anthem.' He laughs. 'In China, we would never ask a foreigner to do that.' 'And that's what we like about Australia,' Xie added, 'that it is multicultural and that people never care who you are, only if you like Australia or not. And we love Australia.'

In October 1994, all three were delighted to be granted permanent residency.

Conductor of the Victoria State Opera, Richard Divall, is likewise delighted. 'They've had a much tougher time than others, having to adapt to Western music. They've had to work harder and that has been to their benefit,' he says. 'Western opera is 100 per cent different to Chinese opera – in vocal style and technique, in music and in thinking. It would be like someone here trying to adapt to ancient Chinese court music, but all three have adapted amazingly well to Western techiques and their professionalism is astounding.

'Each has a different musical quality, a different voice and a different personality but they all work together so well, which isn't surprising as they are all very dedicated. William has a *spinto* tenor voice, Xie a lyric that will go to a heavy lyric and Hao has an amazingly high and intensely agile voice with a phenomenal top F or top G. Together they are a great act – they are terrific.' He makes mention of an international Rotary concert at the Melbourne Tennis Centre, which was a huge success for them, and then the outdoor concert for over 15 000 at the Cataract Gorge in Launceston. 'The crowd absolutely loves them. But the world does love good tenors. I find them very enjoyable to work with and they've got real potential. There's no doubt about that.'

'You have to try hard,' says Xie. That's what keeps him going. That's the only thing he would regret – if he didn't try hard enough, if he didn't achieve his worth. 'I would never forgive myself that – to look back on my life and think I should have done better. Life is like an uncut diamond, one that does not shine. You have to give it a different angle, a different shape to make it sparkle.'

Yet their lives are balanced. As important as their operatic careers are, so are relationships.

'There is a very famous Chinese saying that everyone knows, "At home, you relied on your parents but when you leave, you rely on your friends,"' says William. 'It is very important to keep close family ties and to have friends. You can't live without friends.'

Local Heroes
by Helen Chryssides

This is an honest and warm book, very readable and enlightening.
ELIZABETH JOLLEY, the *Age*

Journalist and former outback dentist, Helen Chryssides, has written 'a warmhearted book' (*Sydney Morning Herald*) that presents intimate and compassionate profiles of ten leading Aborigines, revealing their journeys to prominence both within their own and the wider society. The *Local Heroes* are involved in all aspects of life and culture – dance and theatre, art and music, law and politics, sport and health, education and religion.

The *Local Heroes* are artist **Ian Abdulla**; dancer **Stephen Page**; sprinter and Olympian, **Catherine Freeman**; playwright **Roger Bennett**; bush lawyer **Lorraine Liddle**; coordinator of an alcohol treatment program in central Australia, **Lana Abbott**; star of the movie *Jedda*, former nun and crusader for Aboriginal peoples, **Rosalie Kunoth-Monks**; former stockman **Yami Lester**, who now liaises between government authorities and Aboriginal communities; 1993 Australian of the Year and leader of the rock group Yothu Yindi, **Mandawuy Yunupingu**; and his brother, **Galarrwuy Yunupingu**, the first Australian of the Year and Chairman of the Northern Land Council.

ISBN 1 86371 232 1

CollinsDove
An imprint of HarperCollins*Publishers*